No Child Is an Island: The Case for Children's Literature in Translation

No Child Is an Island: The Case for Children's Literature in Translation

Edited by Pat Pinsent

Papers from the IBBY/NCRCL conference
held at Roehampton University, London
on November 12th 2005

NCRCL papers 12

Pied Piper Publishing

First published 2006 by:

Pied Piper Publishing Ltd.
80 Birmingham Road
Shenstone
Lichfield
Staffordshire
WS14 0JU

www.piedpiperpublishing.com

British Library Cataloguing in Publication
A catalogue record for this book is available from the British Library.

ISBN 978 0 9552106 0 0   10 digit - 0 9552106 0 7

Printed in Great Britain by 4edge Ltd. 7a Eldon Way Industrial Estate, Hockley, Essex, SS5 4AD

Contents

Introduction

Introduction

Pat Pinsent

Holding a Conference about Translation

This book contains the full text of most of the papers given at the twelfth annual conference of the British section of the International Board on Books for Young People, held in conjunction with the National Centre for Research in Children's Literature at Roehampton University. These conferences have always been attractive and well-attended occasions. This time, while the numbers attending were just a little lower than usual, there were more proposals from potential workshop presenters than ever before. The subjects of these included books from areas as diverse as Alaska, Afghanistan, Brazil, Poland, Russia, Hungary, Greece, Uganda, and China, as well as several western European countries. This could possibly suggest that the enthusiasm of academic researchers for the topic of translated fiction has slightly outstripped the interest of children's literature readers in general. If however any of those present at the conference were initially lukewarm about the topic, I am sure they will have been converted into enthusiasts by the end of a very rich day.

Particularly in recent years, a good deal of unfavourable criticism from people interested in world literature has been directed at those seen as responsible for the fact that there is far more translation of children's books **from** the English language than **into** it from other cultures. Is literature written in English really so superior to any other, or is the sparsity the result of the indolence of English speaking readers? Are we so reluctant to read or buy a book by an unfamiliar author with a foreign sounding name that it is not worth publishers going to the expense of producing such books? In the past our literature was enriched by the fairy tales of the Grimms and Andersen, not forgetting *Pinnochio* and *Heidi* and the like. Is the situation today different because English linguistic imperialism has grown as the British Empire itself has dwindled?

The essays in the present collection cannot claim to answer these questions, though they may emphasise the need to ask them. At the conference itself indeed there were more contributions related to translation from English than into it. It is however clear that translators today have a higher profile than at any time in the recent past.

The week preceding the conference did not however bode well. Four separate workshop presenters had to drop out, for a variety of reasons, and at the last moment illness prevented the original keynote speaker, Emer O'Sullivan, from coming. Fortunately, Gillian Lathey, Reader in Children's Literature at Roehampton University, stepped into the breach, and it

1

therefore seems appropriate to include a summary of her paper as part of this Introduction, particularly as it provides valuable historical background material to earlier translations into English.

The Translator Revealed: Making and Altering Meaning[1] (Gillian Lathey)

Writing on translation abounds with references to translators as 'invisible'. In accordance with the low status of children's books, an accreditation of the translated work has always been less likely in translations of children's than of adult literature, so that many translators of children's books into English belong to the great disappeared of literary history. Who were the translators for children of the past? Was translating just a hack job, or did translators exercise some control over the choice of text and manner of translation? Fortunately, a number of translators for children have left behind traces in the form of prefaces, footnotes or afterwords that reveal some surprising insights into translation choices and strategies.

Two translators for children of the late eighteenth and early nineteenth centuries have written commentaries that indicate the translator's power within a given historical period to alter meaning or influence the course of British children's literature. Mary Wollstonecraft, best known as the author of *A Vindication of the Rights of Woman,* expresses a didactic, moral purpose when addressing adults in the 'Advertisement' to her 1790 translation of Christian Gotthilf Salzmann's *Elements of Morality for the Use of Children.* She even inserts into her translation a tale set in the recently fought American War of Independence, representing the humane behaviour of a native American. A translator's reference to the Gulf or Iraq wars in the spirit of Robert Westall's *Gulf* would be a modern equivalent, although Wollstonecraft's purpose was to promote in children a rational, enlightened view of the world rather than to prove a political point. Edgar Taylor, first translator of the Grimm's tales into English (published in 1823), on the other hand, justifies his choice of text from an opposing, anti-rationalist perspective, complaining in his preface that popular tales had been banished from the nursery in the interests of 'scientific learning'. Although the influence of Grimm's tales on British children's literature is well documented, Taylor's pivotal role, his championship of the imagination, and his rationale for bringing these household tales primarily to a young audience, are only rarely acknowledged.

Across history, the translator has also adopted the role of mediator, guiding – or sometimes misguiding – the child towards an appreciation or assimilation of difference. Mary Howitt, first English translator of Hans Christian Andersen, attempts to demystify the foreign in the fey little poem 'To English Children' that introduces her translation of Otto Speckter's fables (1844), while Anna Barwell offers children a patronising summary of the Norway and the Norwegians ('it is very rare to find anyone dull or stupid') in the preface to

2

Hans Aanrud's *Little Sidsel Longstocking* (1923). Prolific children's author Joan Aiken adopts a far more child-centred approach to translation, practising the art of the storyteller in order to beguile her young reader into understanding the French and Russian heritage of the source text author in the lengthy introduction to her translation of the Comtesse de Ségur's *L'Auberge de l'Ange-Gardien* (1976).

The historical examples outlined above demonstrate an alteration and mediation of source texts that reflect changing concepts of what is 'good for the child', as well as the pro-active role that translators have on occasion played in the history of British children's literature. Translators are not mere conduits, nor do they always censor or abridge arbitrarily. Indeed, there are instances where translators have negotiated the cultural transition of texts for the young with great acuity and sensitivity. The reasons behind the frequently criticised manipulation of source texts deserve greater critical attention.

Structuring No Child is an Island

While the nature of the subject of translation means that in effect all the articles in the present volume are interconnected, it has seemed appropriate to divide them into sections, each prefaced by a brief description which reflect on their predominant themes.

The first section, 'Creating a Translated Text', focuses on the authors, translators, and publishers who are involved in the process of bringing translated books to the public, and indeed, in raising the awareness of readers to the existence of such books.

This is followed in Part Two by a collection of material related to the academic study of translation. The most notable topic here is the issue of whether readers should be confronted with the exotic nature of a foreign text by the inclusion of unfamiliar words and concepts, or whether in the attempt to be 'reader-friendly', such elements should themselves be translated into concepts which will carry a similar meaning in the target culture to that which they hold in the source culture.

Part Three focuses on an area which has attracted a good deal of attention - that of the translated picture book or illustrated text. Several workshop presentations looked at the issues such translations may raise, and the motivations behind the enterprise.

Finally, as ever, there are important and interesting papers which cannot easily be constrained into any of these classifications. All focus to some greater extent on how the interplay between cultures is reflected in translated texts.

There were of course many more things going on at the conference which cannot be reflected in this book. Particularly relevant to the theme of the day was the exhibition of the books associated with the Children's Bookshow, described in *Outside In: Children's Writers in Translation*, then newly published by Milet.

At the end of the day, I think that all participants must not only have been better informed about the problems and opportunities involved in the translation and publishing of foreign books for an English speaking young audience, but also optimistic about the wealth of literature which is, so to speak, on our doorstep. I hope that the same effect will be experienced by readers of this collection of papers.

Notes

1. 'The Translator Revealed: Didacticism, Cultural Mediation and Visions of the Child Reader in Translators' Prefaces,' in Van Coillie, J & Verschueren, W (eds.) *Children's Literature in Translation: Challenges and Strategies*, Manchester: St. Jerome, 2006.

Creating a Translated Text:
Listening to the Voices of the Creators of Translated Texts

Voices of the Creators of Translated Books

In order for translated books to exist at all, several agents are obviously essential. There must be **authors** whose books are wide enough in their appeal to attract readers outside their own language and culture. There have to be **translators** who not only have an adequate command of the language in which these books are written, but also can write well enough in their own language to interest readers who are reliant on them. But both these vital agents would be – perhaps often are – frustrated in their efforts if it were not for **publishers** bold enough to commission and produce books for a reading public, which, particularly in the case of children, will have no other way of accessing stories in a language they do not understand.

At the conference we were fortunate to have as a representative of authors with a positive attitude towards translation of their books, Isobel Hoving, winner of a prestigious Dutch award for her novel *The Dream Merchant*. She spoke of how translations need to forge a balance between familiarity and strangeness, observing that she regards the English translation of her book as creating a somehow more 'serious' in impression than the Dutch original. Another author who spoke (though she has not been in a position to supply a paper for this collection), this time as part of the panel, was an Australian, Isobelle Carmody (*The Gathering*); since she spends a good deal of time in Prague, she is in a good position to observe the different effect that encountering a book in another language can have on the reader.

Creators of books also included Dorothy Bedford and Vasiliki Labitsi, artists and researchers, who discussed their project for the creation of a picture book which would enrich young children's knowledge of both Greek and English cultures; they found the many affinities between the stories of Theseus and King Arthur provided them with valuable sources for this project. The project described in another workshop session, by Teri Sloat and Tricia Brown, involved the translation and publication (in bilingual editions) of traditional stories from the Alaskan language, Yup'ik.

Speakers also included two of today's best-known translators of children's books into English, both winners of the prestigious Marsh award, and popular enough in their own right for their names to act as inducements to buyers. Papers from both of them appear in this section. Anthea Bell describes how her life's work of bringing foreign texts to both adults and children in the English-speaking world began almost accidentally, but has continued because of her conviction that her rôle is to enable readers to derive as much pleasure from the text as they would have received from the original. During the last three or four years she has translated more books for young people than ever before – hence her 'cautious optimism.' Sarah Adams is particularly notable for her attention to French colloquial language. Speaking at the end of a long and intellectually demanding day, she managed not only to hold her audience but to electrify them with her recordings of the comments of her teen-age informants (especially about slang) and of songs relevant to the translated texts.

Descriptions of the situation of the translator are also provided by James Riordan, who gives an account of his involvement with the Russian folk tale, which in today's society is something of an endangered species, and Elena Xeni, who unlike the others, is engaged in translation from English. In creating a Greek version of *The Secret Diary of Adrian Mole,* she has had to confront the problems involved in rendering humour from one language into another.

The readership of translated books will however remain small unless these texts are made available to a larger audience by sympathetic publishers. Among the several publishers present were Patricia Billings, the Director of Milet, a leading publisher of translated books, and Neal Hoskins, from Winged Chariot Press; summaries from both of these appear in this section. Additionally Elv Moody, a senior editor at Puffin, spoke from the perspective of a large publisher about the difficulties resulting from the need for foreign books initially to be read and assessed by people fluent in their languages. It had not always been easy to find suitable translators from non-Western-European languages, and this had certainly been a barrier against some books appearing in English editions. Speakers from Frances Lincoln also gave a workshop about their translated picture books (and also made a positive impact on the audience by sponsoring tea with shortbread to launch their new publication, *The Loch Ness Ghost*).

A different slant on the publication of translated books was provided by Annette Goldsmith, whose research has involved interviews with editors at American publishing firms whose books had won the prestigious Mildred L Batchelder Award for outstanding foreign books translated for the US market. Despite admitting that sales were sometimes poor, these editors did express views somewhat like Anthea Bell's 'cautious optimism,' feeling that there is a more positive attitude towards such books within the last five years or so.

Perhaps then there are ground for hoping that both in Britain and the United States, the main nations producing children's books in English in the world today, there is an increased understanding that the search for global unity and peace demands a welcome to books from other languages and cultures. Translators who can make such books equally accessible to their young monoglot English-speaking audiences as they are in their source languages should be recognised as vital in the transmission of cultural values.

Stories for Children: A Cross-Cultural Collaboration

Dorothy Bedford & Vasiliki Labitsi

This paper describes how two art educators who are also artists and researchers worked together to explore cultural similarities and differences between Greek and English stories and illustrations. We aimed to create a book for young children which would enrich the children's knowledge of the two cultures.

Research (Mason, 1999) has identified that cross-cultural learning can make a significant contribution to understanding. The increasingly multicultural nature of British society has emphasised the need for informed teaching and learning about other cultures to constitute part of the curriculum. Art education plays a vital role in this respect. Similarly, education departments in Greece are becoming aware of the way in which such elements contribute to society.

However, investigation of the resources has shown that most of them focus on well-documented but frequently mis-appropriated examples from world cultures (Bedford, 2002). Few are concerned with explaining or respecting the culture from which they have been drawn, preferring to emphasise the perceived design or artistic features of the work. Clearly such judgments have been made from a Western perspective and do little to enable children to acquire a greater understanding of the cultures from which the original texts were drawn.

Factors Involved in Picture Book Creation

Collaborative writing and illustration is almost commonplace; it includes numerous examples of cross-cultural partnerships. However, a partnership between two artist/writers from different cultural backgrounds who have seen the opportunity not only to work together but also to document the research which has underpinned the thinking is perhaps less usual. This paper is a story within a story. It focuses on the research process which has informed the decision making involved in producing a picture book: a book where the story is conveyed through illustration and supported by minimal text. The book is intended as a useful resource for children in primary schools and other learning settings. In particular, it should enable cultural understanding between specific groups of children: Greek children learning English as a second language; children of Greek or Cypriot Greek origin born in or living permanently in England; and children who have an interest in either or both Greek and English culture. The aim has been to enrich the children's knowledge of the two cultures, whilst at the same time encouraging us as writers to think reflectively about our own practice and challenge our preconceptions.

There is huge diversity in the formats that illustrated children's literature can take. Schematically, picture books should be distinguished from children's novels. The latter communicate primarily through the written word and are usually arranged in chapters. Illustrations are used only occasionally to highlight major situations or incidents of the story. Picture books on the other hand rely on the illustrations to convey the meaning with little or no support from the text.

We live in an increasingly multicultural world. It has been estimated that three hundred different languages are spoken by students in London schools. Greek society, which was in the past more coherent and homogeneous, is also experiencing increasing incongruity (Kanatsouli, 2002:.24). Given these changes, it is nowadays acknowledged that understanding, tolerance and respect of each other's culture, beliefs, customs and heritage are important educational aims (Cotton, 2000). A major strength of illustrated children's literature is that it can familiarise audiences with images of their own and other cultures, countries and societies and can offer 'a means of understanding cultural disparity' (Hunt, 1992:110). Contemporary art instruction calls for the incorporation of content that includes art works created by artists who represent a diversity of cultures (Nyman, 2002).

Pictures especially have an inherent and instant attractiveness and can communicate 'more universally and more readily than words' (Nodelman, 1988:5). They have potential that the written words lack, and can communicate descriptive information more easily (Nodelman, 1988:201). They can show what a written text can only describe, developing a story setting and specifying its time and place dimensions. Illustrated children's literature is an effective means for conveying and expressing cultural meanings. Cotton (2000) writes that picture books can both show recognisable aspects of the world children know and expand their understanding about those features outside their own immediate experience.

Picture books are an inviting and diverse art form, and an accessible primary classroom resource, one which is familiar to children (Eubanks, 1999). As Anderson et al. (1998) and Boulanger (1996: 304) have noted, they are inexpensive, 'compact, portable, always available, easy [for children] to use alone or in groups,' and children can return to them again and again. Traditionally, art education has tended to omit children's book illustration from any serious discussion in the curriculum (Johnson, 1994), or has utilised it as a means for developing literacy skills only (Graham, 1990; Marriott, 1991). More recently, the potential of picture books as a resource for art education has been stressed (Kiefer, 1991; 1995) and they are increasingly being used for this purpose (Marantz et al, 1994; Mitchell, 1995).

In Greece almost half the illustrated books for children published each year are translations from abroad, from Europe in particular, whereas in the United Kingdom it is estimated that only one percent of books from non-English speaking countries are published. For Meek (2001:90), the international success of books in English 'seem[s] to have made the British readers more insular and nationalistic.' The outcome is that British children are deprived of the opportunity to enjoy a wider range of illustrative styles and genres or to be exposed to cultural plurality. Indeed, mass-production and international cooperation in the publishing industry may result in a bland, uniform pan-European style, which reflects no tradition or individuality (Cotton, 2000). It was with this knowledge of the field that the collaborative project began.

The Importance of Narrative

Children are exposed to narrative in the form of story-telling from a very young age. 'Nursery rhymes are short narratives; the songs that rock children to sleep are often stories about the future' (Meek, 1991:105). Stott (1994: 245) notes that 'an indication of how basic the activity of storying is can be seen by the fact that the average child entering first grade has consumed as least two thousand stories.' Narrative is 'central to our cognition from earliest childhood' (Plowman, 1996:45). It is 'a means by which human beings, everywhere, represent and structure their world' (Meek, 1991:103). Bruner (1986) considers narrative as one of the two basic and universal modes of thought, or ways of knowing; the other is the logico-scientific mode. But while adults have both modes at their disposal, for organising experiences and for communicating, young children 'may rely on narrative alone' (Wade, 1984: 8). Therefore, being able to make meaning through different forms of narrative is of fundamental importance to children.

Stories are 'part of our common humanity ... All cultures have forms of narrative. Stories are part of our conversation, our recollections, our plans, our hopes, our fears, [they] are part of our first conversation; they create our first memories' (Meek, 1991:105). Through them we discover ways of saying and telling that let us know who we are. Stott (1994) rephrases and extends this statement by explaining that stories address two fundamental questions: 'Who am I?' and 'Where do I belong?' Transferring this statement from the personal to communal level, stories can help us shape our cultural identity. Every culture has its own 'great' stories, its myths and legends. Myths and legends are integral elements of the oral tradition of world culture:

> Our pre-literate ancestors learned what they needed to know in continuous face-to- face encounters with family and neighbours. They were taught ways of remembering who they were, where they came from, how to keep alive. By talking and singing, by

reciting genealogies, they handed down to their children the
history of their tribe. (Meek, 1991:14)

Myths and legends, through their continuous retellings, transmit cultural and
historical knowledge, values, shared experience and collective memories.
Although they were not originally specifically intended for child audiences,
during through their retelling and revisions they have been appropriated as
part of children's literature.

Myth as a Resource

In order to produce a picture book that would develop cross-cultural
understanding and having identified a small niche in the re-telling of
traditional legends, we decided to look for material in the rich reservoir of the
mythologies of our cultures. We chose the stories of Arthur and Theseus as
they are well known and representative stories from each cultural tradition
We were surprised at the shared patterns and motifs: for example, each of
the heroes takes a sword of kingship from under a stone; kills monstrous
men in single combat; unites a kingdom or city; and has overseas
adventures.

The story of Theseus, documented at length by Plutarch in his *Parallel Lives*
in 75 BC, tells that he was the son of the mortal king of Athens, Aegeus - or,
according to some versions, of the sea god Poseidon – and of Aethra,
daughter of the king of Troezen. Theseus grew up with his maternal
grandfather in Peloponnesus. Being extraordinarily strong and clever at
sixteen, he lifted up the rock under which Aegeus had hidden a sword and
sandals and, equipped with these signs of recognition, departed for Athens
to meet his father.

It is hard to unravel the legend of King Arthur because he is credited with
more heroic deeds and battles than any single man could have achieved. It
is thought that the legend may be based on a composite of several people.
In the early fifth century AD the Roman troops who were occupying Britain
finally withdrew to defend Rome itself. The British were left to defend
themselves against the invading Saxons. This signalled the beginning of
what became known as the Dark Ages. It is the early part of this period
which gave birth to the legends of King Arthur. The tales grew and were told
over and over as entertainment. Each story-teller or poet added some
embellishments, helping to give rise to a wealth of beautifully crafted
literature. Consequently there are many versions, probably the best known
being *Le Morte D'Arthur* by Sir Thomas Malory, from whom Rosemary
Sutcliff, amongst many, took her inspiration. It is her work and the numerous
websites which have informed this research.

Our decision to choose the stories of Theseus and Arthur was also made because we realised that the two stories were analogous. Indeed, Anderson (2003:135) claims that we are 'dealing with no more or less than an Indo-European royal heroic kingship cycle, which merely re-invents itself or enjoys a literary efflorescence wherever there is an appropriate written or oral channel of transmission.' These analogies made us look more into theories about the source of the two myths. Littleton and Malcor (1999) develop the theory that 'the Arthurian legend originated in a region known as Scythis or 'sea grass' located in the steppe region of North East Iran and slowly spread to the British Isles through various nomadic groups.

Myths and legends, like all texts, are ideological. Stephens and McCallum (1998:3) alert us that under the guise of offering to their audiences access to strange and exciting worlds, 'they serve to initiate them into aspects of a social heritage, transmitting many of a culture's central values and assumptions and a body of shared allusions and experiences.' Through their retelling, and by offering positive role models, these traditional stories transmit and perpetuate implicit and usually invisible ideologies and assumptions and patterns of behaviour. These ideological configurations are deeply conservative and refer to power (political and personal), hierarchy, gender, class, and race (Stephens and McCallum, 1998).

Both these stories, of Theseus and Arthur, are bound to views of a world which is imperialistic, socially elitist, patriarchal, sexist and masculine, and often militaristic and violent. For example, both Theseus and Arthur are designated as official heroes seeking to counter what are seen as forces of evil; they are used to idealise political order and hegemonic intentions. Their life and adventures legitimate territorial expansion from 'the enemies of civilization.' Both have aristocratic origins: the son of a king or even better of a God is given the unquestionable authority to lead and rule. Their adventures could be read as a symbolic confrontation between patriarchy and matriarchy with the former being victorious.

Hunt (1991) claims that the assumption that stories can be ideologically neutral is a fallacy. We agreed to be consciously aware of the ideological orientations of the original myths and of our own views, beliefs and assumptions, and to be careful with how we dealt and negotiated with them in our retelling.

Part of the concept of myth is that the meanings it communicates are presented as if they are of natural and timeless significance. For Barthes (in Zipes, 2002:209) 'myth is a collective representation that is socially determined and then inverted so as not to appear as a cultural artifact.' Stephens and McCallum (1998) alert us that such traditional stories are subject to implicit and usually invisible ideologies, systems and assumptions of the cultures that produce and retell them. Additionally, Greek mythology and Arthurian legends are produced from and for an androcentric community and are flawed by imperialistic positions. Although our intention has not been to produce radical reversions of the two stories in which these anachronistic ideologies would be directly attacked, we were mindful of the need to be aware of the implicit ideologies.

Cultural Indicators

Our research also indicated that not only does visual text carry meaning, it is also culturally specific and its creators' cultural origins and perceptions of those origins are always present. However, 'some reveal themselves to be more so than others, especially when the culture is made explicit in the book' (Nieres in Cotton, 2000:26). We intend to produce a visual and verbal text, which will manifest itself as Greek and English. As we intend to communicate distinguishable elements of our cultural origins, we have considered the ways in which other illustrators portray and communicate information about their cultures, thus informing our own future practice.

Kanatsouli (2002), Jobe (1993) and Sandis (2004) identify culturally specific elements and categorise them. Although their research is, in the main, confined to literary texts, many cultural indicators seem to apply to visual text also. We have identified the following categories that were significant for us through our investigation of picture books from Greek and English sources and offer some examples: environment; climate; everyday activities; style; and design.

Environment: Geography, Flora and Fauna, and Architecture

Granpa, a picture book by John Burningham (1984) 'tells through economical pictures and apparently random scraps of text, of the joys and sorrows in a friendship between a small girl and her grandfather which comes to an end with the old man's death' (Graham, 1990:108). The geographical and architectural details of the setting locate the story in England. The distinctively white vertical cliffs and the pier in the background of the book cover refer visually to the south coast of England, despite the simplification and abstraction which the illustrator's personal style donates to the picture. Grandpa dozes in his deckchair with a knotted handkerchief on his head to keep off the sun, while the child builds sandcastles at his feet. A picnic basket from which a thermos flask protrudes is behind them. Similarly, in Scullard's *The Great Round-the-World Balloon Race* (1990), the visual indicators in the depiction of an aerial view of landscape with green patchwork fields bounded by hedgerows, white cliffs and a choppy sea, are clearly English.

The Greek landscape is one of the preoccupations of Greek illustrator Fotini Stefanidi. The end papers of a book series which retells traditional Greek folk

14

tales for children show landscape with flowers and tree shapes typical of the Greek landscape, set against a pure Mediterranean sky with glimpses of the sea. According to the artist, the intention was to take children out for an excursion and show them the Greek landscape and light. Maritime and island landscapes also appear in modern Greek literature for both adults and children (Zervou, 2002).

Architecture of the built environment and depiction of recognisable historical monuments are strong cultural markers in children's book illustration. In both English and Greek picture books there is an abundance of such visual indications. For example, Papanikolaou (1995) uses white houses, terracotta tiles and window shutters to depict Cycladean traditional architecture. The neat patterns of vineyards on the nearby hills, set against blue sky and sea, are typical of Greek coastal landscape. In *The Castle that Flew* (Mela, 1999), two storey houses are built amphitheatrically, with a castle at the top of the hill, as in many towns of the Aegean islands. Two typical wooden fishing boats complete the scene. However, the illustration of this book is 'far removed from any kind of picturesque and tourist atmosphere' (Zervou, 2002, p.9). The dark and dramatic colour scheme corresponds with the book theme. The castle becomes a place of conflict; the town elders, despite the objections of the children, want to turn it into an enormous hotel and generate profits.

In the picture book *Little Stowaway*, Browne (1997), narrating the life of fishermen on the North East coast of the British Isles, depicts quite elaborately the harbour and fishing boats and architecture. Included in the scene are a red brick church and the gothic window shapes of a ruined edifice on the hillside. Another British artist, Charlotte Voake (1990), even retells the Aesop myths in an English setting, the effect being marked by her linear spontaneity and at the same time her lively and humorous style in the tradition of Quentin Blake and Edward Ardizzone. Architectural elements, such as house façades, roofs and chimneys, and mazes, remain faithful to a typically British atmosphere.

Famous landmarks are also used to identify place. In *The Good Wizard Leloublin Moves to Athens* (Kunturēs, 2002), the arrival of the Wizard in the city of Athens is confirmed visually by the depiction of the Parthenon, its diachronic symbol. Equivalently, Buckingham Palace is depicted by Shepard (1924) and Foreman (1995) and is an unquestionable London landmark. Typical English urban landscapes can also be found in a collection of nursery rhymes (Marks 1991), as well in the appearance of an English school. Depictions of buildings that refer to classic and traditional Greek architecture are drawn on in Vasiliki (1999): remains of an ancient temple and an open theatre in the bottom of the sea, a typical two-storey traditional house from Northern Greece, a mainland mountain village, a white Cyclades island church are all included.

Weather Conditions

Although depiction of particular weather cannot signify a specific country, the treatment of Aesop's fable *The North Wind and the Sun* provides an interesting example of cultural specificity. In the British version by Rackham (1867-1939), one of the most talented and influential English illustrators, a fierce wind dominates the scene. Although the outcome of the fable is known (the sun wins), in this illustration it appears that the opposite is taking place. In the Greek version by Andrikopoulos (1995), a contemporary Greek illustrator, the wind is struggling against a larger, brightly coloured and confident sun surrounded by blue sky. In the illustration, a traveller is so sure of the outcome he takes a nap under a wide sun hat. Unlike the Rackham version, the sun's victory looks certain.

Environmental issues are very often touched upon in contemporary picture books. Kanatsouli (2002) considers them as an additional though less explicit indicator of culture in national children's literature. For example Maroylakis (1993) composes a powerful depiction of a problematic contemporary Greek city (possibly Athens) through the repetition of identical blocks of flats and TV aerials. There is an atmosphere of pollution, and a lack of open spaces and trees.

Everyday Life: Food/ Activities/Objects

The Three little Wolves (1993) is a picture book created through an interesting and unusual collaboration between the most popular contemporary Greek children's book writer, Eugene Trivizas, and the well known British illustrator, Helen Oxenbury. It was published in the United Kingdom and then translated into Greek, where it instantly became a best seller. It is a radical retelling/reversion of the tale of the three little pigs. A vicious pig threatens to destroy the houses that three peaceful young wolves built one after the other. The illustrator chooses to represent activities considered to be typically English. For example, the three wolves play croquet in the garden of their wooden house, and in the last illustration share afternoon tea with the big bad pig who by then has been tamed. While in the Greek version of the text the writer refers to both English and Greek food, such as strawberries and cream as well as 'loukoumathes' and 'xalvadopita', the illustrator depicts only a bowl of strawberries. Other examples of activities perceived as typical of everyday life are olive gathering in Andrikopoulos (2000) and villagers joining in a Greek dance in Mela (1999).

Within the illustrations, cultural indicators such as flags, heraldic ornaments, banners and crowns give clues as to the country of origin. In the same way, symbols such a crown of bay leaves or a pomegranate on a plate allude to a particular cultural tradition. Cultural attitudes depicted in posture, position, and social conventions are also apparent. Costumes also inevitably play an important role in the depiction of cultural specificity. With incredible accuracy and care, Barrett (1997) dresses the emperor in new clothes of the Georgian period.

Art/Style

Artistic style is a significant cultural indicator in children's book illustration. Nodelman (1988) writes that stylistic references to the art of a particular historical period or culture give authenticity and historic accuracy to the visual narrative. He adds that because style conveys meaning, illustrators must choose theirs in the context of their intentions. Stefanidi (2003), an acclaimed Greek illustrator with a fine art background, often uses a technique based on Byzantine iconography to add authenticity. She builds human faces and bodies from a basic layer of opaque dark colour; this is then partly covered by a second layer of lighter shades. This technique has been used extensively by Greek painters to express a particular Greek aesthetic.

Walter Crane (1870), one of the most popular English illustrators of children's books in the late 19th century, was also one of the earliest exponents of the coloured picture book (Carpenter and Prichard, 1984). In his famous illustration of the encounter between the wolf and *Little Red Riding Hood,* he anthropomorphises the wolf, raising it on its hind legs and dressing it in peasant clothes, holding a stick. The straight stick and the tree behind separate the wolf from the girl. In *The Tunnel* (1989), Browne draws directly on this rich illustrative tradition, creating complex symbolisation. He takes the shape of the wolf from Crane's illustration and incorporates it into the bark of a huge and overpowering tree; this assumes sinister proportions in comparison with the fleeing child.

Design of the Book

Our research has identified several examples of illustrated stories about Theseus or King Arthur in both Greek and British children's literature. We have not, however, been able to find any evidence of the two stories being incorporated in a single book. The next stage therefore, was to undertake research to determine the design of our book.

Children's books have been illustrated at least since Comenius, who in 1658 published *Orbis Pictus,* an illustrated alphabet book. According to Whalley and Chester (1988), this is generally accepted to be the first book specifically for children. However only during the last four decades has there has been significant growth and expansion in the field of children's book illustration in the western world. This is in part due to impressive developments in printing

17

technology. This growth has been characterised as 'one of the conspicuous changes in the child's world and one of the achievements of art in our era' (Schwarcz, 1982: 2).

A basic characteristic of contemporary picture books is that they have simple texts but 'very sophisticated and highly accomplished pictures' (Nodelman, 1996: 244). When the number of illustrated 'scenes' is large, the visual sequence of the story happenings and events is more coherent and the story can be followed even when the reader cannot comprehend the written text. The use of continuous narrative where one character is portrayed in more than one place in a continuous picture plane, and of other techniques that derive from cartooning, is very effective in supporting the narrative structure of the illustrations.

Furthermore the presence of a strong visual narrative alongside a brief and simple text in a language that children cannot read can facilitate basic linguistic awareness. Linguistic development is not a primary aim of our project. However, language is a basic cultural component; thus we acknowledge this potential, which has also been recorded in relevant literature. In the research project 'Picture Books Sans Frontieres' Cotton (2000) used fifteen picture books, each from a different European country, to develop upper primary school children's awareness and understanding of the languages and cultures of their European neighbours. Workshops in classrooms showed that, with the aid of the visual narratives, children were enabled to decode words or phrases in the accompanying minimal text, although this was written in a language unknown to them.

As we identified visual narrative as the primary vehicle for the telling our two stories with a picture book format, there were choices which had to be made. We decided that it would be profusely illustrated (every double spread to contain illustrations) and support a clear visual narrative structure. It would contain short text, to be written in simple language, set in a large typeface in a larger than standard-size book (Shulevitz, 1996).

Another decision that had to be made was how the written texts and visual narratives of the two stories would be placed within the book. A simple solution would have been to place one after the other, as it is the case in conventional or traditional collections of stories, myths or legends. But this design would have divided the book into two independent sections and urged the readers to perceive the two texts as two separate units, each taking place in its own time and space. In order to suggest the similarities and common patterns in the two stories we had to consider alternative design solutions.

Contemporary (or post-modern) picture books often break the traditional linear story grammar and allow multiple stories to coexist within one text (Goldstone, 2002). A consideration of one such case shows its implications for our project. *Black and White* is an experimental picture book written and illustrated by David Macaulay and published in 1990. Each double spread is divided into four equal rectangles, illustrated in different styles, colour schemes and techniques, and which seem to tell four independent stories. A warning on the title page alerts readers to this:

> This book appears to contain a number of stories that do not necessarily occur at the same time. Then again, it may contain only one story. In any event, careful inspection of both words and pictures is recommended (Macaulay, 1990: 1)

As the book is read it becomes apparent that there may be some common elements in the four stories such as the setting, the characters and the elements of plot. Towards the end of the book, parts of one picture drift from one rectangular frame to another. Finally the reader is confronted with a black and white unified double spread and it becomes apparent that the four stories are part of the one, 'which is an interruption in commuter train service and its impact on people's lives' (Anstey, 2002).

Could we apply elements of the design and concept of *Black and White* to underline the similarities in the two stories we had chosen to illustrate? One possibility would be for the stories to start, develop and end simultaneously, sharing each double spread and separated one from the other with some sort of framing device. Selecting some moments when the two stories seem to come closer to each other, we could at intervals break the frames and 'melt' the two illustrations into one, thus working together on the same illustration plane.

Another example we considered was a device similar to that which John Burningham uses in *Time to get out of the Bath, Shirley,* which narrates two contrasting stories. On the left pages, the mother asks her daughter to get out of the bath. On the right Shirley lives her own private fantasies in vividly coloured plates. A similar design is adopted by Jan Brett (1989), in *The Mitten,* an adaptation of a Ukrainian folktale. A boy wears his new snow white mittens and goes out for a walk in the snow. He drops one of them and unaware of the loss he continues his walk. The mitten becomes the cosy and warm house for a number of wild animals. The bear, tickled by the whiskers of a mouse, sneezes and shoots the mitten up into the sky. On his way back, the boy finds it again. The picture book is arranged in double spreads split into a main central rectangular space and two smaller peripheral spaces. Each of these areas is used to narrate visually incidents of the story taking place simultaneously or in sequence but representing two different points of view: the animals in the mitten and the boy in his walk.

Another solution we considered was that used in *Where are you going? To see a friend* (2003), by Eric Carle and Kazuo Imawura, a story in two languages of a friendship. This collaboration between an English and a Japanese illustrator solves the problem by starting from opposite ends of the book to tell the story of two dogs meeting friends on each page and finally meeting one another with all their friends in a glorious centrespread party.

So, one possibility was to develop our two stories in the same unified space but to give each a separate space. Another concern, which inevitably added a new dimension to the book design, was how additional reference material about the two target cultures might be included. For example, should we include visual and textual information about contemporary Greece and United Kingdom to enable the readers to create links between the historical and contemporary aspects of the two cultures, thus avoiding the production of a text which gave idealised and nostalgic perceptions of the two cultures?

Conclusion

All of the above issues posed many challenges to both of us as illustrators and called us to develop new design skills and collective practices. Additionally, a text with a complex narrative structure and page design was seen to be more demanding on the reader, who will be called to engage in an active search for meaning making. This opens opportunities for children's development of visual literacy skills. We also appreciate that if the book is to be used in educational settings, teachers need to be aware of these complexities. The research has proved informative, and we hope that the result in terms of the book will be equally illuminating to readers of all ages from both cultures.

Bibliography

Primary sources *(referenced under illustrator name)*

Aggelidis, N (1993) H *Kurani toy Dasous,* Athens: Alexandria

Andrikopoulos, N (1995) *Ena proi me ton Aesopo*, Athens: Patakis

Andrikopoulos, N (2001) *To Thaumasto Tajidi tou Geggariou Stin Gi*, Athens: Ellinika Grammata

Barrett, A (1997) *The Emperor's New Clothes*, London: Walker Books

Brett, J (1989) *The Mitten*, London: Simon & Schuter
Browne, A (2000) *Willy's Pictures*, London: Walker Books

Browne, A (1989) *The Tunnel*, London: Walker Books

Browne, J (1997) *Little Stowaway*, London: Little Fox

Burningham, J (1978) *Time to Get Out of the Bath, Shirley*, London: Red Fox

Burningham, J (1984) *Granpa*, London: Jonathan Cape

Clark. E (1995) *Something Rich and Strange: A Treasury of Shakespeare's Verse*, London: Kingfisher

Drosinis, G (2000) *Four Fairy Tales*, Athens: Agyra

Foreman, M (1993) *Grandfather's Pencil and the Room of Stories*, London: Red Fox

Foreman, M (1995) *After the War Was Over*, London: Puffin Books

Kunturēs, M (illus.) Mpulōtēs, C (text) (2002) *Ho Kalos Magos Lelumplin Metakomizei stēn Athēna* (*The Good Wizard Lelumplin Moves to Athens*) Athēna: Minōas

Labitsi, V (1999) *One Time One Nest*, Athens: Minoas

Labitsi, V (1999) *The Clam and the Crab*, Athens, Minoas

Labitsi, V (1996) *The Sadtown that Became Again Flowertown*, Athens: Minoas

Macaulay, D (1990) *Black and White*, New York Houghton Mifflin Company

Marks, A (1991) *Ring-A-Ring O'Roses, A Book of Nursery Rhymes*, New York, London: North-South Books

Maroylakis, N (1993) *Ena Dentro Zitaei Auli* (*A Tree Seeks a Garden*), Athens: Minoas

Mela, E (1994) *Kalimera Eirini,* Athens: Sugxroni Epoxi

Mela, E (1999) *To Kastro pou Petakse* (*The Castle That Flew*), Athens: Sygxroni Epoxi

Oxenbury, H (1993) *Ta Tria Mikra Lykakia* (*The Three Little Wolves*), Athens: Minoas

Papanikolaou, K (1995) *H Porfurenia kai to Mandolino tis,* Athens: Alexandreia

Rackham, A (1912) Illustrations to *Aesop's Fables,* London: Westminster Budget Books

Scullard. S (1990) *The Great Round-the World Balloon Race,* London: Dutton Children's Books

Shepard, E H (1924) *When We Where Very Young,* London: Methuen and Co Ltd.

Stefanidi, F (2003) *O Kleftis ton Karpoyzion,* Athens: Patakis

Thomopoulou, E (1999) *I Fantasia, I Elpida kai oi Koukles,* Athens: Ellinika Grammata

Tsaknia, E (2000) *To Miso Pithari,* Athens: Ellinika Grammata

Voake, C (1990) *The Best of Aesop's Fables,* New York: Candlewick Books

Zarabouka, S (n.d.) *Mythologia 6: H Ios, O Ilios, O Faethon, H Selini, kai o Pan* (*Mythology 6: Ios, Sun, Faethon, Moon and Pan*), Athens: Kedros

Zarampouka, S (1997) *H Aliki stin Chora ton Marmaron,* Athens: Kedros

Secondary sources

Anderson, C, Kauffman, G and Short, K (1998) 'Now I Think Like an Artist: Responding to Picture Books' in Evans, J (ed.) *What's in the Picture,* London: Paul Chapman Publishing

Anderson, G (2003) *King Arthur in Antiquity,* London: Routledge

Anstey, M (2002) 'It's not all Black and White: Postmodern Picture Books and New Literacies', *Journal of Adolescent and Adult Literacy,* Vol.45, No.6

Bedford, D (2002) 'Craft Education in the 1990s: Provision and Practice at Key Stages 3 & 4' Unpublished PhD thesis. London: Roehampton University

Boulanger, S (1996) 'Language, Imagination, Vision: Art Books for Children', *The Horn Book Magazine,* May-June, pp.295-304

Carpenter, H and Prichard, M (1984) *The Oxford Companion to Children's Literature,* Oxford and New York: Oxford University Press

Cotton, P (2000) *Picture Books Sans Frontieres*, Oakhill: Trentham Books

Eubanks, P (1999) 'Learning to Be a Connoisseur of Books: Understanding Picture Books as an Art Medium', *Art Education*, Vol.52, No.6, pp.38-44

Goldstone, B (2002) 'Whaz Up with our Books? Changing Picture Book Codes and Teaching Implications' in *Reading Teacher*, vol.55, no.4, pp.362-371

Graham, J (1990) *Pictures on the Page*, Sheffield: The National Association for the Teaching of English

http://www.learningbenefits.net/Publications/OtherReports/NoteOnFamilyLearning

Hunt, P (1992) *Literature for Children: Contemporary Criticism*, London: Routledge

Jobe, R (1993) *Cultural Connections: Using Literature to Explore World Cultures with Children*, Markham, Ontario: Pembroke

Johnson, P (1994) 'Illustrated by Children' in *Journal of Art and Design Education*, Vol.13, No.1, pp.21-32

Kanatsouli, M (2002) *Amfisima tis Pedikis Logotechnias*. Athens: Sinchroni Orizontes

Littleton, S & Malcor, L (1999) *From Scythia to Camelot*, London: Garland Science

Marantz, K, et al (1994) *The Picturebook: Source and Resource for Art Education*, Reston: The National Art Education Association

Marriott, S (1991) *Picture Books in the Primary Classroom*, London: Paul Chapman Publishing

Mason, R (1999) Multicultural Art Education in the Millenium: Where to Now? *Journal of Multicultural and Cross-cultural Cultural Research in Art Education* Vol. 17, Fall, pp. 57-71

Meek, M (1991) *On Being Literate*, London: The Bodley Head

Meek, M (2001) *Children's Literature and National Identity*, Stoke on Trent, UK: Trentham Books

Mitchell, F (1995) 'Art Education and Children's Literature: An Interdisciplinary Approach for Preschool Children' in Tompson, C (ed.) *The Visual Arts and Early Childhood Learning*, Reston: NAEA

Nodelman, P (1988) *Words about Pictures*, Athens, Georgia: The University of Georgia Press

Nyman, A L (2002) Cultural Content, Identity, and Program Development: Approaches to Art Education for Elementary Educators, Gaudelius, Y & Speirs, P (eds.) *Contemporary Issues in Art Education*, Upper Saddle River, New Jersey: Prentice Hall

Sandis, D (2004) 'Proposing a Methodological Paradigm for the Study of Literary Nation(ality)', Conference Paper; *The Child and the Book Conference*, University of Surrey, Roehampton, UK, April 2004

Schwarcz, J (1982) *Ways of the Illustrator, Visual Communication in Children's Literature*, Chicago: American Library Association

Shulevitz, M (1996) *The Secret Room: Books For Children*, New York:Farrar, Strauss and Giroux

Stephens, J & McCallum, R (1998) *Retelling Stories, Framing Culture: Traditional Story and Metanarratives in Children's Literature*, London: Routledge

Stott, J (1994) 'Making Stories Mean; Making Meaning from Stories: The Value of Literature for Children' *Children's Literature in Education*, Vol.25, No.4

Wade, B (1984) 'Story at Home and at School' *Educational Review Occasional Publication,* Birmingham, UK: Birmingham University Press

Zervou, A (1997) *In Wonderland: The Children's Book as a Meeting Point between Children and Adults*, Athens: Patakis

Zervou, A (1993) *Censorship and Opposition in our Childhood Texts: Robinson Crusoe, Alice in Wonderland, and Penelope Delta's Nameless Tale,* Athens: Odysseas

Zervou, A (2002) 'Ancient and Modern Greek Tradition in the Illustrated Childrens' Book: Case Study: Sofia Zarambouka', Conference paper: *Society for Children's Book Writers and Illustrators*: Hydra Island, May 31-June 2, 2002

Zipes, J (2002) *The Brothers Grimm: From Enchanted Forests to the Modern World*, Hampshire: Palgrave MacMillan

Returning Home: Creating Children's Books in Alaska's First Languages

Tricia Brown and Teri Sloat

A Brief History

Tricia

Alaska's story is one of cultures in conflict. Although indigenous people have populated the region for millennia, the first contact with foreigners occurred in 1741 when European explorer Vitus Bering arrived. At that time, more than 40 languages were spoken by Alaska's various people groups, who lived within well-defined homeland boundaries and saw little intermarriage, despite much trade across their borders. These people included the Iñupiat, Yup'ik, Siberian Yupik, Alutiiq, Aleut (or Unangan), Eyak, Athabascan, Tlingit, and Haida; the Tsimshian people were not to settle in Alaska for another century. Since Bering's arrival, waves of outsiders have descended on Alaska, from the earliest Russians, who came to get rich on the fur trade, to the churchmen, gold miners, military personnel and white settlers who followed. The effect on the Native cultures as each new wave forced their rule and customs on to the indigenous people was devastating. Diseases also wiped out great numbers of Natives. But it was the US government's plan for assimilation through education that may have done the greatest harm.

In 1884, twelve years after the United States purchased Alaska from Russia, a Presbyterian missionary named Sheldon Jackson was selected as US General Agent of Education. Jackson was charged to establish an educational system for all children, regardless of race, on the meagre budget of $25,000. His territory was so large - 570,374 square miles, or nearly 1.5 million square kilometres - that its land mass equalled one-fifth of the continental United States. So Jackson relied on the then-common custom of funding missionary schools through government contracts. To stretch his budget, he divided Alaska into segments and invited church groups to open and operate schools. Many government authorities agreed with Jackson that the lives of Native children would improve with immersion into English and American ways.

However frugal the plan, under the umbrella of missionary schools, generations of Alaska Native children were compelled to learn English and abandon their first languages. In many villages, mission teachers prohibited 'potlatching', thus taking away one of the most significant traditional celebrations, and restricting the use of language, with its rhythms and innuendoes, in song and dance. It also removed one of the main sources of teaching traditions to youth. During this massive assimilation, children were

26

forbidden to speak their heritage languages within schools and churches. The great-grandparents of today's school children were humiliated, sent home, or even punished physically if they used their Native tongue. This continued until the latter half of the twentieth century.

Cultural Rebirth

In the 1960s, young leaders hungry for traditional knowledge began to look to their elders for direction. Artisans asked older craftspeople to teach them to weave, carve, or sew skins. Potlatching, with its song and dance, slowly returned to some areas, and stories were collected from elders. This process was accompanied by the revival of language.

Nowhere was this effect felt more than on the Yukon-Kuskokwim Delta, where Yup'ik was the first language in 22 villages and was a strong second language in the remaining 30 to 40 villages. Linguist Irene Reed and others began working with Yup'ik speakers to help preserve their language. As an oral language, it needed a written orthography, which was developed through the Alaska Native Language Center. By the early 1970s, educators were becoming aware of the problems of forcing children to abandon their heritage languages upon entering school. A move toward bilingual education began.

The Bi-lingual Movement: From English to Yup'ik

Teri

The Bethel Agency Bilingual Program, the second bilingual programme in the United States, was funded in the early 1970s. For the first three years children with Yup'ik as their first language would be taught in Yup'ik for four to five hours per day. The goal was a comfortable beginning to formal education and a fluency in Yup'ik, with a smooth transition to English as a second language. Educators like myself, and translators with classroom experience, were hired not only to create a new curriculum based on local culture and environment, but also to develop and print materials in Yup'ik to support and enhance that curriculum.

The programme required collaboration and compromise between two cultures, between oral and printed language, between what was known at an academic level about a language and how that language was played with and developed orally between parent and child within a Yup'ik family. The program faced many challenges:

- There were no previously developed books for children in the Yup'ik language

- The written Yup'ik orthography had only been in place for about five years and had yet to be standardised

- Translators faced many dialects begging to be represented

- Translators who were aware of child development and the pleasures of reading were culturally hesitant to suggest changes to translators whose approach was more literal

- The staff of the bilingual centre was responsible for developing, printing, binding and shipping materials to support a curriculum, and for developing a testing method. As teachers and translators we were all called into positions with no role models

- The quality of materials reflected this stiff learning curve. The materials the children received did not compare with commercial products

- The collaborative language of the staff was English, which meant that our materials, though produced in Yup'ik, were still translations of English thought processes

But it was a beginning. Young children could now enter school speaking the language they spoke at home, while learning English as a second language. And, for the first time, they began to have books that reflected the language and environment of their homes, villages, and surrounding areas. Along with dictionaries, picture dictionaries, classroom materials, we created:

- Illustrated anthologies printed in black and white;

- Individual picture books printed in two colours, with stories pulled from folklore and from everyday village life;

- Full-colour anthologies of tales from around the world;

- Concept books to support the curriculum;

- A series of basal readers with controlled language development and a collection of characters that would reappear throughout the first three grades;

- Yup'ik translation 'paste-overs' for a growing number of commercial trade books of higher quality.

Creating in Yup'ik: From Literal to Literary

Although the 'paste-overs' interrupted the art of the commercial picture book, the translation of quality trade books gave the translators an opportunity to look at children's literature and its wording as an art, and in turn they began to reach for a more literary use of their language. It brought an overall awareness that the Yup'ik children needed to see their own stories presented with the same written and illustrative appeal as the commercially produced books they saw with English text.

All of us on the staff were aware that some of the appeal of the stories was lost by first writing a Yup'ik story in English, then translating it to Yup'ik. One of our translators brought the story of *Aguagaakaaq* (*The Hungry Giant*) to the collaboration table. She presented it to us in Yup'ik first so we could hear the fun she had with the language and the repetition. One of the other translators began collaborating and when they were done playing with the story orally, they shared it in English.

In retrospect, it seems like a small step, but *Aguagaakaaq* led the way to creative play with language among the translators and away from such literal translation. The process then of retelling rather than translating the story into English allowed us to look at the different structures of the languages, and a conversation began about the word patterns, innuendoes and feelings attached to objects in stories.

Betty Huffmon, a Yup'ik educator and burgeoning storyteller, began working with us to create stories that involved language play, presenting us with a series of fables in which repeated sounds, plus the subtleties of how something was said, provided much of the pleasure of the story. The project was the beginning of a collaborative friendship between Betty and myself that has lasted for thirty years.

The programme has continued on a regional level for over thirty years now, and has been transferred to state control, but for Betty and me there was a need to move toward the world of commercial publishing. Along with Helen Morris, director of the bilingual centre for many years, we felt a desire to put books of commercial quality into the hands of the children in the village and to have them written in their language.

Reaching a Larger Audience

While the books produced by the bilingual program filled a need and were constantly improving, our mandates made it difficult to take the time needed to create books of commercial level quality. My experience at the bilingual centre helped me make the move to the world of commercial publishing. After my first success in that area, I began to work with Betty once again, to retell *The Eye of the Needle*, with the hope that we could create a story of high quality with appeal to both her culture and mine. We wanted it to reach the Alaskan villages in English, then have paste-overs in the Yup'ik language. Both Betty and I were looking at what made a universal story as well as at the ingredients of a commercially successful book. The children in the villages deserved reading materials in their language that matched the quality of books they saw during the ESL part of their day.

In the early 1990s, there was a hunger within US publishing for folklore, and *The Eye of the Needle* was published with Dutton. Betty and I learned that there are phrases in English that lend themselves to a Yup'ik story, and some that do not. She was the storyteller, and I was the writer. She helped me turn a traditional oral story into a western-formatted story suitable for commercial publishing. She had the cultural confidence to change the ending of the story from one of disaster to the more universal theme of the forgiveness of a grandmother. Asked for another Yup'ik tale, I turned back to the story of *Aguagaakaaq*. It had all the elements of a good universal story for children. It was about a giant and children who did not mind their parents. With Lillian Michaels' permission, the story was published with Dutton as *The Hungry Giant of the Tundra* (now in paperback through Alaska Northwest Books).

I took greater liberties with the retelling, checking with Lillian to make sure that the book 'felt' like the same story. Because of a lack of marketing by large publishers to rural areas, it took a long time to get either book into the hands of rural children.

Collaboration between Writers from Different Cultures

Betty and I began working on another collaboration based on an oral tale that explained the creation of berries on the tundra in four sentences. It was about a grumpy old woman with four daughters who turn themselves into berries. This time we wanted to work together as co-writers, both working to iron out the text. We joined our imaginations for another fun ride. Our goal was to stretch the story into one of substance that all cultures could share. The powerful Anana replaces the grumpy mother by a young woman (a good shaman in our minds) who realises she has the ability to create new berries for the village. She sews four dolls and slips a different *platuuk* (scarf) over each one's head, and takes them up to the top of a hill in the moonlight. Laying down her bag, which has grown suspiciously heavy, she dances as four little girls pop, one by one, out of her bag and turn into the different berries on the tundra. We see the girls flying around the tundra at night making more berries, then she presents the berries at the fall feast in the traditional dish of *aguutaq* (Eskimo ice cream). While writing, Betty searched for Yup'ik terms and words that brought pleasure to both Yup'ik and English speakers. In the quest for language that could be shared, a phrase which means 'Berry, Berry, Be a Berry,' is translated to *Atsa-ii-yaa, Atsa-ii-yaa, Atsaukina!*

When Betty and I collaborate, she is cultural safeguard for both the writing and the illustration, feeling accountable to her own people. But we share a love of words, sounds, rhythm of language, and the world of the picture book, and she understands that my job is to push the story as far as possible towards a book with universal appeal. Even though we work together in

30

English, we have to find terms and phrases that 'sound' right to both cultures. We search to find a variety of ways to say the same thing. Eventually one of those ways will translate into the same feeling and image for both of us and for our audience. Both of us push for the way we want the story to sound to the reader. As the illustrator as well as the co-writer, I check with Betty to make sure what I am illustrating is not so generalised as to create the feeling that it could not come from her area; we seek to enhance the story with cultural details, but not to make the details become the story itself. As a writer from 'outside' the culture, my job is to find the things that an observer of the culture could learn from and to incorporate them into the story and the artwork.

As in any collaboration, we need to address the inevitable feeling of discontent when the same words mean different things to people with different backgrounds. So we talk about where we feel the discontent. 'In the throat' means that one of us is trying to take-over the story and make it our own, and a compromise needs to be found. 'In the stomach' means that one of us has pushed the story away from its culture or away from the quality it could have, which could have the effect of making the other person regret having her name attached to the project. It is a time for rethinking and explaining. 'In the head' means we have wandered off track from the original pleasure and spirit of the story or have become hung up on details of wording something, which means it is a good time to let the story rest for a while.

After *Berry Magic* was completed we began to search for the right publisher. The first offer came from a house that wanted to take away a lot of the language pleasure; the second offer came from a house that would publish it but could not actively market it in the north. With the efforts of Helen Morris, a bi-lingual programme director, we connected with Tricia Brown from Alaska Northwest Books. She shared the vision of putting quality trade books into indigenous languages and getting them to the children waiting in the villages. Not only would they publish the book in English, but they were also willing to find a way to publish the book in Yup'ik.

The First Languages Program

Tricia

Not long after Alaska Northwest Books published two of Teri's books in paperback, she brought us a new book idea titled *Anana's Gift*. Collaborating with Betty Huffmon, Teri had produced a wonderful creation story about Alaska's berries. It was a perfect fit for our catalogue. But Teri, Betty, and their colleague, Helen Morris, also had a unique vision for this book - they wanted to see it published in Yup'ik. From that seed - a book later entitled *Berry Magic* - I developed the First Languages Program. With the company's support of the vision, my executive editor devised a return on investment plan that allowed for a very narrow profit margin so we could offer the books at a deep discount. The buyer would translate and proofread the text, so we would not be responsible for any spelling errors or disagreements over word choices. We could open our rich backlist of books to Native kids in their own language. Additionally, thanks to fairly recent changes in printing technology, it had become easier to do what we wanted. The designer could make changes on the computer screen and simply output new files.

Originally, I wanted to release *Berry Magic* simultaneously in English and several Native languages. But there were obstacles for the Native groups that I contacted, such as:

- Storage. The buyers would own the entire print run, and would have to find a place to keep a couple of pallets of books

- Distribution. Beyond meeting the needs of their people, did they want the hassle of selling to interested urban bookstores?

- Minimum print run was 1,500 books. It was the only way to make the finance work, but it might be more than they wanted

Just as the English edition was going to press, the Yupiit School District (YSD) said they had some grant money and wanted books in Central Yup'ik. (Ironically, the combined populations of the three villages that comprise the district - Akiachak, Akiak, and Tuluksak - was 1,455, virtually identical to the minimum print run.)

When the Yup'ik edition of *Berry Magic* was released, YSD invited us to fly out and celebrate with book signings, writing workshops, and community events at the libraries. We flew between villages in tiny planes, landing on snowy airstrips. In each village, the little libraries were packed. Every child got a free book. In one third-grade classroom, I invited a Yup'ik aide to read the story aloud to the children in their language. I loved to watch the kids following along as he read, and then he'd pause, ask a question in Yup'ik, and get answers in Yup'ik and English.

Since *Berry Magic* was released, we've been able to produce more books in Yup'ik, including Teri's *The Eye of the Needle,* and a Native-written book, *Kitaq Goes Ice Fishing.* Another buyer, the Lower Kuskokwim School District, has ordered more titles, including *Kumak's Fish* and *Big-Enough Anna.* My book *Children of the Midnight Sun* is also on their 'to do' list. Even though these stories hold subjects of interest to Native people (fishing and dog mushing), what binds them is that none is a Native legend or tribal story. They're stories that hold the interest of any young reader.

Yup'ik and Other Languages Today

Tricia

Alaska's Natives continue to straddle the centuries, cherishing the ways of their ancestors and practising much of what has been handed down through the centuries. That may include taking and sharing food from the natural world, celebrating through specific traditional means, honouring the wisdom of elders, and teaching children how to survive in a landscape where success is measured so differently. Cultural pride is high on the list of priorities.

It's only been about 130 years since Sheldon Jackson divided Alaska among the churchmen. The deconstruction that began with the first fur hunters and traders has completed its turn, and revival is a continuing process. A level of fluency in Yup'ik now exists across the Yukon-Kuskokwim Delta, along with a basic level of Yup'ik literacy. It is reflected in radio, TV, newspapers, and the Internet. Other developments among Alaska's Native languages include:

- The Alaska Native Language Center continues to preserve twenty languages through dictionaries, curriculum materials, and grammar guides as well as personal works. It stores copies of all Native-language books by other publishers.

- Alaska Native Studies degree programmes at the University of Alaska include language components as well as studies of children's literature.

- There are teaching tools on the web for parents, teachers, and librarians. The Alaska Native Knowledge Network and alaskool.org both offer Native perspectives and materials for teaching history, language, and culture.

- The Nallunairvik Yup'ik Literary Board, a professional group of Yup'ik people, publishes online critical reviews of children's books with Yup'ik content. Their website says: 'It is not the traditional Yup'ik custom of our people to be critical of other people's work. This task has been extremely difficult for us, but we want our future descendants to read literature that reflects accurately and positively the Yup'ik culture.'

- Native-taught classes have students answering specific questions as they read books, such as 'Is the continuity of the culture represented with values, morals, and an outgrowth of the past, connected to the future?'

- Children's literature is being studied as a part of Yup'ik studies for the first time. Students are learning the process of reviewing. Right now the reviewing process is critical. As a larger quantity of books becomes available the reviews will look beyond individual fears and protectiveness and toward the universal elements of good literature in any language.

We who are non-Native are involved for complex reasons. One of these is that we're in a position to help. Publishing is powerful. But ultimately we share the same values: teaching children who they are by looking back as well as by anticipating the future. Another value is that of being rooted to a place: the instinct toward 'returning home,' just like a salmon, lies in all of us.

A Hope for the Future

Teri

Many cultures, like the Yup'ik and other cultures of Alaska have experienced language oppression and a loss of stories. It is a loss to the whole world. The stories from these areas often reflect our basic connection to the earth and teach those of us in more urban areas some of the basic tenets of life. Betty and I share a hope with Tricia that the publication of quality trade books in indigenous languages will encourage new writers with a love of language and word play and a desire to describe their world to the rest of us. While there are many emerging linguists, there are few emerging writers from the rural areas of the north and they need encouragement, workshops for translators, and publishers like Alaska Northwest who will cater to smaller language bases. And while Betty and I work on picture books, it is our hope that longer stories will begin to be translated for young adult readers so that they have the opportunity to stretch their language to a new level.

Those of us who are working to provide commercial quality trade books to indigenous language groups know the importance of publishing at a regional level. Bilingual programs are springing up in many places. They provide the opportunity to take language to a new level as well as to satisfy curriculum needs and provide a place to protect stories. Regional efforts provide an opportunity for improving writing, translation and illustration skills, and knowledge in child development. The regional effort gave Betty and me confidence to extend our work to a commercial level. There are others who have taken that leap and there will be many more in the future. As workshops for translators take hold in the state, as the quantity of books grows, so will the confidence to improve their quality and to take the chances with imagination that make for good children's literature in all cultures.

Betty and I are beginning two new stories. One is a story she grew up with. But the other is a new kind of story for us. It is not based on folklore but on the imaginations of two cultures coming together to create a good story that neither could create on their own. Betty Huffmon's mother was one of the few women in Alaska who owned her own reindeer herd. My husband and I have a reindeer bell found on the tundra. Betty jokingly said that maybe it was her mother's. I told Betty that after finding the bell I wanted to write a story about a woman who chooses Santa's reindeer from the herd she owns. Of course, after our discussion, it will be based on her mother's reindeer herd. We are starting a story of our own, based on the reality of her history, the traditions of our cultures and the fact that I always wanted to know how Santa chose his reindeer. We will write it in a way that satisfies both her culture and mine, and hopefully the universal imagination of children that exists in all cultures. We also hope that when this is completed the story will find its way, not just into English publication, but into translation for indigenous cultures of the North. Wish us luck!

Bibliography

Bania, M (2004) *Kumak's Fish: A Tall Tale from the Far North*, Portland, Ore: Alaska Northwest Books

Brown, T & Corral, R (1998) *Children of the Midnight Sun: Young Native Voices of Alaska*, Portland, Ore: Alaska Northwest Books

Flowers, P with Dixon, A (2003) *Big-Enough Anna: The Little Sled Dog Who Braved the Arctic*, Portland, Ore: Alaska Northwest Books

Haycox, S W 'Sheldon Jackson in Historical Perspective: Alaska Native Schools and Mission Contracts, 1885-1894,' *The Pacific Historian*, Vol. XXVIII, No. 1, pp 18-28

Mitchell, D C (1997) *Sold American*, Hanover, New Hampshire: University Press of New England

Nicolai, M & Rubin, D (2002) *Kitaq Goes Ice Fishing*, Portland, Ore: Alaska Northwest Books

Sloat, T & Huffmon, B (2001) *The Eye of the Needle*, Portland, Ore: Alaska Northwest Books

Sloat, T & Huffmon, B (2004) *Berry Magic*, Portland, Ore: Alaska Northwest Books

Sloat, T & Sloat, R (2001) *The Hungry Giant of the Tundra*, Portland, Ore: Alaska Northwest Books

Websites

Alaska Native Heritage Center:
www.alaskanative.net/

Alaska Native Language Center:
www.uaf.edu/anlc/

Alaska Native history, education, languages, and culture:
www.alaskool.org

In Praise of Imperfect Translations: Reading, Translating, and the Love of the Incomprehensible

Isabel Hoving

'Oh, how I wish things could be different!' A sensation like this must have coloured and shaped the childhood of many of us, and sometimes can be a very strong and overwhelming feeling. At first sight, there is nothing remarkable about this desire to be different, to live in a different world, as it simply seems to be related to the fact that children are growing up, and that they are therefore inevitably trying to imagine the possibilities of what they may become. But I think there is more to it, and that it is a rich emotion we should treasure.

The interest in, and the desire for, difference may be an indispensable talent in a multicultural, globalising society. The philosopher Martha Nussbaum (1997) suggested that we should teach our young people the ability to develop an intercultural imagination and to identify with people from different backgrounds. Following her lead, I will argue that the practice of translating to which this book is dedicated is closely related to the project of stimulating the intercultural imagination. By way of an example, I'll tell you my own story, and I'll explain how my own childhood sensitivity to otherness was kindled by my experience as a young Dutch reader of translated books. Next, I will use the example of my own translated youth novel, *The Dream Merchant,* to show how the practice of translation interferes with the way in which the novel addresses the issue of translation, interculturality, otherness, and the incomprehensible.

Identification

A few years ago I heard an excellent talk about translation by Susan Bassnett. It brimmed with tall tales about the East, cruel, man-eating monsters, large sheep, Mongol emperors, frightened travellers, and travel-writers such as Sir John Mandeville. One of the things she said stuck with me. People love to read travel stories written by their own compatriots about far away countries, but they are not interested in reading the stories that the inhabitants of those countries write about their own countries. Perhaps I should add that she said that this applied especially to the British (Bassnett 2003). My British readers will know better than I whether she was right. Her talk made me think about the relation between identification and the desire for otherness. It seems that there are different patterns of identification. Philosopher Max Scheler (1874-1928) defined one specific type of identification as that achieved by the imitation of the other, that is, in its most radical form, letting the self be overcome or devoured by the other. In contrast, he defined a type of identification through which the self is

37

assessed by the absorption of the other – the most extreme form of this type might well be called the cannibalistic mode of identification.

In my novel, *The Dream Merchant,* I have tried to explore what it means to follow either one of these strategies. Listen to the words of the Great Devourer, Satura, the Mother, the Snake that is the End of Time, when she discusses the issue with one of the heroes of my story. First, this hero, Teresa, tells her:

> 'Satura, Satura, you breathed light into the darkness where you lay, and children came forth from your starlight, and you found them lovely and multicoloured, and you allowed them to grow in thousands of different shapes and a rainbow of hues ... But then, Satura, then your children grew to adulthood. They grew as big as you and as proud as you, and they no longer obeyed your laws ...'
> 'So,' asked Satura severely, 'what did I do then?'
> 'You were about to devour them,' said Teresa. 'You were going to devour them, the way you devour all your children the moment they grow too powerful!' (Hoving, 2005: 586-87)

After this Teresa asks Satura: 'Isn't it horrible to devour your children and lay waste to what grew and bloomed so beautifully, in thousands of different shapes and sizes?' To which Satura, reluctantly, answers: "You spoke truly,' Satura blew back softly. 'It is horrible" (Hoving, 2005: 588). Satura stands for all parents who insist on identifying their children as their exact likeness, and who do not allow their children to differ from them. This is the cannibalistic strategy of identification. My story criticises it, to a certain extent, but it also explores this strategy in different ways. The main theme of my novel is *greed* – a theme addressed together with the theme of the origins of commerce and capitalism, and of the world market. Greed, that primal cannibalistic drive, is not simply evil. It is an ambivalent force. My story tries to unravel its cruel and its wonderful sides, showing how greed influences our attitudes to things and to people.

Very often it strikes me that people assume that this cannibalistic drive is the primary strategy – that human beings would naturally wish to appropriate and absorb otherness. This assumption would also apply in innocent fields like that of translation. Thus, a translation is often praised by saying that it creates the effect of reading a novel in the original. My novel, which was originally set in Amsterdam, has been tele-transported to London, and I must say that, in my eyes, even if I felt ambivalent about this decision, it has been very well done.

However, what about the opposite strategy? It seems to me that the wish to identify by letting oneself be overcome by others is especially strong in

38

children. I know this wish can be dangerous, as it can leave children vulnerable to abuse, and it can be an obstacle to their development as independent adults. Yet I also see the productivity of the pleasure that young readers take from otherness, and I would like to sing the praise of that desire – which is both psychological and sensual. To make my point, I will stick to what I know, that is, my own personal experiences as a child. I was very much in the grip of the childish wish to disappear into the heroes I was reading about, and I wanted them to be as alien, far away, and unlike my own condition as possible. I wanted the books I read to be about far away places, long, long ago.

Reading translated books

Perhaps it was less the kind of books I read, as a child than my way of reading them. I read virtually anything I could lay my hands on, but was forever editing my readings, exaggerating, colouring, exoticising them. As a child, I especially loved what I came to see as 'English' books. There was something immensely exotic for me in this Englishness: the castles; the hearth fire; the four o'clock tea; the endless rainy hills; the smell of autumn; the boarding schools; the horses; the knights; the forests - the melancholy. For me, then, the physical strangeness of what I thought of as Englishness was primarily a deep sensual delight: Elizabeth Goudge, Hilda Lewis, C S Lewis, and, later, Terence White, J R R Tolkien were some of the authors who contributed to it.

An added delight, which I could not quite put into words at the time, was the curious rubbing against each other of language, in the Dutch translations, and the story. Something seemed to be wrong: reading these translated books was like squinting, and adopting double vision. The Dutch names did not fit the English characters. The villages with their very ordinary Dutch names were all too obviously not Dutch. Nothing was quite right: the prices in the shops, the public transport, the meals, the time of leaving school. Everything was lopsided, twisted, queer. Being a child, I took this as it came, without really criticising it. I was aware that I knew something the book did not want me to know: I had discovered the book's artificiality. I had discovered that the translation was covering up a real, genuine, more adult world.

Through translations, then, I obtained that crucial insight that we all obtain when approaching adulthood: the awareness that there is not just one reality, one truth. But translations (and especially *bad* translations) taught me something else as well: that being aware of different realities *at the same time* brings a certain pleasure. The very effort of erasing that other reality behind the translation made it all the more visible. In addition, the mismatch between words and the things to which they referred, was in a curious way exciting. I realised that some words were wrong, and others were awkward, old-fashioned or inappropriate. In other words, I discovered *style*.

This sensitivity, this awareness of doubleness, came to its full maturity when I was sixteen and read, in English, *The Lord of the Rings,* after having read the trilogy a few times beforehand, in Dutch. I am sorry to have to use such a hackneyed example, but here it is. The Dutch translation is excellent. Max Schuchart's translation is creative, effective, rich, and his translated names are perfect matches with the world they refer to. However, when I read the English original, something unexpected happened. I did not simply enjoy the reading – I was shattered by it. The characters underwent subtle but incredibly meaningful changes. Something huge was added; the proverbial Dutch preference for diminutives and the everyday was now replaced by the suggestion of seriousness and magnificence, even in the heart of the everyday. Whereas Aragorn, in Dutch, had been known as Stapper – which is a very down-to-earth name, a silly name really, more suitable for an animal than for a man – he suddenly emerged as Strider. A simple, reductive name too, indeed, but much more serious than its Dutch counterpart. In the English book Aragorn rose, then, from an accessible person who would accept the disguise of being a humble laughing-stock, to a more magnificent kind of hero, who might go undercover, but would never be ridiculous. It was as if someone I had been close to, with whom I had been playing with when I was young, who had been dirty and disgusting and funny at times, suddenly visited me again as an adult, a stranger who had done very well in society. He had become a stranger, someone different from what I had imagined, a richer, larger *English* character, not to be appropriated.

I am not exaggerating when I say that the discovery of the English original of Aragorn's name resulted in three days of adolescent ecstasy. I had not *lost* the original Dutch hero; he had acquired a new dimension, a doubleness, a new potential. I had won something wonderful: I had understood that a slight change in language is capable of creating great changes in the representation of the world. Change three letters in a name, and not just the bearer of the name, but the whole world changes its colour, mood and rhythm. This story of adolescent epiphany is simply the discovery of the fact that our worldview is only a construct – and, apart from that, and equally important, the discovery of style. The translation impressed on me, in a deeply sensual way, that different languages and styles create different worldviews. This is not an adult discovery - it builds on the childish desire for otherness, the childish delight in being overwhelmed by otherness, instead of wanting to appropriate that otherness. This childish attribute can be a great asset in trying to create the intercultural imagination.

Gaining Weight: How a Winged Cat Became a Dream Merchant

My own story, *The Dream Merchant*, is a quest of sorts, in which a twelve-year-old boy enters a dream world, composed of all the dreams about the past. Josh Cope and his friends discover that some dreams evoke a certain historical period as happy and bright, whereas other dreams about the same period are nothing but nightmares. Obviously, black people remember the days portrayed in the early parts of *Gone with the Wind* quite differently from those whose ancestors lived in those great mansions. Whilst Josh is trying to find the exit to the dream world, the story shows different ways of imagining the past, and reveals that many of these imaginative constructs conflict. Jumping from one dream to another, Josh learns that he himself is also able to see the world in different ways; he learns how to see through his first impressions, and thus discovers something about the multiplicity and multiculturality of the world, as well as the fact that our worldview is often distorted by fear and stereotypes – to our disadvantage.

This is the story. Understandably, I was very excited when an English publisher decided to translate my novel about multiculturality – and my story could not have come to more able, respectful, caring and sincere publishers than Walker Books. With the thrill of this turn of events, came the additional thrill of seeing how my book turned out in English. When I read the final version of Hester Velman's translation from beginning to end, I found that the story appeared to be a flowing epic with a sustained rhythm, with an unmistakably melancholy undertone. Even if I could have expected this, having read other English translations, I was surprised. The original story had been written in a subtly different tone. The original everyday language was ever so slightly off-key. I had done my best to disturb the flow of the text from time to time, to create a counter-rhythm, to insert short staccato beats here and there. To my own ears, the Dutch story is less serious; it is lighter, closer to the banality of everyday life, and there is more humour. To my satisfaction, though, the first American review (in *Kirkus Review*) praised the story as 'offbeat.' Though I am not completely sure how I should understand the description, this was literally what I had intended: a counter-rhythm. I wanted to write a story that would be not just be a traditional quest, but rather an improvisation on a quest. My reason for doing that was that the traditional quest does not answer the needs of today's multicultural readership. There was, perhaps, something else as well. What I had really intended to do, without knowing it, was to write a book that would already seem to be a translation – that would suggest that a smooth, flowing story cannot capture the polyvocal, multiple, wayward, present-day world. This is the very theme of the novel. It argues there is not just one way to look at the world, and that trying to look beyond the stereotypical ways of seeing the world is difficult. I wanted to reflect the unease, the strangeness of intercultural meetings, and I wanted to spark the imagination of readers in order to make them wonder: what if? Is it possible to see the world differently? Or is every effort at representing otherness doomed to be nothing but an appropriation?

Another question is equally important to writers and publishers: how much strangeness can a reader appreciate? A story has to offer the opportunity for identification if it wants to be breathlessly exciting, which was my intention. I wanted enough realism to allow my readers to identify, but I also wanted to show that realism does not get us everywhere; our own, trusted language and worldviews do not enable us to grasp the otherness of alien cultures.

These contradictory aims proved to be a source of problems and conflicts, not only in my own mind, but also in my negotiations with my publishers. In an effort to show that some worldviews are not accessible to those who do not speak the appropriate languages, I had invented a mythical language to be used by the people who carry the key to the solution of the plot. This was not a great success, and both my Dutch and my English editors cut out some of this language. Another way in which I had tried to keep my distance from realism was my decision to use unusual names for my heroes. To my delight, the names also became a point of debate between my English editor and myself. The endless debates I had with editor Chris Kloet of Walker Books about appropriate translations were almost as enjoyable as the writing of the book itself. I had the same excitement as I had experienced years before, when confronted with different sets of names in Tolkien's work. My characters acquired new depths, as they turned into Josh, instead of Jasje, Mervin instead of Herman, Marmaduke instead of Joost, Baz instead of Bors. It seemed as if they suddenly entered a new imaginative universe on their own. They gained new independence, new symbolic weight. But my experience of the effect of this translation was different from my adolescent experience with *The Lord of the Rings*. Something was lost in the translation of the names – and what was lost was exactly my decision to distance my heroes from realism, from 'real life.' My hero, Josh, was originally called Jasje, a name which does not exist in the Netherlands. It means 'Jacket,' it is a funny diminutive, which also makes it an endearment. But just like Josh, who has not yet quite entered the adult world, and will not be able to do so until he has faced his fears, the name exists just outside the real adult world order. This is just a tiny detail – but you see how small decisions like this change the story from one that is hovering on the brink of reality, into one that is more firmly set in reality.

In this manner, the translation has slightly changed one of the themes of the story – the story's resistance to realism has been reduced, some of the unease with reality has been smoothed over. In the Dutch original, the theme (that there is more than just one way to see reality) is not just addressed explicitly, in the description of different people with different value systems, it is also addressed in the style, in the play with an incomprehensible language, and in the names. Some of these elements have vanished in the translation. But because these elements and references were fairly implicit, the story has lost some of its ambiguity, has gained more consistency and clarity. Perhaps that is not such a bad thing for a juvenile novel.

Yet if I think back to my experience of reading translated novels as a child, I would be sorry if all translations were to become excellent. I would deplore the loss of all traces of the incommensurability of languages: the artificiality, clumsiness and inappropriateness. The imperfect translations of the past were dear to me, as they taught me so much about the gap between languages and cultures, about the essential otherness, the untranslatability, the *opacity* of other cultures. Why not grant our children the immense pleasure of experiencing the taste of other, unpronounceable, names? Why not allow them the pleasures of losing themselves in otherness, instead of just the pleasures of cannibalising others?

The answer, of course, is not straightforward. One answer was given by a group of young Dublin readers, who told me that were rather sorry that my novel was now set in London. They would have preferred to read a story about Amsterdam. Leaving aside the political dimensions of their preference, this taught me how difficult it is to maximise a story's potential for identification. I think it is a safe bet to assume that people – and especially children - do not want simply to recognise themselves in stories. Turning back to the political dimension, I would add that our children's strategies of identification may differ vastly from those of their parents; they may identify with their own multi-ethnic peer group, which will be organised around a certain style of music, for instance, rather than round an official national identity.

All writers and translators have to strike a balance between the wish to seduce readers with familiar images and words, and the wish to offer them the pleasure of otherness and opacity. The question is how to present strangeness in such a way that readers will at the same time find it fascinating, relevant, pleasurable – and impossible to appropriate. All of us are trying to find our own answers to this impossible question. Let me end by arguing again that we should take the many merits and pleasures of opacity as seriously as possible. Building on that sensitivity is the surest way of developing our children's intercultural imaginations. We may of course find that in this aspect many of the young readers of the twenty-first century are already ahead of the writers who are trying to convey to them the interculturality and globalisation of the world.

As for me, I am infinitely grateful for the joy that my publishers in England and abroad have given me by letting me savour the new names and rhythms in my translated story. It is wonderful to imagine that their willingness to translate my book has brought it into a much wider world than before, perhaps inciting people to ponder issues of difference and translation, just as we are doing in the pages of this book.

Bibliography

Bassnett, S (2003), unpublished paper at the conference *Inside the Whale*. University of Northampton, 11-13 July 2003

Hoving, I (2002) *De Gevleugelde Kat*, Amsterdam: Querido

Hoving, I (2005), *The Dream Merchant,* London, etc: Walker Books

Nussbaum, M C (1997), *Cultivating Humanity: A Classical Defense of Reform in Liberal Education*, Cambridge Massachusetts: Harvard University Press

Grounds for Cautious Optimism?

Anthea Bell

That cautious title just about sums up what I'd like to say in this paper. I was invited to the IBBY conference, I imagine, as someone supposed to have specialised in the translation of books for children and young people. In fact I did very little such work for many years, for the simple reason that over a long period, English-language publishers were unwilling even to consider foreign books for the young. Notoriously, far more in every genre, adult as well as juvenile, was and still is translated out of English than into it.

Becoming a Translator

A relatively large number of books for children was being translated when I began working as a translator, which I did entirely by accident. I have never studied the theory of translation – not, of course, that that has prevented me from forming theories of my own about it, but they derive from practice rather than academic discipline, for the simple reason that translation studies didn't exist when I was an undergraduate. I might not have headed for the subject anyway, since I never set out to be a translator, and my degree isn't even in modern languages but in English. It was a hard choice between languages and English – you had to make such a choice in those days, and could not opt for both – but there was a course at Oxford where I could study the history of the development of the language, and that was what I wanted to do. In this course Milton was the cut-off line for literature, but that was all right, since I would be reading later English and American literature for pleasure anyway (just as I went on reading French and German books), but here was my one chance to study a highly non-vocational subject for the sheer fun of it. Charles Clarke, when minister of education, went on record as saying he didn't mind having a few medievalists around for ornamental purposes; I hate to think what his opinion of that Oxford course in the philology of the English language would have been. Still, one does wonder what happened to the pursuit of knowledge purely for its own sake.

When I was a schoolgirl, it was to get at what was inside the foreign books on the library shelves which I couldn't read that I made a rapid assault on the languages in which they were written. And may I add a rider to the title of this conference: no child, obviously, should be an island, but if he or she does want a private island then books are ideal. I was miserably unhappy at my boarding school – in that respect I am amazed by the Harry Potter phenomenon, which apparently attracts young people to the boarding-school ethos – and I found consolation in reading. I still remember my delight when I could tackle not just a school exercise but a real book in French – it was Théophile Gautier's picaresque novel *Le Capitaine Fracasse,* and I picked it off the library shelves because it was temptingly long. I wanted to read the books in their own languages – it is thus, I suspect, that those who would rather read the original than a translation inadvertently qualify themselves to be translators.

And we all need translators, however little we may know it. Even astonishingly prolific and knowledgeable translators, like my friend Michael Henry Heim of the University of California who translates from eighteen languages, cannot know **all** the tongues in which books are written. It is my personal regret that I have not a word of any Slav language, and I am grateful to translators for allowing me to read the great Russian novels. Once Michael Heim and I were on a panel at a day on translation organised by English PEN. Just before our own part of the proceedings, a famous pundit spoke; she arrived in a hurry, read a poem in Spanish without offering any hint of its meaning to non-Spanish-speaking members of the audience, delivered a diatribe to the effect that all translation was bad and useless, and swept out again leaving no time for questions, let alone protests. It was then for our panel to pick up the pieces as best we might. Much more constructive was a talk earlier in the day by Michael Ignatieff, who pointed out that anyone drawing up a list of the great international literature that an educated person might be expected to have read would probably include names such as Homer, Virgil, Ovid, and, moving on from the ancient world, perhaps Rabelais, Cervantes, Dante, Boccaccio, Goethe and Schiller, Heine, Flaubert and Victor Hugo, Proust, Thomas Mann. I need hardly go on, for I think the gist of his remarks is obvious. And I haven't even included any figures of the same stature writing in the English language, because Ignatieff's point was that translations are essential for many readers if they are to have access to the books at all. So if translators are an evil, as the pundit strongly implied, they are a necessary evil. I remember saying so on that occasion in our defence.

The same is true, perhaps particularly true, of children's literature. When I accidentally fell into translation, it was because my then husband and I knew a publisher's editor who asked if we could advise her as to someone who could read German and give her an opinion on a German children's book. I diffidently said that I expected I could do that. I don't think I recommended it, but one thing leads to another – the grapevine operates very efficiently in publishing, I have always found – and the first book I ever translated was a book for children, Otfried Preussler's fantasy *The Little Water-Sprite*. I did it literally on the kitchen table, with my baby asleep in a basket beside me. This, I repeat, was at a time when English-language publishers were reasonably open to foreign books for young people.

Translating for Children

Even later, when there was much less likelihood of a foreign title's being published in translation, I still felt that it was particularly valuable for children to have access to the best books written for them in languages other than their native tongue. For one thing, it ought to encourage the habit of wide reading as an adult, of the kind suggested by Michael Ignatieff at that PEN seminar. I make no apology for offering you a quotation that I have cited before, from Dr Johnson, who, when asked what books he would give a boy to read first, said with great common sense:

I am always for getting a boy forward in his learning; for that is a sure good. I would let him at first read any English book which happens to engage his attention; because you have done a great deal when you have brought him to have entertainment from a book. He'll get better books afterwards.

We may forgive Johnson, in his period, for specifying boys only; by better books, I suspect he meant the Greek and Latin literature that an educated person of his time would read. The equivalent today might be the major literary classics of other modern languages. And how better to make young people receptive to those classics than by introducing them to books from other countries while they are still young?

I was at a seminar in Oxford some eighteen months ago where it was mentioned that there did seem to be a certain upturn in the translation of certain genres, for instance crime fiction, which is perfectly true, and children's books. Now I do not like describing literature for children and young people as a single genre – suggesting that, say, Lewis Carroll, Enid Blyton, Astrid Lindgren, Philip Pullman and indeed all other writers for the young can placed in a single category, whereas young people relish responding to different genres as much as adults do. But for some years past I have definitely found a greater willingness on the part of English-language publishers to consider books from other languages seriously. And translations will be necessary – particularly given the parlous state of modem language teaching in the United Kingdom at the moment. German in particular, the language from which I chiefly translate at present, seems to be in decline in schools, which is a humbling thought when one considers that, conversely, the Germans are teaching English in their own primary schools now. I was charmed when quite recently that first-ever translation of mine, the Otfried Preussler book, was reissued in a teaching edition for use in schools by Preussler's German publishers, and I have translated a couple of other books into English for another German publisher, for the same purpose. They appear with comments and explanatory notes in German by a German teacher of English. There is quite a lot of similar activity going on; I know others who have translated German children's books into English for use in German schools. Compare and contrast – or perhaps don't – the fact that at that Oxford seminar only eighteen months ago, a young lecturer in German said she had recently found that most of her modern language students were reading their literary texts not in the original but in English translation. And this was at Oxford, supposedly one of the great seats of learning in the United Kingdom! There was a moment's stunned silence before someone faintly observed that at least the undergraduates **were** reading them, which was better than nothing. I spoke up here and asked in that case, where was the next generation of practising translators going to come from?

Translation is a low-profile profession, and in my view it ought to be; I adhere to the old school of invisible translation, which is not fashionable today, but I am absolutely delighted if someone says that he or she didn't realise a book was a translation at all – I have even heard a secondary school head teacher, no less, say she had no idea the 'Asterix' series was not written in English in the first place, which astonished me, for you would think those stories had 'This is French' written all over them. I think therefore that the translator's profile **should** be low; the idea is not for the translator to go on an ego trip, but for the reader to have as far as possible the same pleasure from reading a book in translation as readers of the original. All the same, we do have a function in the literary world, perhaps more than ever in a time when learning modern languages is perceived as difficult – back in my own student days the subject was notoriously considered a soft option.

I see no difference in kind between translating for adults and for children. I have been asked if I adopt a different approach for children's books from that for adult books, but no; I adopt a different approach for **every** book, because the translator is trying to be someone else the whole time, much like an actor. I am very happy to move between adult and juvenile literature. During almost a couple of decades when few foreign books for the young were translated into English, I would be asked now and then to speak or write as a translator of children's literature, and had to point out that I wasn't in fact translating any, barring a picture book here and there and the new 'Asterix' title whenever one was published. It is odd, I think, that children's books should be perceived as different in kind from just books, full stop. They have often been placed in a kind of ghetto – and when you consider the comparative reluctance of the English-speaking world to publish any translations at all, translation in itself has been in a ghetto, so translated children's books have been banished to a ghetto twice over.

I believe, cautiously, that they are on the way out of it. The advent of the so-called crossover title may have something to do with it – although frankly only the term is new. The *Children's and Household Tales* of the Brothers Grimm, and other collections of folk and fairy tales in general, particularly from the nineteenth and early twentieth centuries, could claim to be quintessential crossover texts, since they were not deliberately aimed at children in particular. Some critics have attacked the reading of young

48

people's books by adults as a symptom of dumbing down in general, but I don't agree; surely Philip Pullman's *His Dark Materials* trilogy, for instance, is far more grown-up than many an adult bestseller, and he'll even have people re-reading Milton yet. In real life, surely you should never be told that you cannot read something because you are either too young or too old for it. I recollect weeping tears of fury at my school when, aged eight, I was not allowed to borrow Rudyard Kipling's *Thy Servant a Dog* because it was in the senior library and I was only a junior. The reading child can and surely should be allowed to read anything – I also made my way at around eight or nine right through the magnificent Authorised Version of the Bible in English, full of stories that when you come to think of it are in theory highly unsuitable for the young mind - when I came to Rahab the harlot helping Joshua's men into the city of Jericho and didn't know exactly what a harlot was, I did not ask anyone for enlightenment, just filed the word away in my mind for future reference, and at some point, lo and behold, I had read enough books to know what a harlot did. Conversely, why should not adults feel interested in, even challenged by, works for young people?

I feel it is not entirely due to those involved in adult literature, incidentally, that there is a certain entrenched concept of the juvenile market as separate and on its own. My dear friend of many years, Klaus Flugge of Andersen Press, seems to have wondered how I had kept body and soul together when no translations for children came my way for some years, but then he chanced upon my translation of the late W G Sebald's *Austerlitz*, and realised that I had in fact been busy on other works during that time. And once I fixed to meet another old friend, Ron Jobe, who will be well known to many involved with IBBY, in Cambridge where I live: 'We'll meet outside Heffer's main bookshop,' I said firmly. Waiting there for ten minutes, I thought there was no sign of Ron – until I glanced across the road, and there he was fifty yards or so off, waiting patiently outside Heffer's Children's Bookshop. That, to him, **was** the main bookshop, and perhaps he was right.

When I was fortunate enough to be awarded the Austrian State Prize for Literary Translation for 2003, I was particularly pleased and honoured to hear from the President of IBBY, who I believe is Austrian himself, that he regarded the award as a recognition of translated children's literature. As it happens the specifically Austrian books I have translated include a number of adult titles – a volume in the New Penguin Freud series, several novellas by Stefan Zweig, on whom I am very busy at the moment, a long and ingenious novel by Lilian Faschinger – but I am very happy to be thought of as a translator of children's books. Again, when you come to think of it the difference is not so very great. After I had translated that Freud volume, I found myself saying, if asked, that my work ranged from versions of Sigmund Freud to Asterix the Gaul. It then occurred to me, since my Freud volume was *The Psychopathology of Everyday Life*, that when you are translating puns and wordplay, as you must in something like the Asterix *bande dessinée* series which is full of such verbal games, you are trying to do on purpose what Freud describes as the verbal slips we all perpetrate by accident. A Freudian slip is a pun gone wrong, or possibly vice versa. In the course of my translation of that title, whenever I caught myself out in the famous Freudian slip, I wished I could ring Freud up a hundred years back: 'Here's another for your collection, Professor.' For he was scrupulous in that particular volume about using material only from his own experience and that of colleagues, not from his patients.

Recent Developments

So the difference between translating for adults and for children is not as great as it may seem, and it is encouraging to see a revival of interest in foreign books for young people. I like to think that among the reasons for this revival are initiatives such as the Marsh Prize for Children's Literature in Translation, in essence the brainchild of Kim Reynolds here at the Roehampton Institute, along with the distinguished author Aidan Chambers, and I was privileged to be among the company invited to discuss the project on that first occasion. Later in the day, this seminar will hear from Sarah Adams, winner of the latest award with her impressive translation of the French author Daniel Pennac's wonderful story *Eye of the Wolf*. Sitting on the jury panel, I was delighted to find a whole sixteen titles offered to us on that occasion – many more than when I had last had the honour of serving on the jury. I have the strong impression that the Mildred Batchelder award in the States always has more entries.[1]

There is, of course, something of a downside to the increasing willingness of English-language publishers to look at foreign material: translators like me do a good deal of reading for publishers too, and it is depressing to see many hopeful offerings that have obviously been deliberately concocted with a view to the international children's bestseller market, especially in the currently popular field of fantasy. J K Rowling's Harry Potter books have worked wonders in making reading a trendy activity among the young, boys as well as girls. But Harry Potter is also unwittingly responsible, as far as I can see, for a belief that all you have to do is collect as many familiar fantasy ingredients as possible, shake them up together like a cocktail, and hey presto, you have manufactured an instant bestseller, usually threatening to turn into a trilogy. (Whatever happened to the one-off title?) We get a number of these fantasies offered to the twice-a-year journal *new books in german (nbg)*, published for the London and Frankfurt Book Fairs, which aims to interest English-language publishers in just that, recent or forthcoming German publications in various fields; the editorial committee likes to include at least a couple of children's books whenever possible. We are offered some sixty titles for each issue, of which about twenty will ultimately be included and reviewed in the journal, so the standard has to be high. For the recent Frankfurt issue of autumn 2005 I read a very disappointing fantasy, which therefore was **not** included. It was disappointing because it was by a well-established author whom I won't name, writing out of her usual age-range; I suspect that her publisher had said: why not have a try at an older children's fantasy, you of all people can do it? It was a dragon story, and as there are any number of dragon stories around at the moment they need to have something special about them, which this one didn't. A tell-tale sign of deliberate manufacture for an international bestseller market was also the fact that the proper names and place names were English. So I drew the short straw there, but rather late in the day a good futuristic novel for young people came along, about cloning and the ethical and medical problems it poses. Both our editor Rebecca Morrison and I liked it, and it was in time to go into the journal.

Names were also designed to be as international and mainly English as possible in another fantasy we saw for *nbg* a couple of years ago. That one did go into the journal because our interim editor liked it, although she freely admitted that she knew little about books for young people. I had my doubts at the time, although of course the *nbg* editorial committee cannot all read all the books offered, and we have to rely mainly on the opinion of our readers. When I did come to read it for a publisher I found those doubts confirmed. The ingredients in that one were lavish indeed, comprising parallel worlds as in Philip Pullman; an Arthurian theme with the figure of a wounded Grail king in both worlds; ponies and a riding school for pony-mad girls; thirteen sinister Black Knights, thus numerically trumping Tolkien's Black Riders; ruins and tunnels, stone knights and even topiary dogs coming to life and chasing the heroine, and a recurrent phrase in which she thought, in italics, *But that's just not possible!*, a sure sign that it was about to happen next minute. The whole thing was set in – guess what – a boarding school, where the teachers were on opposing supernatural sides; I couldn't help thinking that someone should explain why so many hereditary champions of good and evil were gathered in this one tin-pot educational establishment – did the rest of the world just have to fend for itself? – and thought that the parents of pupils would have had good grounds to sue for return of the school fees, since so little of the prosaic business of teaching went on. I saw, looking out that report the other day, that I read it for Walker Books, who had told me what they had forthcoming, and said they were hoping for a good German title to add to their foreign books. I had to conclude my report: 'I fear this is not one of the gems you are looking for, and would not be a worthy companion to Pennac and Hoving on your list.'

There **are** good fantasies to be translated, but they have to have something extra, and do more than reshuffle the familiar ingredients, which simply does not work. I would like also to mention a few others: Cornelia Funke, whose books published by Scholastic and the Chicken House are extremely popular, particularly in North America, and who I think has done a great deal to make English-language publishers more willing to contemplate a foreign title; Kai Meyer, this year's winner of the prestigious Corine prize in Germany in the young people's category, a prize previously won by Rowling and Funke (Meyer is in the process of publication in English by Egmont); Lene Kaaberbøl's delightful self-translated Danish series from Hodder; and a long French fantasy by Anne-Laure Bondoux, *The Princess and the Captain*, coming from Bloomsbury next year. And when, as a reader, you do come upon something that can really be recommended, it is most encouraging, and makes looking at the duds worth while.

Moving between Adults' and Children's Books

As a translator, I myself actively enjoy moving between the adult and the young people's markets; I was surprised recently, talking about the subject to Mareike Weber, who is extremely knowledgeable about both German and English children's literature, to hear her say that in Germany doing this was uncommon. In fact when I mentioned her comment to Emer O'Sullivan, Emer immediately came up with the name of Mirjam Pressler, distinguished author and translator for adults and children alike, besides being editor of the Critical Edition of the diaries of Anne Frank. And Mareike herself has mentioned to me the name of Harry Rowohlt, who also translates for adults and young people, but those sound like exceptions. The practice is unusual in general, she tells me, and it is even possible for German translators to specialise in a particular genre within the children's market, for instance historical novels for young adults. It would hardly be feasible for a translator to concentrate on such a clearly defined area in the English-speaking world, for of course so much more is translated **from** English than **into** it. But in the UK we do have a number of good translators who are happy to translate for both the adult and the juvenile markets, including Sarah Adams who translates from French for adults too; Adriana Hunter, also translating for both fields from French; and John Brownjohn, whose wonderfully ingenious versions of Walter Moers's novel *The 13 ½ Lives of Captain Bluebear* and its sequels may be considered genuine crossover books, disproving both the common misconception that the Germans have no sense of humour, and the other misconception that humour in general cannot be translated - something which the same translator again disproves in his versions of the amusing stories of Dietlof Reiche. Patricia Crampton, who says she now considers herself at least partly retired, has made fine contributions to translated children's literature, working mainly from German, Dutch and Swedish, and has won both the second Marsh Award for her version of Gudrun Pausewang's moving Holocaust novel, *The Final Journey*, and the Schlegel-Tieck award for translation from German for Wolfgang Hildesheimer's *Marbot*. At the moment I am engaged on the translation of a marvellous novel by the Syrian-born German writer Rafik Schami, *The Dark Side of Love*, a family saga spanning some seventy-five years of the twentieth century, almost 900 pages long and told in many short chapters, each of which is almost like a short Arabian Nights story in itself. Only two weeks ago, at a dinner in London for Cornelia Funke's recently published *Inkspell*, I mentioned this book to her when she asked what I was working on, and she immediately said, oh, he was a friend of hers, and they had a flourishing correspondence, which did not surprise me at all – both are born storytellers. Schami is an author who moves happily between writing for adults, as here, and writing for young people. I hope I do the same as a translator. I am delighted to reflect that in the past three or four years, I must have translated more books for children and young people than in the two preceding decades. We would all here today like to see translated children's literature move out into public view; I do see a distinct tendency that way, and may it long continue.

Notes

1.   See Annette Goldsmith, 'Found in Translation' in the present volume.

Bibliography

Bondoux, A-L (2004) *La Princetta et le Capitaine*, Paris: Hachette

Freud, S (1901) *Zur Psychopathologie des Alltagsleben, Leipzig: Monatschrift für Psychologie und Neurologie*; Eng. Bell, Anthea (trans.) (2002), *The Psychopathology of Everyday Life*, London: Penguin Books

Funke, C (2005) *Tintenblut*, Hamburg: Cecilie Dressler Verlag; Eng., Bell, Anthea (trans.) (2005), *Inkspell*, Frome: The Chicken House

Gautier, T (1863) *Le Capitaine Fracasse*

Goscinny, R & Uderzo, A (1961—) *Astérix le Gaulois*—, Paris: Dargaud, from 1981 Les Editions Albert René; Eng., Bell, Anthea & Hockridge, Derek (trans.) (1969—) *Asterix the Gaul*—, London: Hodder & Stoughton, from 2001 Orion)

Grimm, J & W (1812 first ed.) *Kinder- und Hausmärchen*

Hildesheimer, W (1984) *Marbot*, Frankfurt am Main: Suhrkamp Verlag; Eng., Crampton, Patricia (trans.) (1984) *Marbot,* London: Dent

Hoving, I (2002) *De Gevleugelde Kat*, Amsterdam: Querido; Eng., Velmans, Hester (trans.) (2005) *The Dream Merchant,* London: Walker Books

Kaaberbøl, L (2000) *Skammerens Datter*, Copenhagen: Forum; Eng., the author (trans.) (2003) *The Shamer's Daughter*, London: Hodder Children's Books

Meyer, K (2001) *Die Fliessende Königin*, Bindlach: Loewe Verlag; Eng., Bell, Anteha (trans.) (2005), *The Flowing Queen*, London: Egmont

Moers, W (1999) *Die 13½ Leben des Käpt'n Blaubär*, Frankfurt am Main: Eichborn; Eng., tr. John Brownjohn (2000) *The 13 ½ Lives of Captain Bluebear,* London: Secker & Warburg

Pausewang, G (1997) *Reise im August*, Ravensburg: Ravensburger Taschenbuch; Eng., Crampton, Patricia (trans.) (1998) *The Final Journey,* London: Viking

Pennac, D (1984) *L'oeil du Loup*, Paris: Editions Nathan; Eng., Adams, Sarah (trans.) (2002) *Eye of the Wolf,* London: Walker Books

Preussler, O (1957) *Der kleine Wassermann,* Stuttgart: K Thienemanns Verlag; Eng., Bell, Nathea (trans.) (1960) *The Little Water-Sprite*, London: Abelard-Schuman

Pullman, P (1995–2000) *His Dark Materials* trilogy, London: Scholastic

Schami, R. (2004) *Die dunkle Seite der Liebe*, Munich: Carl Hanser Verlag

Sebald, W G (2001) *Austerlitz*: Munich, Carl Hanser Verlag; Eng., Bell, Anthea (trans.) *Austerlitz*: London, Hamish Hamilton

Mind the Gap

Sarah Adams

This, the last talk of the day, is given in that crepuscular hour the French refer to as 'entre chien et loup' – the twilight zone when it's hard to tell between whether what's out there is a dog or a wolf; which is worrying given that part of this talk is about a book called *The Eye of the Wolf*. There are no bullet-point projections.[1] But if I manage to keep technically on top of things, I'm hoping to do a spot of DJ-ing and you'll be able to listen to some music and radio clips instead...

I've been visiting primary schools around London recently for The Children's Bookshow. In the workshops I've been running with Year 3s, we've been talking about Pennac and *L'Oeil du Loup*. It's the tale of a young orphan called Africa and a wolf from the freezing wastes of the 'Barren Lands.' These two characters find themselves staring at each other through the wire meshing of a city zoo cage. Technically, their worlds and life experiences are such poles apart that they have everything and nothing to say to each other. When the wolf, for instance, stares into Africa's eye and sees projected onto the boy's iris, or the twinkle of his pupil, as if onto a cinema screen, the arid wastes of the Sahara, his only means of interpreting what he sees is as 'Big hills of snow, as far as the eye can see. A strange, yellow kind of snow that creaks and crunches with every step, and slides in patches like the snow in Alaska.'

This impasse of comprehension reminds me of a quote I once came across from the anthropologist Claude Levi-Strauss – whose observation went something like this. He argues that there's no point in travelling, because either you encounter something so extraordinarily different from what you know that you have no means of assimilating or understanding it; or else you engage with something compatible with what you already know, and you instantly homogenise it. Either way, Levi-Strauss would argue, why leave the armchair? Why not, I might counter. But of course it's not always practical to leave the armchair, and that's where translators come in – as voyagers in language whose job it is to bring the meaning back to you. To ferry it over. To go-between. To dialogue.

Of course, Africa and Blue Wolf, as we discover the wolf is called, *do* find ways of communicating and making sense. They do this through the power of storytelling, through flexing their imagination, and through the understanding that our ability to imagine ourselves into someone else's shoes is just that, a muscle, that requires flexing and discipline and practice, as well as beefing up or making more sinuous. And they communicate despite the wolf's handicap of only being able to use one eye. In fact, dialogue can only open up once Africa of his own volition closes one of his eyes too, in sympathy, so that suddenly communication can begin to happen from a level starting point.

But none of this necessarily made life any easier for me when I found myself faced in a London school with a class of predominantly Bengali Year 3s. They were already adept translators and interpreters at home, even if they didn't think of themselves as such, but story-telling in French was possibly not first on their hit-list of useful life skills.

As is so often the way, the best workshops are the ones that take you totally by surprise. Precisely because second and even third languages were a given, the children at Columbia Road primary had already put aside all prejudices about strange new sounds passing through their lips. They were very ready to play the game of communication in another linguistic incarnation. They were riveted when I read a chunk of the story in French – because we'd laid down enough story-telling blocks for them to build on, and because they were open enough to the idea that sometimes you can catch sense from the sound and flow of words, even if you don't have a talking dictionary to hand.

And so it was through *sound* that I tried to open the doors of Frenchness and, beyond that, to Francophonie to them. I may not have couched it in these exact terms, but my point was that to get to grips with contemporary French is to access that whole world of French-speaking countries that is the legacy of colonial history. So we embarked on a geography discussion as I explained that Daniel Pennac is a Corsican, born in Casablanca, Morocco, who grew up in Africa and South East Asia and who now lives in the multicultural district of Belleville in Paris. And I suggested that his taste for cultural mixity or 'métissage', for 'not being surrounded by people just like me' - which is so prevalent in his writing – could as well have been reflected in, say, the music he listened to as a child.

Inside his childhood bedroom, in Casablanca, I suggested, he might have heard something as quintessentially French as *George Brassens Chante les Chansons de son Enfance...* Lean out of that very same bedroom window, I went on, and he might have heard something altogether different sounding. I was admittedly cheating a bit, since the extract I played them was care of the contemporary Grenoble-based group Gnawa Diffusion (whose name loosely translates as 'broadcasting desert rhythms'). Lead singer and politicised lyricist Amazigh Kateb[2] is the son of Algeria's late great novelist, poet and playwright Yacine Kateb. But Gnawa's musical spirit – as with the Paris-based 'Orchestre Nationale de Barbes' (which is comparable to calling yourself 'The National Orchestra of Brixton') - is rooted in that century-old encounter between North African desert or mountain music and the big city.

So, lean out of his Casablancan bedroom window and Pennac might have heard the raw ingredients for if not the literally breathtaking sound. Suddenly, back in the classroom, there were ripples of excitement at the introduction of familiar sounds, and we were talking about Arabs and Berbers and Kabylia as well as West Africa, rather than just 'le Metropole.' World music was beginning to create a framework for approaching world books.

At a later stage in the workshop, I used film-style subtitles I'd blown up big for some of the questions that Africa got asked on his first day at school, when all the other children at school refused to believe that someone could be named after an entire continent. One of these questions: 'Tu sais jouer au Belvedere?' is a self-consciously invented question by Pennac. It refers to the made-up or group-specific games that help define a child's sense of group identity. I was asking my workshop participants to come up with suggestions for names of games they might ask Africa if he knew how to play? At first, the usual sporting contenders were offered up: volleyball, football, tennis, hockey…What about games other people haven't heard of, I prompted them? We progressed conservatively to hide-and-seek, bulldog … Still no deviation from public meaning. Then, little by little, the children began to realise they were free to suggest precisely the kinds of playground-specific names that were usually discouraged from letting through into classwork: 'satsuma' and 'duck-duck-goose' are the two that stuck in my head. In this translation game of creativity and complicity, the children understood the crucial leap any translator must make in terms of re-visiting and inhabiting the original word, capturing its playfulness and sense, and finding a way to make it speak in a new language. This is the point where the Sahara ceases being just 'yellow snow' and becomes a whole new concept: desert sand.

Back up in Kentish Town, at another workshop, the unforgettably named Godswill from the Congo asked me why I was a translator. I offered up something about loving dialogue and exclamations in different languages, and the challenge of finding a way to make that work in English. The example I gave was of getting across, say, the sense of 'Oh dear!' 'Oh la la la la la la…' I riffed, trying to show how much you can play with the musicality of sound in the French. And I pointed out how I also had a lot of fun with the ping-pong ball equivalent in Greek: 'Po po po po po po po.' There was a broad grin on Godswill's face and his hand shot up: 'I know how to say 'ouch' in my home language' he announced. 'What's that, Godswill?' his teacher asked. 'Ai!!' Now we were talking.

Communicating across the Peripherique

Today, more than ever, there are two versions of France – on the one hand *la belle vielle France:* the 'old skool' baguette and beret on a clapped out bike of George Brassens' childhood; and on the other, for example, Gnawa

Diffusion's spirit of francophony. Indeed, in the headgear of lead-singer Amazigh, you can see this very spirit of fusion embodied: he wears a traditional Berber head-dress topped off with a Rastafarian hat.

The dismal events of autumn 2005 revealed the breakdown in communication between these two Frances. What we have is the legacy of friction between the Metropole or Hexagon of the mainland versus the DOMs and TOMs (overseas domains and territories) as well as the former colonies. More topically, the contradiction is between the wide-rise sprawling ghettos of 'challenging' *banlieues* (a term we might translate as 'suburban inner-city' where tower blocks are horizontal bars, sometimes stretching as far as 200m in length and which have been designated such an uninhabitable catastrophe they're now being dynamited) vs the manicured town centres of urban architects such as nineteenth-century Haussman. In Paris, at the time of the riots, I detected in a twenty-first-century city - divided from the 'cités' or projects by the peripherique - something positively medieval. It was as if that ring road had morphed into ramparts.

The implications of this divisiveness are no less significant when it comes to language. Ironically, a word such as 'racaille' – which we might translate as 'scum' or 'vermin' or 'hoodlums' or, more kindly, 'rabble' or 'riff-raff', and which was so inflammatorily used to describe the residents of the banlieue by France's Interior Minister Nicolas Sarkozy – is the very kind of word (usually in the mouths of the CRS, the riot squad police) that I agonise over how to translate when I'm on my home-ground of dealing in the business of slang.

More than ever, it is essential to get a handle on slang, to try to get it right, or, failing that, at least to have a sense of where it's coming from. Yes, of course, we must accept slang's whip-lash effect, the in-built obsolescence that goes with the territory; we must recognise that sometimes the best translation of slang is alternative humour or silence, or italics, or terse contraction or a shift in syntax or capturing the same dynamic by saying it otherwise. But whichever way we look at it, there is, undeniably, work to be done. Indeed, the poet Carl Sandburg once described slang as 'language that rolls up its sleeves, spits on its hands and goes to work'.

When I was researching the Youth language for the *Golem* series, I did so both in the Algerian quarter of Marseille and around the Tulse Hill Estate in Brixton where I was living. I'd like to quote directly from Paris-born, Stockwell-based Cleo Soazandry:

Sarah: So Cleo, you're bilingual in French and English?

Cleo: Mm hm, yes I am. I'm bilingual in French and English. And, um, basically back in France their slang is totally different, they actually talk backwards. So let's say, um, if you wanted to say 'hello' they will say 'lo-hey'! But obviously in French it sounds much better, and it's much funnier.

Cleo: Yeah, so… [coming] back to here now, and having, um, different words actually just put together, our slang it's fun but I just prefer the French slang.

Sarah: So, was French the first language that you learned to speak, or did you learn both English and French at the same time?

Cleo: No, French was my first language that I learned obviously back over there...
It's only when I came over here at the age of 12 that I went to school and everything and learned the language. And it was a bit tricky at first, you know having to keep up, and obviously coz I couldn't speak the language I did get into a lot of fights because I couldn't, you know, cuss back or anything, so I had to use my fists… [*laughter*] to get my point across. But then obviously, um, after that my mum did tell me that I had to stop because it's not a really good thing to fight. So the years after that, you know, I stopped fighting, just going into a bit of arguments but coz I was able to express myself, didn't have to go to that hooligan side of me [*laughter*]

Sarah: So are you trying to tell us that learning slang rescued you from being a hooligan? [laughter]

Cleo: Yes, I've got to admit that learning slang did rescue me from becoming a hooligan!

I'd also like to give you a fine example of one of the definitions from Live's slang dictionary: 'Flossin' vb – wearing lots of expensive clothes and jewellery: 'The Queen is always *flossin.*"

Of course, Live's references are often to Jamaican influenced-slang, (although there's plenty of crossover from East End 'Benglish' or Bengali-influenced slang too, with exclamations like 'nang!' or 'gully!') And it would, in the main, be inappropriate for me to square the circle by translating North African street culture into Jamaican or Bengali patois, thereby hatching some glorious turkey of an Ali G hybrid.

But that's not to say the research journey isn't a useful one. Or that developing knowledge of youth slang and an understanding of its shifting position in relation to the mainstream isn't crucial when it comes to having your finger on the pulse of current and accessible language.

Take the relationship of French *verlan* or backslang to race, for example. Far more frequently than in Anglo-Saxon texts, French characters are referred to by their racial origins. What this means when it comes to slang is that someone 'Arabe', given the backslang treatment, is referred to as a 'Beur' (or, for a woman, beurette) by slicing the word down the middle, flipping it and then playing with it some. Except that 'Beur' has now become such a staple of the mainstream term, the slangstas have flipped it again, transforming it into 'rebeu'...

Another word that fascinates me is 'Le Bled', which originates in the Arabic. For Caucasian French-speakers, this has come to mean 'a godforsaken village in the middle of nowhere'; while for Maghreb immigrants it refers to nothing less than the homeland or mother country. This startling semantic paradox was wonderfully encapsulated by the title of a shop near where I lived in Marseille. In a dazzling stroke, guaranteed to confuse, it called itself 'Ici le Bled': here is home (or alternatively, 'here is a godforsaken village in the middle of nowhere'). Because what both definitions agree on is the fact that wherever this elusive Bled may be, it's most certainly *somewhere else*.

So what is my point here? Why LIVE magazine? Why the intricacies of slang? The answer is really very simple. I just don't think we can ever over-state the importance of keeping up with both the contexts that we, as translators, are building bridges between. To know of what we speak and translate, to publish books about contemporary urban life for young people - with all the multi-ethnic questions about identity that implies, to keep current, be actively more accessible, more in a position to speak to young people, we don't just have to do our research – we have to be in dialogue with them.

And that is precisely the moment in Daniel Pennac's *The Eye of the Wolf* when we learn that the wolf is neither myopic nor partially sighted – he has chosen to close one eye because the world as he knew it didn't seem worth viewing in glorious technicolour. It is the moment at which he has the *largesse* of spirit to open his eye in order that the boy Africa can see again. And, unsurprisingly, the world looks a whole heap more interesting when you choose to take it all in, eyes wide open, and recognise that what you thought was the periphérique was actually the optical illusion of a blind-spot – although no less real for all that.

Notes

1.   There were however some music and radio clips.

60

2. Amazigh is the Berber word for 'Berber', whereas the name we are familiar with is a bastardisation of the Roman word for barbarians.

The Problems of Translating Humour: A Case Study of Adrian Mole

Elena Xeni

Introduction

In this paper, I shall focus on the problems which arise in attempting to render a humorous text from one language into another, looking in particular at the novel *The Secret Diary of Adrian Mole, Aged 13 ¾,* a book which has attracted an audience which ranges from teenagers to adults.

The Need for Humour

Humour, making a person laugh or smile, is the key to solving many problems; its importance in child development has often been emphasised by theorists (Ross, 1998; Katsiki-Gavalou, 1993). Adolescent school-children face many difficulties, both social and personal and often feel the need to understand or interpret particular situations. Reading humorous literature can provide one of the best answers to these needs. It excites, entertains, but most of all it can help them to eliminate problems and difficulties (Michailidou, 1998). Inglis observes, 'Laughter puts a meaning on the world. It is self-confident. A funny story is a way of turning things upside down in order to understand them better' (1981: 309). A further advantage of translated books in this area is that they expose readers to a wider range of cultural values than material from their own background would be able to do. Experts in multicultural education frequently emphasise the importance of using literature to increase cultural awareness (Tway, 1989). Norton (1983) indicates that the use of multicultural literature can extend students' knowledge about parallel cultures by exposing them to the differences and similarities between their culture and that of other groups. Incorporating literature from different cultures into the curriculum can expand students' awareness and decrease negative stereotyping of individuals from other cultures (Litchner et al., 1973).

Problems in Translating Humour

Translators always have to contend with aspects of lexis, grammar and syntax that need to be rendered in a way that will communicate with children who are unfamiliar with them, and humour tends to pose more difficulties than do most areas. But perhaps the first requisite is to attempt to define what humour is. However commonplace it is in everyday life, humour seems to be rather elusive as a theoretical concept. One of the difficulties in defining it derives from the fact that the terminology used to describe it is not explicit. I have suggested (Xeni, 2005b) that humour coheres in utterances which are identified by the analyst on the basis of paralinguistic prosodic and discoursal clues, as invented by the speakers in order to be amusing, and

62

which are also perceived to be amusing by at least some participants. I have also observed that a wide range of contextual and linguistic clues are relevant to identifying instances of humour, including laughter, the speaker's tone of voice and the audience's auditory and discoursal response (Xeni, 2005a). Put more simply, I would suggest that humour is whatever seems to be funny and whatever evokes laughter, and thus can be detected by its effect (2005c, 2002). This is the definition that the present piece of work will accept, even though several limitations derive from basing research and pilot studies on a definition as such.

According to Holmes (2005), several problematic areas can arise derive from attempts to accept definitions like those mentioned above. Even if humour is whatever is intended to be funny, it may not always be perceived or interpreted as such. Much depends on whose perspective the definition focuses on: the speaker's, the audience's, the addressee's, or even the analyst's. The definition also does not give a basis for distinguishing between various forms of humour, such as jokes, sarcasm, irony and witty comments. Additionally, as Holmes suggests, accepting the particular definition means that queries regarding 'failed humour' also come up. Explaining that failed humour occurs whenever there is no response or when people feel amused, but do not show it, Holmes supports her views by pinpointing the results of recent research on 'Friends' episodes shown without the laughter track, where the particular audience fail to laugh or respond to the humorous sequences shown.

Priego-Valvere (2005) suggests that for humour to be justified, it is necessary to take into account the amount of humour and its different types and styles. Throughout the years, there has been research into such types as repressive, contestive and supportive humour, which have been judged as important, whereas Priego-Valvere talks about sick humour, family humour, black humour, death humour and teasing humour. Many styles of humour are also to be found in conversation, where differences may occur between single utterances and extended sequences, and between a collaborative and a competitive style. Different tones have also been researched; Holmes (2005) indicates that humour can have a teasing or friendly tone, whereas Priego-Valvere (2005) suggests the addition of black humour to these.

Last but not least, the role of humour is an area much discussed throughout the years. Being viewed as a cultural characteristic or element of humanity, humour has been studied for many years now in every part of the world. The academic study of humour cuts across many disciplines, as scholars explore the notion of a few traits common to humans across both time and distance. Humour has mainly been approached from educational, sociological, psychological and linguistic angles in relation to its entertaining and healing roles, whereas nowadays there is a trend to conduct research regarding its communicative role (Xeni, 2006a).

Humour in Literary Translation Studies

Humour is a challenging topic, and there is no doubt that it can be described as a specific genre of translation studies, raising several problematic issues, as happens with the translation of all culture-bound and languaculture specific elements (Xeni, 2006b & 2006d). Research shows that translators of humour have less latitude with a humorous text if they want it to function for the Target audience in as close a way as possible to how the Source text does for its audience. A successful translator will attempt to re-communicate in the Target Text those features of the Source Text which are relevant for the text to evoke laughter, even if this may mean departing from a strictly literal approach to translation.

The whole issue of translating humour is particularly complex, because a translator not only has to judge whether the Target Language Culture (TLC) reader understands the particular humorous situation in a given text, but also to know or guess whether that humorous situation functions as humour in the TLC. Thus, as humour is presented as a social languacultural characteristic/ element/ tool, the translation of humour needs to follow the norms accepted in the TLC. Balancing between Source Language Culture (SLC) restrictions and TLC demands, the translator of humour is engaged in what could be compared to an exercise in tightrope walking and the immediacy of effect can easily be lost (Xeni, 2005a & 2004b).

In the case of Literary Studies (Xeni, 2000), humour can bring up several issues when translated. In providing a commentary on the translations of three humorous books (corresponding to three age groups of children's literature), I found that humour translation presents both general (text type, style and register) and specific problematic areas. These latter generally involve lexis, and occur particularly in the field of the translation of poetry, colloquial speech (slang, argot, jargon, dialects, vulgarism, the vernacular, curse words, swearing language, etc.), and figurative language (proverbs, metaphors, irony, idioms, fixed expressions, similes). Idioms, fixed expressions and various cultural references are often encountered. Below, as a case study, is a discussion of a humorous novel, which is a challenging translational task, followed by some brief analysis of specific problematic areas that were encountered.

The Case of *The Secret Diary of Adrian Mole* from English into Greek

The book under consideration is a work of fiction, a fictional diary, written in reality by a middle-aged British Writer. Its target audience consists largely of teenagers and young adults, though it has also been widely enjoyed by readers older than this. Written in the style and conventions of a diary, it is

64

about an adolescent male growing up in England in the eighties, who keeps a diary with vivid details of the events of his everyday life, expectations and ambitions. I selected this book because of the universality of its appeal. It has met with great success all over the world and sold more than a million copies within a very short period, being translated into all European languages, and broadcast in 1982 on Radio 4 in the UK (Thomson, 1999). What made the novel an even bigger success was its humour, a culture-bound element that has been studied in every part of the world.

Adrian Mole is an adolescent boy growing up in a working-class community. He worries a great deal about his appearance and the development of his body, and though he is doing relatively badly at school, he nevertheless thinks that he is an intellectual and a talented poet. Readers join his Diary on New Year's Day, when he decides on his new year resolutions. The next few months see him getting involved in several comic events, and the account is peppered with humorous comments on modern life. When life's frustrations and inconsistencies become too much for him, he can always fall back on the intellectual medium which is the haven of all great writers like himself (in his own judgment): the poem.

Sue Townsend, the author, began writing the book after joining a Writer's Group in 1978. Much of the appeal of the character derives from the way he displays characteristics common to many adolescents: Hatherall comments, 'After all we all have been there (or somewhere close) already' (1997:30).

General and Specific Problems in Translating *The Secret Diary of Adrian Mole, aged 13 ¾* from English into Greek

Among the specific and general problems I encountered while attempting a translation of this novel, the fact that much of the original is very culture-bound and culture-specific presented a considerable challenge. Aiming at maintaining the identity of the original text and at the same time bridging the cultural gaps, as well as various linguistic differences arising when translating humorous extracts from English into Greek, I applied several approaches and did my utmost to provide a good quality translation. Additions, omissions, as well as reductions and shifts were applied in descriptions and dialogues in an attempt to create a humorous text.

An example of the kind of material which creates challenge occurs in a fairly typical passage of narrative and description, where Adrian describes a shopping expedition:

> We went to Sainsbury's this afternoon. My father chose a trolley that it was impossible to steer. It also squeaked as if somebody was torturing mice. I was ashamed to be heard with it. My father chose food that it is bad for you. I had to put my foot down and

insist that he bought some fresh food and salad.when we got to the check-out he couldn't find his banker's card, the cashier wouldn't take a cheque without it, so the supervisor had to come and stop the argument. I had to lend my father some of my birthday money. So he owes me eight pounds thirty-eight and a half pence. I made him write an IOU on the back of the till roll.

But I must say that I take my hat off to Sainsbury's, they seem to attract a better class of person. I saw a vicar choosing toilet paper; he chose a four-roll pack of purple three-ply. He must have money to burn! He could have bought some shiny white and given the difference to the poor. What a hypocrite!
(*The Secret Diary of Adrian Mole, aged 13 ¾*, 1991:58, April 4th)

Every generation has slang words and expressions distinguishing adolescent users from both younger children and adults. Slang is linguistically related to young people since 'it generally sounds odd on the mouth of an older person' (Holmes, 1997: 183) and is ephemeral, since 'it is sensitive to time and local culture' (Newmark, 1988: 95). In Adrian's diary my aim as a translator was to introduce the readers to the 'exotic of other cultures and times; (Bravo-Villasante in Klingberg, 1978: 49) as well as humour and the language of the particular social group. Based on these principles, I tried to find corresponding expressions. However, in some cases it was impossible to find a fully adequate equivalent in this form of colloquial speech, so I decided to make the Target Text less colloquial, since according to Leighton 'although attempts in recreations of colloquial speech can enrich a translation, they can also irreparably harm it' (1991: 126).

In the passage quoted above there are several instances of slang and colloquial language, something that occurs throughout the book as a whole. Among the many other examples of words being used in a colloquial and non-literal way are for instance, 'massive' in 'He said he couldn't see a spot, but he was just being polite because the spot is massive today' (1991: 20, Jan 17th); the word conveys Adrian's panic at a pimple which we learn later is actually quite small. Adrian often uses the word 'dead' with the sense of 'very', as for instance in 'Art was dead good' (1991: 25, Jan. 27th). A slang word which occurs very frequently is 'yukky', as in 'The vet showed me a plastic bag with lots of yukky things [objects that have been extracted from the stomach of the dog!] in it' (1991: 17, Jan 10th) and 'She [his grandmother] gave us a cup of Bovril and a piece of yukky seedcake' (1991:40, March 5th). In instances such as these, the translator may not always be able to find equivalents which will generate a similar degree of humour for the target language readers, and is unlikely to provide exact equivalents. In this instance, these three slang words related to teenagers' language were translated as following: 'Massive' → 'τεράστιο' [literally 'huge'], 'Yukky' → 'απαίσια', ['horrid'] and 'Dead' → 'πολύ' ['much'].

This passage also includes several instances of idioms, such as: 'I had to put my foot down,' 'I take my hat off,' and 'He must have money to burn,' all of which, if translated literally, could present a real problem to a reader unfamiliar with British culture. Fixed expressions – Adrian constantly uses 'Just my luck,' for instance, twice on the first page of the text, Jan.1st and 3rd (1991: 14) – demand from the translator a decision as to whether to search for something similar in the target language, or to widen the understanding of target language readers by translating literally and engendering a sense of the 'foreign'. Thus, I found myself applying Baker's (1992) suggestions for translating idioms and fixed expressions corresponding to three possible strategies: (a) finding an idiom / fixed expression of the same meaning and form; (b) finding an idiom / fixed expression of the same meaning but different form; and (c) finding an idiom / fixed expression of similar meaning but dissimilar form. Based on these principles, the idiom 'I take my hat off' translated as 'βγάζω το καπέλο' ['I take off the hat'] is an example of the first strategy, whereas the idiom 'It shared the fate of' is translated as 'Είχε την ίδια μοίρα' ['It had the same fate']. 'He must have money to burn,' translated as 'αυτός θα πρέπει να έχει λεφτά για πέταμα' ['he must have money to throw/waste'] and 'I had to put my foot down,' translated as 'Χρειάστηκε να πατήσω πόδι' ['I needed to step on a foot'], are idioms of the second translation strategy. Finally, the idiom 'to spill the beans,' translated into its target language equivalent 'να τα ξεφουρνίσει όλα' ['to take everything out of the oven'] is an example of the third strategy.

Taking into account that Baker (1992) treats both idioms and fixed expressions the same way when refers to their translation, the humorous fixed expression 'Just my luck' translated as 'Τι ατυχία' ['what unluckiness'] is an example of an expression that shares the same meaning when translated but a dissimilar form, leading to the third translation strategy.

Cultural references, a category consisting basically of proper names referring to places, magazines, items and social groups, also involve the need to consider whether to translate the actual words, or to take a parallel instance in the target language. There are many such examples in *Adrian Mole*, such as 'Sainsbury's' in the passage above, and the names of newspapers ('the *Morning Star*,' 1991: 25, Jan 6th), cigarettes ('Woodbines', 1991:28, Feb.3rd), and comics ('the *Beano'*, 1991: 21, Jan 18th). Aiming at providing 'knowledge of the ST languaculture and in an effort to maintain any humorous elements, I transliterated the names of the places and applied additions identifying what these are in the ST languaculture. These additions have either the form of a simple word addition, as in the first three examples below, the form of explanatory translation (addition of phrases within the text, as in the fourth example), or footnotes (addition of information out of the text).

Sainsbury's → η υπεραγορά Σαίνσμπουρυς (the supermarket Sainsbury's)
Morning Star→ η εφημερίδα Μόρνιγκ Σταρ (the newspaper Morning Star)
Woodbines → τα τσιγάρα Γούντμπαινς (the cigarettes Woodbines)
Beano annuals→τα κωμικά περιοδικά Μπινόου (the comic magazine Beano)

Translating Poetry

Poetry has always been an area of particular difficulty for the translator. Adrian's 'poetry' is of course (by the intent of the author) very far from a classic text, but it nevertheless presents the translator with the need to decide whether to attempt to capture elements such as rhyme and rhythm in the target text, even though the 'poems' have an informal style and fairly low register.' An example of a poem is this, followed by the Greek translation in which I managed to keep the same rhyme scheme and create a humorous impact, largely because of freedom with the vocabulary, generally less controlled in literature for young adult readers.

The Tap, by Adrian Mole

The tap drips and keeps me awake
In the morning there will be a lake
For the want of a washer the carpet will spoil
Then for another my father will toil.
My father could snuff it while he is at work
Dad, fit a washer don't be a burk!
(1991: 18, Jan 13th)

Η βρύση, του 'Αντριαν Μολ

Η βρύση στάζει, ξύπνια μ'αφήνει
Κι ίσαμε το πρωί θα υπάρχει λίμνη
Για ένα λαστιχάκι το χαλί θα χαλάσει
Και για ένα άλλο ο μπαμπάς θα κοπιάσει
Μπορεί να το φτιάξει καθώς είναι στη δουλειά
Μπαμπά, φτιάξ' το λαστιχάκι, σταμάτα να χασομεράς!

[The tap drips, leaves me awake
And until the morning there will be a lake
For the want of a washer the carpet will spoil
And for another one my father will toil
He can fix it while he is at work
Dad, fix the washer, stop wasting time!]

Conclusion

The discussion above has revealed some of the major problematic areas I encountered while translating the humorous novel *The Secret Diary of Adrian Mole aged 13 ¾* from English into Greek. In fact, the list of areas that arose for discussion while translating humorous material from English into Greek seems endless; there has been no opportunity here to discuss the translation of pronunciation; political, social or further cultural factors; connotations; taboo language; sex and religion; or grammar and syntax issues (class shifts, unit shifts, intra-system shifts, structure shifts and punctuation).

It is obvious that literature for children and young adults can meet some of the essential needs of this readership. Research shows that it is easier for children and young adults to assimilate new information when it is presented within the structure of a story. Thus, storytelling is a beneficiary activity which can meet their needs and help them to answer some of their questions about life. It is also clear that the translation of literature is an activity that gives a larger audience a chance to experience the benefits of what has been written in another language.

There are many other issues which would benefit from further research, such as consideration of the translation of the diary form; how literature can aid interdisciplinarity, multiculturality and cross-culturality; how literature for children and young adults can be related to heritage maintenance; the translation for children and young adults of material related to new technologies. Translation is an act which can lead to increased cross cultural understanding. Humour translation in particular can be a re-communicative act which can aid efforts to eliminate failures of communication between peoples.

Bibliography

Primary Text

Townsend, S (1991; first published 1982), *The Secret Diary of Adrian Mole aged 13 ¾*, London: Methuen

Secondary Texts

Anderman, G & Rogers, M (eds.) (1999) *Translation for Professional Purposes*, University of Surrey: GITS

Babiniotis G (1998) *Lexico tis Neas Ellinikis Glossas*, Athens: Kentro Lexicologias

Baker, M (1992) *In Other Words: A Coursebook on Translation*, London: Routledge

Bravo-Villasante, C (1978) 'Translation Problems in My Experience as a Translator,' in Klingberg G et al (eds.) *Children's Books in Translation: The Situation and the Problems,* Stockholm: Alqviste & Wiksell International, pp46-50

Catford, J (1989) 'Translation Shifts,' in Chesterman A (ed.) *Readings in Translation Theory,* Helsinki: Oy Finn Lectura Ab, pp 70-79

Collins *Cobuild English Dictionary* (1998) London: Harper Collins

Durham, A (1978) 'Translation-Art, Science or Craft,' in Klingberg G et al (eds.) *Children's Books in Translation: The Situation and the Problems,* Stockholm: Alqvist & Wiksell International, pp104-112

Fry, S (1998) 'The Development of Personal Meaning and Wisdom in Adolescence: A Reexamination of Moderating and Consolidating Factors and Influences, in Wong, T P & Fry, P S (eds.) *The Human Quest for Meaning: A Handbook of Psychological Research and Clinical Applications,* Mahwah: Lawrence Erlbaum, (pp.91-110)

Hatherall, G (1997) 'Adrian Mole: 'Coping with Cultural References: What are Woodbines in French, German and Spanish?", *Linguist* 36/2, 30-33

Holman, M (1998) 'Of Pasternak and Parsnip or What Translators do with Names,' in Anderman G and Rogers M (eds.) *Translation for Professional Purposes,* University of Surrey: GITS

Holmes, J (1992) *Introduction to Sociolinguistics,* London: Longman

Holmes, J (2005) 'Humour, Gender & Communities of practice', *3rd European Workshop on Humour Studies,* University of Bologna, Bertinoro, Italy, May 2005

Holmes, J & Schnurr, S (2005) 'Politeness, Humour and Gender in the Workplace: Negotiation Norms and Identifying Contestation,' *Journal of Politeness Research* 1, 1: 73-93

Hoff-Ginsberg, E (1997) *Language Development,* Florida: Florida Atlantic University

Hunt, P (1994) *An Introduction to Children's Literature,* Oxford: Oxford University Press

Hunt, P (1991) *Criticism, Theory, & Children's Literature,* Cambridge: Basil Blackwell

Inglis, F (1981) *The Promise of Happiness: Value and Meaning in Children's Fiction*, Cambridge: Cambridge University Press

Katsiki-Givalou, A (1993) *Children's Literature: Theory and Practice*, Athens: Kastaniotis

Klingberg, G et al. (1978) *Children's Books in Translation: The Situation and the Problems*, Stockholm: Almqviste & Wiksell International

Knowles, M & Malmkjaer, K (1996) *Language and Control in Children's Literature*, London: Routledge

Leighton, L (1991) *Two Worlds, One Art*, Illinois, US: Northern Illinois University Press

Litchner, J H, Jonson, D W & Ryan, F L (1973) 'Use of Pictures of Multiethnic Interaction to Change Attidutes of White Elementary School Students towards Blacks,' *Psychological Reports*, 33, pp 367-372

Michailidou, M (1998) *Seminar: D1010: Children's Literature*, Nicosia: Paedagogical Institute of Cyprus

Nash, W (1985) *The Language of Humour: Style and Technique in Comic Discourse*, London: Longman

Newmark, P (1998) *Approaches to Translation*, Oxford: Pergamon Press

Newmark, P (1982) *A Textbook of Translation*, London: Prentice Hall

Norton, D E (1990) 'Teaching Multicultural Literature in the Reading Curriculum,' *Reading Teacher*, 44, 28-40

O'Connell, (1999) 'Translating for Children,' in Andreman G & Rogers M (eds.) *Word, Text & Translation*, Cleveland: Multilingual Matters, pp208-216

O'Dell, A (1948) *Socialisation through Children's Literature*, Cambridge: Cambridge University Press

Oittinen, Riita (1993) *I am Me - I am Other: On the Dialogics of Translating for Children*, Tampere: University of Tampere

Pargament, K I (1999) 'The Psychology of Religion and Spirituality? Yes and No,' *International Journal for the Psychology of Religion*, 9, pp3-16

71

Priago-Valvere, B (2005) 'Humour', *3rd European Workshop on Humour Studies*, University of Bologna, Bertinoro, Italy, May 2005

Rasinski, T V & Padak, N D (1990) 'Multicultural Learning through Children's Literature,' *Language Arts*, pp576-580

Ross, A (1998) *The Language of Humour*, London: Routledge

Stafylides A (1994) *Hyper Lexicon English/Greek-Greek English*, Athens: Stafylides EPE

Stavropoulos G (1998) *Oxford Greek-English Learner's Dictionary*, Oxford: Oxford University Press

Thompson-Wohlgemouth, G (1998) *Translating Literature for Children*, University of Surrey

Thomson, L (1999) 'The Grit beneath the Froth', *The Independent* 16 Oct.1999

Xeni, E (2000) *Translation of Children's Needs for Literature and Problems Related to their Translation*, University of Surrey

Xeni, E (2002) 'Minimizing Children's Worries, Anxieties and Fears through Translation: The Case of Translating Humour from English into Greek,' *The First International Research Summer School in Translation and Intercultural Studies*, The University of Manchester, July 2002

Xeni, E (2004a) 'Facilitating Cross-Cultural Communication and Understanding through Diary Humor Translation: The Case of *The Secret Diary of Adrian Mole, aged 13 ¾* by Sue Townsend,' *International Conference of Literatures in English*, Chennai, India, December 2004

Xeni, E (2004b) 'Translating Humour for Teenagers and Young Adults & Cross Cultural Communication,' *International Conference on Applied linguistics,* Victoria University, Wellington, New Zealand, Aug-Sep 2004

Xeni, E (2005a) 'Didactics of Translatology: Attempts to Investigate the Gap Between Academic-professional Translation from English into Greek,' *50th Anniversary of the Institute of Translation and Interpreting*, Monterey, California, USA, September 2005

Xeni, E (2005b) 'The Challenges of Translating Figurative Language as a Cross-Cultural Activity', *4th International Maastricht-Lotz Duo Coloquium on Translation and Meaning 2005*, Department of Translation and Interpreting,

Maastricht School of International Communication, Maastricht (The Netherlands), May 2005

Xeni, E (2005c) 'Humour Translation Challenges: The Case of Humorous Languacultural Elements/Situations from English into Greek', *3rd European Workshop on Humour Studies*, University of Bologna, Bertinoro, Italy, May 2005

Xeni, E (2006a) 'Think Aloud Protocols and the Translation of Literature for Teenagers and Young Adults,' *University of Ghent*, Brussels, January 2006

Xeni, E (2006b) 'Investigating Creativity Competence in Humor Translation: A Pilot Study Report,' in *Conference Proceedings on Translation and Creativity*, Portsmouth University. UK, November 2005

Xeni, E (2006d) 'Didactics of Translatology: Attempts to Investigate the Gap between Academic-professional Translation from English into Greek,' *Conference Collection - 50th Anniversary of the Institute of Translation and Interpreting*, Monterey, California, USA, September 2005

Communicating Russian Folk Tales

James Riordan

Priskazka [Prologue]

I have a confession to make. It was ˋlittle water' or vodka (voda means ˋwater', so adding the suffix ˋka' makes it into a diminutive - ˋlittle' or ˋdear little water') that first led me into the realm of Russian folklore. I was part of what was known in those days (1969) as a ˋfriendship delegation' to the Urals city of Yekaterinburg, then Sverdlovsk. To my everlasting foolishness I took Russians on at vodka swilling, matching them tumbler for tumbler, straight down the hatch. During the next three bedridden days in my hotel, I was visited by a headmistress, Anastasia Bushuyeva, and her eleven-year old pupils who sat by my bed, closed their eyes and told me folk tales of the Ural Mountains - of the Mistress of the Copper Mountain (who could turn into a lizard or a beautiful maiden), of the Malachite Casket and The Little Stone Flower.

I cannot say this was the best cure for a hangover, but it was far more of an unforgettable experience than bending my elbow. So grateful was I to the head and her young charges that, once home, I spent every spare moment writing down the stories from memory and checking them against a Russian version of Pavel Bazhov's *Uralskie skazy* (Urals Tales, translated Riordan 1974). My intention was to produce a collection that children could enjoy, while trying to be loyal to the Russian original - not an easy task, as many ˋtranslators' have discovered. Incidentally, I dislike the word ˋtranslator'; it does not do justice to someone who provides a folk tale text in another language. Maybe ˋcommunicator' is more appropriate.

My book, *The Mistress of the Copper Mountain: Tales from the Urals*, came out in 1974. I had never published a book before, and I clearly remember my excitement as I checked my name and dedication to those Russian schoolchildren in the few copies on the shelves of W H Smith's. Some time later I was awarded the Urals Peace Prize for the book and, more important, was made ˋFriend Number One' of Railway School No.1 in Sverdlovsk. My most cherished award!

After completing my degree I returned to Russia, this time to Moscow where I lived, first as a student, then as a translator, for the next five years. During that time and subsequently over twenty years I took part (you don't simply ˋlisten' to real folk-telling) in folk tales in Russian cottages from the Moscow region to Yakutsk in north eastern Siberia, from the shores of the White Sea to Russian hamlets in Tartary - told with all the naïve enthusiasm that I was later to witness amidst North American native peoples and the folk of southern Ireland. There followed other books in English of the popular

74

treasures of not only Russians and other Slavs (Ukrainians and Belorussians), but of Siberian tribes and the peoples of Tartarstan (Riordan 1976, 1978, 1989, 1990 & 2000).

As any `communicator' of folk tales knows, to speak the language is not enough; you must know the culture and the soul of a people, live cheek by jowl with them and, as the Russians say, consume a pood of salt with them.

Some Peculiarities of Translation

Like most folk tales, Russian stories have their own peculiar vocabulary and grammatical structures, what the great folklorist Alexander Afanasiev (1826-1871) called `folk tale rites'. It is impossible here, to non-Russian speakers, to explain these in full, but some oddities are translatable.

The tale often begins and ends with a special prologue/epilogue, on occasion totally unrelated to the rest of the text and the tale proper. The prologue, the priskazka, is often a device to get attention and to remind the audience that, if they want to hear the main or another story, they must pay up or at least give the storyteller a drink. A common postscript is as follows:

I was there, drank mead and yet,
N'ere did get my whiskers wet.

Or,
It was at the feast I heard this tale,
There it was I drank mead ale.
Though it flowed down my beard, my mouth stayed dry,
For never a drop passed my lips, swear I.

In other words, if you want to hear more stories, the storytellers needs to wet his whistle. Stock descriptions also exist for a whole range of actions: saddling a horse, the hero's journey, a hut on hen's feet, the witch's words at a new arrival, and so on.

There are also a number of details typical for the folk tale, such as: the execution of difficult tasks with the aid of various magic objects, such as a ball that rolls off into the forest showing the way; a doll that acts as a guardian angel; a magic table cloth; the water of life; a ring that transfers the hero to another place, etc. Further, in common with other European folklore, Russian folk tales abound in the rule of three: three sons or daughters; three tasks to fulfil; three wishes; a three-headed dragon; or a multiple of three. Thus `to the ends of the earth' in Russian is `beyond the realm of three times nine, in the kingdom of three times ten'.

Much of the vocabulary contains many obsolete and regional words and expressions. Among the grammatical peculiarities of folk tale language are the following:

- the wide use of suffixes that give an affectionate or diminutive tone: bratets (little brother), sestritsa (little sister), synok (little son), dedushka (Granddad), solnyshko (little sun), matushka (little mother);

- the use of pairs of nouns with virtually the same meaning: put-doroga (path-way), zhili-byli (there lived, there was), rat-sila (power-strength);

- the universal use of the second person singular (thou, thine) in addressing people;

- the use of a wide and rich variety of stock epithets: dremuchi les (dreamy wood), kosoi zayets (cross-eyed hare), sery volk (grey wolf), yasen sokol (clear-eyed falcon), dobry molodets (bold youth), krasnaya devitsa (fair maiden).

It is important to remember that the tales were often sung or narrated in a sing-song voice, so the word order and `standard' grammar are changed at will to fit the rhythm and mood of the storyteller. Of course, many of the `oddities' are no more than ordinary peasant speech that may be heard in any Russian village today (at least by the older people unaffected by the standardisation brought by television).

Three Genres of Tales

The folk tales of the Russian people are part of a heritage unparalleled in the oral literature of the world. Probably no other nation has preserved by word of mouth such an exuberance of tales, songs, proverbs, laments, riddles, topical humorous and satirical songs (chastushki), heroic poems, sayings, lyrical and historical ballads. Since this paper is concerned with folk tales, attention will be focused on three principal genres: fairy, animal and everyday. Each of these has its own distinct style, themes, scenarios, origins and audience. Occasionally actors and themes intermingle - for example, a princess may wander into an everyday tale, or two peasants tangle with the magic elements. But this inter-marriage is rare.

1. Fairy Stories

The traditional fairy stories are full of fantasy and stock descriptions: the heroes and heroines are bold/innocent young men and innocent/bold maidens, assisted by helpful beasts and magic implements; the villains are dragons, witches, sorcerers and evil kings. And the lucky number is three, thus presenting triads of witches, tasks, sons, princesses, nights and dragons' heads. Many themes and characters belong to Russian peasant myth and are undoubtedly as ancient as the inhabitants of the Great Russian

Plain. The greatest of all Russian poets, Alexander Pushkin (1799-1837), mentions some - the storytelling cat, the woodsprite and mermaid, *Baba Yaga* (the Russian witch) and *Koshchei Bessmertny* (Old Bones the Immortal) in the prologue (*priskazka*) to his long verse tale *Ruslan and Ludmilla*, set in pagan Russia, upon which the first great Russian composer, Mikhail Glinka, based his famous opera.

An oak tree green at river's bend
Its band of gold doth there suspend
Chained to a cat as wise as can be
Who day and night walks round that tree.
To the right he treads - a song to sing,
To the left he springs - a tale to spin.

Wonders abound: a woodsprite flits,
A water nymph in the branches sits;
And there amid the trampled ferns
Lie trails of beasts of yore;
A little hut on hen's feet turns;
No windows, nor a door.
There, forest and glade in marvels abound;
At dawn waves swish in gentle sound
Dancing lightly in rippled ring,
And thirty handsome heroes leap
In turn from glistening waters deep
Chasing a demon river king.
Lo! A bold young prince comes swiftly riding
Hard on the heels of an evil tsar;
There in the clouds a wizard is hiding
Waiting to seize a noble boyar
And bear him over the steppe afar.

In a dungeon deep a princess pines,
A big grey wolf his captive minds;
There, Baba Yaga in her mortar looms
Sweeping her traces away with her brooms;
There, Old Bones the Immortal hoards his gold,
There's Russian blood, there's Rus so old!

And I was there, I drank mead ales,
Under the oak tree great I sat
And listened while that wise old cat
Told me these ancient fairy tales.

Although not strictly folklore, this prologue provides an appropriate introduction to the heroes and demons of Russian fairy tale. We meet Baba Yaga, the witch who dwells in a revolving hut on hen's feet, sometimes with and sometimes without windows or doors. Typically, this old hag sits on a bench or on the stone stove, one leg curled beneath her, the other dangling, her hooked nose reaching to the ceiling. She rides through the air in an iron mortar propelling herself along with a pestle and sweeping her tracks away with a broom, stirring up terrible storms and leaving a trail of disease and death in her wake. She is, of course, a cannibal, specialising in devouring young children.

It is noteworthy that, in several tales, the witch is helpful (see *The Frog Princess*, and *Fenist - the Bright-Eyed Falcon*), thereby reverting to her earlier functions in the Mother Age of Folk Tales when she represented the priestess in whom all love and religion was embodied. The strong matriarchal influence on Russian folk tales is further apparent in that the main role is frequently played by the woman - who may be a bold warrior in the case of Marya Morevna, a wise maiden like Fair Vasilissa, or an enchanted wife like the Dove Maiden or the Frog Princess.

In most non-Russian variations of the Frog tale, the frog is a man, a prince; in the Russian version, the frog is a bewitched princess brought back to her proper form by the man's kiss. Similarly in west European versions of *Sleeping Beauty* and *Snow White*, the princess is awakened with a kiss; in the Russian equivalents, it is the man who is awakened with a kiss from the maiden who has had to undergo many difficult adventures to reach her destination.

With social change that made man the centre of the social group, especially as a result of Christian influence, the power and knowledge of women were broken down and the priestess (village herbalist, midwife, storyteller) became the wicked witch; her superior wisdom - dabbling in witchcraft - was reason enough to have her burned at the stake or, in Russia, set loose across the steppe tied to a horse's tail.

Another purely Russian fairy tale villain is Old Bones the Immortal who carries off fair maidens. Chained and imprisoned (as in Marya Morevna), he features in a forbidden chamber incident, common to the Bluebeard cycle of European tales. His Russian name *Koshchei* appears to derive from either the Old Russian or the Turkish (*koshchi*) meaning `prisoner'. The constant struggle between Russians and nomadic Turkic tribes, including the Polovtsians and Tartars, has bequeathed many names and figures to Russian tales. The name *Koshchei* became confused with the Russian word *kost*, meaning `bone' and so he also came to mean a skeleton or miser. The epithet `Immortal' means that he can only be killed in an exceptional manner, since his death is usually at the end of a needle, which is in an egg, the egg is in a duck, the duck in a hare, the hare in a stone chest and the chest at the top of an oak tree.

This brings us to another feature of Russian primitive belief: that the soul or heart dwells outside the body in some special place. In some tales, trees and plants are tenanted by the souls of the dead, thus becoming personified and endowed with human qualities. This superstition led to certain trees being regarded as sacred, to the legends of the speaking or bleeding plants, and to the planting of trees as life tokens. Even today in Russia, the silver birch is generally accepted as personifying women, and the maple or lime represents men. Memories of holy trees and groves are recorded (in English) in the name Holywood and Holyoak. Trees and other objects also feature as life tokens: if the hero dies, the tree falls or, as in *Marya Morevna*, the birds' feathers become bloodstained - because the hero's soul resides in them. In another version of this story, Prince Ivan leaves his silver spoon, fork and snuff box with his brothers-in-law and the implements, by their tarnishing, indicate his death. These primitive beliefs are associated with the present-day notion of breaking a mirror and, in Russia, a person whistling indoors - both said to summon up the devil and presage a death.

On the other hand, today's lucky charms, crosses, icons and other miraculous objects may be compared with the magic swords, self laying tablecloth or sack in the tales. A black cat or flying cranes today play similar roles to the helpful beasts of the tales - the grey wolf (in, say, *The Firebird*), the pike fish (in, say, *The Fool and the Magic Fish*) or the horse (in, say, *Chestnut Grey*). The probable significance of these animals is totemistic – that is they indicate a belief in the sacred nature of certain beasts and plants from which we claim descent.

The point of departure for all `fortunate youngest son' stories (which are common in Russian folklore) lies in the fact that the youngest born was originally the heir - a position which he gradually lost with changing social conditions. He would therefore be regarded by many as an heir deprived of his rights, so that a sentimental feeling for him would arise. This is evident in both *The Firebird* and *The Frog Princess*, in which the elder brothers try to deprive the youngest brother of his inheritance or some other prize. *Puss-in-Boots* is a well-known Western example. Similarly, it was once the last born in Russia who, when his parent died, performed the funeral rites; it was he who watched by the grave. When the other brothers refuse to take their turns at watching by the father's grave, it is the youngest who keeps the vigil or, as in *The Firebird*, guards a golden apple tree.

2. Animal Tales

Animal tales are said by the Russian folklorist Yuri Sokolov in his book *Rusky folklor* (Russian Folklore) to constitute about ten percent of the entire Russian stock of folk tales, a much smaller proportion than in Western Europe. Further, of the seventy themes in the Russian stories about animals, half are common to West European tales, the rest belonging exclusively to Russia. This relatively small place given to animal tales is due to the special nature of the medieval literature of Russia where, unlike Western Europe, the animal epos never gained great popularity - partly owing to the fear that most Russians had of wild animals (wolves, bears, even tigers) that inhabited the Russian forests.

To the mind of the primitive Slav, as of all primitive peoples, beasts with human attributes seemed perfectly natural. They shared the world with them, on their own level, and they admired the animals, feared them, respected them, ascribed to them the power of speech and a nature resembling their own. As the Polish anthropologist Malinowsky observed in his book, *Magic, Science and Religion* (1933):

> By their general affinity with man - they move, utter sounds, manifest emotions, have bodies and faces like him - and by their superior powers the birds fly in the open, the fishes swim underwater, reptiles renew their skins and their life and can disappear in the earth - by all this the animal, the intermediate link between man and nature, often his superior in strength, agility and cunning, usually his indispensable quarry, assumes an exceptional place in the savage's view of the world.

In the folk tale, therefore, each animal is distinguished by a certain characteristic and its own name. The heroine of Russian tales in the crafty fox or vixen, known as Liza (from *lisa*, the Russian for `fox'). Her patronymic is Patrikeyevna (though Goodness knows how an Irish father got mixed up with a Russian vixen!). She is variously known as the beautiful fox, the fox with an oily tongue, the gossip, the godmother, little sister, a deceiving midwife, a smooth-tongued seller of Communion bread or a mother-confessor. Unlike most Western tales (*Reynard the Fox* or *Brer Fox*), the Russian fox is female - perhaps another indication of the proximity of Russian tales to the Matriarchal Age.

By contrast to the sly fox is the stupid wolf, Levon, the grey fool, the stupid old wolf, the victim of the fox's tricks. The bear, Mikhailo Ivanovich or Misha, is the twig-crusher, the old grey peasant, clumsy and slow-witted, but also kind-hearted. The hare is a coward, the little grey fellow, the cross-eyed one. The cat is often the purring one (i.e. the storyteller), the zither player. She is known as Catafay Ivanovich. The cock is fearless, Petya (from *petukh*, the

Russian for `cock'). The goat is Kozma, from the Russian word for a goat, *kozyol*; and the ram is Baran Baranich, from *baran*, meaning ram.

Some of the tales are peculiar to Russian folklore, while others are more or less universal and may be found in the fables of the Greek slave Aesop and of Lafontaine, and in the tales of Uncle Remus, the Grimm brothers and Charles Perrault. Russian animal tales are usually short, related mainly for children and in the form of a dialogue in which the storyteller sings the little songs and imitates the voices and actions of the animals.

3. Everyday Tales

The third group of tales concerns everyday life; the stories are recounted in the form of anecdotes featuring peasants and soldiers, priests and merchants, rich and poor. Rarely do the characters have names: the most usual appellation is Lord, Priest, Soldier, Poor Man, Peasant. In this dream world it is the poor peasant or soldier who gets the better of the rich, the bigoted and the selfish. Authority is satirised in comical vein; the story is recounted for what it is worth, sometimes badly and starkly, without the ceremonial trimmings of the fairy tale or the childlike simplicity of the animal tale. Indeed, some everyday tales are definitely not for the ears of children, telling as they do of the amorous adventures of a priest, peasant or soldier.

Typical of this genre are the soldiers' tales, normally told by soldiers about soldiers. The hungry, homeless solider, going on leave or after discharge from the army, told his stories to gain a supper and a night's lodging. Like many other vagabonds of old Russia, he had to be cunning and resourceful to stay alive. Before the reform of military service in 1872, army recruits were taken only from the lower classes and military service lasted for as long as 25 years! This often meant forsaking one's village and family, mother and girl friend, for ever - a heart-breaking affair which gave birth to a special form of folklore: the laments for departing soldiers. In his tales the Russian soldier expels devils and punishes witches and mean old women. Being accustomed to all kinds of people and the rigours of army life, nothing surprises or frightens him: dead bodies, devils, witches, wizards, unclean spirits, even death itself. It is an interesting observation that devils in Russian tales are usually comical, hard-done-by figures, not the invariably evil and fearful objects they are elsewhere. As Afanasiev (1855-67) comments:

> In the greater part of tales featuring unclean spirits, the devil is not so much a fearsome tormentor of Christian souls as a rather pitiful victim of tricks played by wily heroes or heroines; he falls victim to a clever wife, he is beaten by a soldier's rifle butt, he comes under the blacksmith's hammer or he is cheated by a peasant out of his hoard of gold.

Tales of the mean, stupid and lustful priest abound in Russian folk satire, although few such tales passed the censor prior to 1917, the year of the Russian Revolution. In pre-revolutionary Russia, every village had its little church with its onion-shaped steeple and its married priest or 'pope'. The Russian peasant, though exceedingly religious and superstitious, regarded the priest more as a prayer leader, a necessary personage for births, weddings and funerals, than as a spiritual guide. The flock required only that he have a majestic manner, a fine beard and a deep, strong voice. By popular repute he was often greedy (being quite poor and having to bargain with the peasant for his fees), a boozer and a womaniser (life in the village being hard and dull). According to the philosopher Alexander Hertzen (1874): The Russian peasant is superstitious but indifferent in religious matters which are, in general, incomprehensible to him. He ritually performs all the rites, the entire external aspect of the cult. But he despises priests as greedy and indolent, living at his expense. The priest, deacon and their wives are invariably the butt of the mockery and scorn in all indecent folk tales and street songs.

Hence the proliferation of satirical stories about the clergy. For greater effect, the storyteller would often intone the words of the priest or deacon in the manner of the church liturgy, while singing those of the congregation in the manner of a folk tune. Devices resorted to by priests to extract donations from parishioners supply another common object of satire.

Tales on the 'rich and poor brother' theme highlight the problems of economic inequality between rich and poor peasants, even within a family - although family in this sense is more likely to be the extended family of the old Russian village, so that a 'brother' may be a distant cousin. Nevertheless, by contrast to tales which pit the peasant against the squire or merchant, the tales of discord between brothers heighten the intense feelings of greed, cruelty and disdain even for family ties. In the folk tales, the themes are usually of good and evil, with the poor man eventually becoming rich, and the rich man poor. Tales of corrupt judges who inadvertently help a poor man evade his fate are numerous; they often revolve around the poor man who conquers fate and a greedy, merciless rich brother who treats misfortune as a crime.

These everyday tales make up the majority of Russian folk tales, constituting about sixty percent of all material. Much of it is uniquely Russian, thereby providing a useful source of social investigation, a mirror of Russian peasant values.

The Storytellers

The unique artistry of Russian folk tales must in part be attributed to the storytellers (*skomorokhy*) who cultivated their storytelling art and passed down stories by word of mouth from generation to generation. These minstrels, jesters, blind peddlers, vagabonds of every sort, masters of the telling of a tale, were most welcome in the remote settlements. Some were so adept at their craft that they were able `to relate not only the whole night through, but for several days together'. So says Professor Yuri Sokolov in *Russky folklor* (1950/66).

At a time when modern life had not yet spread into the remotest corners of the countryside, storytelling was a favourite entertainment in the quietness and monotony of the long winter evenings, in a land where snow and ice cover earth and water for half the year. When the Sokolov brothers were recording folk tales, they recalled that fishermen would come and bargain with the storyteller who pleased them most, promising him a portion of their catch if he would accompany them on their fishing expeditions.

It is interesting that in Russia folk tales were for so long not simply tales to amuse the common people, but to entertain gentlefolk too. A good storyteller was a much-prized possession in many well-to-do homes, including that of the emperor or empress her/himself. The first Russian tsar, Ivan the Terrible, was said to be a great admirer of folk tales and had at Court three blind men who would take turns at his bedside, telling stories to lull him to sleep. The Russian poet, Alexander Pushkin, acknowledged his debt to his childhood nurse Ariana Rodionova for his great love of folk tales. Count Leo Tolstoy, as a child, fell asleep to the stories told by an old man who had been purchased by his grandfather for his skill at storytelling.

Folk tales recounted by serf nurses to young aristocratic gentlefolk provided themes for innumerable Russian masterpieces - from the music of Pyotr Tchaikovsky (*Sleeping Beauty, Swan Lake, Nutcracker*), Rimsky-Korsakov (*Sadko, The Snow Maiden, The Golden Cockerel, Sheharazad*) and Stravinsky (*The Firebird, Petrushka*) to the writings of Pushkin, Gogol, Aksakov and Yershov). Indeed, there can scarcely have been a Russian writer or composer of any stature whose work was not inspired at one time or another by memories of folk tales told in childhood.

But storytellers had not always been welcome. The tsar Alexei Mikhailovich, father of Peter the Great, had the *skomorokhy* rounded up and their tongues cut out. In the famous royal edict of 1649, as quoted in Zenkovsky (1963), it was proclaimed:

> Many persons stupidly believe in dreams, in the evil-eye and bird-song; and they propound riddles and tell fairy stories. By idle talk and merrymaking and blasphemy they destroy their souls.

Ironically, it was during the reign of Tsar Alexei Mikhailovich that the first records of oral Russian tales were made. But they were not published in Russia or in their mother tongue; ten tales were recorded by an Englishman, Samuel Collins (1619-1670), who worked in Moscow as royal physician during the 1660s. His stories, along with travel notes, were published in London in 1671 under the title `The Present State of Russia'. It was to be nearly two centuries before a collection of Russian folk tales was published in Russia.

Why, in the land of its birth, were records of the Russian folk tale so late in appearing? After all, Charles Perrault began publishing his French fairy tales in 1697 (*Contes de ma Mere l'Oye*) and the brothers Jacob and Wilhelm Grimm their German tales in 1812 (*Kinder und Hausmarchen*). The answer to this Russian riddle also explains why Russia's voice was silent for so long in literature generally. While other nations had their Shakespeare and Chaucer, Dante and Cervantes, Corneille and Racine, it was only in the 19th century that Russian literature came to life. An explanation for this late start must be sought in the role of the Church in Russia.

By its control of printed literature, the Russian Orthodox Church was able for several centuries to prevent the literate from reading the `fables of men'; they were not to be deflected from the `Divine Scriptures'. In any case, the idea of using written Russian, so intimately associated with the Church, for the coarse peasant language of the oral tales was thoroughly alien to the Russian tradition. Even when Pushkin attempted to imitate the folk tale, he was condemned for intruding peasant vulgarity into refined aristocratic society. Like other writers to follow, he was compelled to `prettify' the folk tale, often having to draw on Western sources, before it could be accepted. It was perhaps hardly surprising that the priests and nobility should find themselves lampooned by the folk whose lore they sought to suppress, or even by eminent Russian writers in their stylised folk tales. For example, Pushkin's satire on the clergy, `The Priest and His Workman Balde', was banned during his short lifetime, then published four years after his death as `The Merchant Ostolop and his Workman Balde,' and was only restored to its original version some forty years later.

Despite the dead hand of Church censorship, the l9th century saw the intensive recording and study of folk tales. In 1838 there appeared the first attempt at a collection of true folk tales - five stories under the title `Russian Folk Tales', by Bogdan Bronitsyn (1838), taken down, the Preface says, `from the words of an itinerant storyteller, a peasant from the Moscow region, to whom they had been related by his father as an old man'.

But the first significant and unsurpassed collection of Russian folk tales was that made by Alexander Afanasiev, whose vast enterprise appeared in eight volumes between 1855 and 1867, and contained as many as 640 tales - by far the largest collection of folk tales by one man anywhere in the world. Unlike the Grimm tales, Afanasiev's stories were taken down second-hand - from the records of other people. Only about a dozen stories were recorded personally by Afanasiev himself. Yet this modest lawyer from the Voronezh region became one of the most influential figures in Russian national culture. Generations of Russian authors, composers, artists and sculptors have drawn upon his subject matter and been inspired by it.

Afanasiev's interest and pride in the intrinsic beauty of Russian peasant language, at a time when aristocratic society was aping foreign fashions and conversing in French, brought him to admire folklore for its rich musical quality, its poetic artistry, sincerity, purity and childlike simplicity. He would surely have agreed with Pushkin (1841) that:

Our language is inherently beautiful and nowhere has it such breadth of expression as in folk tales. How marvellous they are - each one a poem! We must learn to speak and love Russian, not simply to admire its tales.

To Afanasiev, folk tales were primitive people's story of Nature: the heroes are the gods of sun, sky, light, thunder and water, while their foes are the gods of darkness, winter, cold, storms, mountains and caves. Because of this mythological approach, Afanasiev attached no value to information concerning the storytellers from whom the stories had been taken. He did not think style of delivery important, since folk tale, like language, was to his mind a product of collective work over the ages. Moreover, he saw nothing wrong in a stylistic revision of a tale, although he did not go so far in this respect as his principal model, the Grimm brothers. In fact, his editing is clinical; he does not seek to prettify his stories, to make them interesting for children. In at least a third of the tales he does not even indicate where the tales come from.

Beside fairy stories, his work contained many satirical animal tales and anecdotes. Not all of them evaded the censor and those that were published stirred up opposition in some quarters. The Moscow Metropolitan Filaret declared:

The legends published by Afanasiev are thoroughly blasphemous and immoral; they offend pious sentiment and propriety. Religion must be safeguarded from such profanity.

To this Afanasiev replied indignantly:

There is a million times more morality, truth and human love in my folk legends than in the sanctimonious sermons delivered by Your Holiness.[1]

But the tide of official encouragement was now turning and many in authority inclined to the view that the folk tales tended to corrupt by their coarseness, their satire (particularly against the clergy and nobility) and their peasant wit. In 1860, the censor responsible for vetting his works was dismissed and the police raided the printing works which published the tales. The owner was arrested and the second edition of the tales was confiscated and later burned. Soon after, Afanasiev's house was searched and he was summoned to appear before a special investigating commission. Afanasiev found himself disgraced, dismissed from his job and deprived of his Moscow house. At the end of 1865 Russia's greatest folklorist and eminent historian at last found work as a humble assistant clerk in a Moscow court. His home was now a cramped and damp room and this, along with hard work, caused his health to suffer.

More and more Russian writers, however, were acknowledging their debt to the man who had brought to light the prodigious repertoire of tales of the Russian people. In the spring of 1872, the eminent novelist Ivan Turgenev wrote a letter from Paris to the Russian authorities declaring that Afanasiev's literary work gave him the right to receive financial assistance for `security from hunger, cold and other discomforts.' He could not have known that Alexander Afanasiev, at the age of 45, had died of consumption in poverty and virtual obscurity six months previously.

Conclusion

With the march of time the old storytelling traditions seem to be fading in modern Russia. In town and village Russian children are more likely these days to cluster round the television set than to sit at the feet of *babushka* - `grannie', that last great font of oral magic. Such is progress. In Soviet times, children probably had more communion with folk art - tales, songs, dances and crafts - than did their sisters and brothers elsewhere in the industrialised world. Folk tale books, often exquisitely illustrated, were printed in abundance and formed the most popular category of children's literature. Afanasiev's collection, last published in three volumes in 1977 (in a printing of 150 000 copies), is today one of the most precious acquisitions of any library. New collections appeared, like that of Pavel Bazhov, which is where I started my acquaintance with Russian folk tales in that Urals hotel room.

Somewhere, perhaps in the depths of Siberia, the tales live on. More read than recounted, they remain a colourful part of Russian life and language, the heritage of a people proud of the folklore that originated with the early Slav tribes on the Great Russian Plain.

Notes

1. Quoted in Produminiski (1974)

Bibliography

Afanasiev, Alexander (1855-1867) *Narodnye Russkie Skazki v 5 Tomakh,* Moscow/St Petersburg

Bronitsyn, Boris (1838) *Russkie Narodnye Skazki,* Moscow/St Petersburg

Collins, Samuel (1671) *The Present State of Russia,* London

Hertzen, Alexander (1874) *Byloye i dumy - My Past and Thoughts,* London

Malinowski, Bronislaw (1933) *Magic, Science and Religion,* Cambridge: Cambridge University Press

Produminski, Vladimir (1974) *A Rasskazat vam Sskazku?* Moscow

Pushkin, Alexander (1841) *Russkie Skazki,* Moscow/St Petersburg

Riordan, James (1974) *The Mistress of the Copper Mountain. Folk Tales from the Urals* by Pavel Bazhov, London: Frederick Muller

Riordan, James (1976) *Tales from Central Russia,* London: Kestrel Books

Riordan, James (1978) *Tales from Tartary,* London: Kestrel Books

Riordan, James (1989) *The Sun Maiden and the Crescent Moon: Siberian Folk Tales,* London: Canongate

Riordan, James (1990) *Russkie Narodnye Skazki,* Moscow Russky Yazyk; London: Collets

Riordan, James (2000) *Russian Folk-Tales,* Oxford: Oxford University Press

Sokolov, Yuri, (1950/1966) Smith, C R (trans.) *Russian Folklore,* Hatboro, Pennsylvania, US: Folklore Associates

Zenkovsky, S A (ed.) (1963) *Medieval Russia's Epics, Chronicles and Tales,* New York: Dutton

Found in Translation: How US Publishers Select Children's Books in Foreign Languages

Annette Y Goldsmith

Introduction

Literary translations (both fiction and nonfiction) serve an important purpose in connecting young readers in the US with stories from the wider world. In translations, children can discover worldviews different from the ones they already know. Translations introduce children to authors they would not otherwise be able to read, unless they read in the original language and have access to books in that language. According to Jella Lepman, founder of the International Youth Library (IYL) and the International Board on Books for Young People (IBBY), books from other countries, including translations, build international tolerance and understanding through 'a bridge of children's books' (Lepman, 2002). Lepman's post-World War II vision of furthering international understanding through children's books has been carried on by the institutions she founded, and continues to influence the contemporary children's book world (Tomlinson, 1998; Jobe, 1996; Jobe, 2001; Joels, 1999; Freeman & Lehman, 2001; Lo, 2001; Stan, 2002; and Roxburgh, 2004). If anything, this mission has grown in importance in the increasingly globalised world.

Why So Few Translations?

Though translations fill a unique information need, pitifully few are published in the US Tomlinson (2002: 14) states that translations probably make up no more than 1% of US children's book production. In their annual report on the state of US children's publishing, the Co-operative Children's Book Center notes only 13 translations published in 2004: 'six novels from France, three from Germany, one each from Belgium, Denmark, Israel, and Italy.' (Horning et al., 2005:16) In continental Europe, by contrast, 30 to 70 percent of publishing for young people consists of translations (Jobe, 2001:782). Jobe actually says 'European countries,' but it is clear from his comments about the notorious lack of interest in translations on the part of the English-speaking world that he is referring to continental Europe.

Publishing children's translations is generally considered a money-losing proposition: translations 'tend to be expensive, time-consuming, and unsuccessful in the marketplace.' (Roxburgh, 2004:48) Though the following excerpt refers to publishing in the United Kingdom, it also describes the situation in the US:

> But these days, more and more mainstream publishers are owned by big multi-national corporations that are interested only in profit,

and in nothing else whatsoever. And it costs money to translate books, because it's a demanding intellectual activity and there aren't many people who can do it well, and publishers are reluctant to spend money on producing books that booksellers won't sell, and booksellers are reluctant to give space to books that readers don't want, and readers don't want books they've never seen reviewed, and literary editors won't review books if the publishers don't spend much money on advertising. And it all goes round in a circle, and outside the circle is the rest of the world. (Pullman, 2005: 23)

Scope and Purpose of the Study

I am concentrating in this paper on how US editors acquire and publish English translations of books in foreign languages, so the publishing of translations in continental Europe is beyond the scope of my study. Several of the editors I interviewed raised the issue of Americanisation of texts from other English-speaking countries. This is an important aspect of translation, but peripheral to this study, and so omitted from my discussion.

In spite of all the obstacles mentioned above, some US publishers take risks to bring translations to young readers. How do they do it? There is anecdotal information on the process (for example, Bean, 2003), but no systematic research. Klingberg (1978) polled participants at a landmark symposium on children's books in translation in order to identify the areas they thought were most in need of research. 'Ways of selecting books for translation' was one of the five topics identified.

To the best of my knowledge, my study, 'Found in Translation', is the sole response to Klingberg's call for research on this topic. It is a qualitative, exploratory study that investigates how successful acquisitions editors, the gatekeepers most directly responsible for publishing translations, make their decisions. Editors whose houses had won the Mildred L Batchelder Award (described below) were considered successful at publishing translations. The qualitative data from this study will also be used to develop a web-based questionnaire to be sent to US children's book publishers about their attitudes towards publishing translations. By using both qualitative and quantitative approaches, a fuller picture should emerge.

Mildred L Batchelder Award

The Mildred L Batchelder Award is an American Library Association (ALA) award given annually to a publishing house for an outstanding children's book originally published in a foreign language in a foreign country and then translated into English for the US market. Books must have cultural context; folk tales and most picture books are not considered. The Association of Library Service to Children (ALSC), a division of the ALA, administers the award, which was first given in 1966; honor books were added in 1994. 'ALSC gives the award to encourage American publishers to seek out superior children's books abroad and to promote communication among the peoples of the world' (ALA, 2006). ALSC defines children as aged 0-14. The Mildred L Batchelder Award winners and honor books typically also appeal to young adults, defined by the Young Adult Library Services Association (YALSA), another ALA division, as 12-18 year olds. Most of the books discussed fall into the 12-14 children's/young adult crossover category. I will henceforth use the term 'Batchelder books' to refer to both the winners and the honor books.

The Interviews

A purposive sample of five key informants (two women and three men) was drawn from the different publishing houses that had most frequently won the Batchelder Award. They were all very experienced children's book editors, with an average of 22 years in the industry. In the case of small houses, or imprints of larger houses, the editor who acquires the book may also be the publisher. All described themselves as monolingual; most had some knowledge of languages other than English, but not to the level of fluency. These editors constitute elite subjects, so appropriate interviewing techniques were used. 'Elite individuals are considered to be the influential, the prominent, and the well-informed people in an organization or community and are selected for interviews on the basis of their expertise in areas relevant to the research' (Marshall & Rossman, 1995: 83). The advantages of elite interviewees applicable to the publishing field are that they have possibly unique, valuable information; can often provide the 'big picture'; are more likely to be familiar with the legal and financial side of publishing; and will be conversant with policies and plans. The disadvantages are that they may be inaccessible without an introduction; may take charge of the interview; and generally place greater demands on the interviewer (Marshall & Rossman, 1995: 83). I also used the techniques of unstructured interviewing (Fontana & Frey, 1994: 366), which allow the flexibility of adjusting one's questions and adding prompts and probes as necessary.

The study's interview guide was pre-tested with two Canadian editors of comparable status to the US interviewees so as not to use up the fairly small pool of US editors. Adjustments were subsequently made to the interview guide. The questions were individualised and provided in advance. Allowing the editors preparation time meant that I could extract the most information possible out of the short time we had for the interview. There was an added bonus: one editor went back to his files and produced his reader's report, so did not have to rely on memory for his initial reaction to the book in question.

After obtaining permission from my university's Institutional Review Board, and informed consent forms from the interviewees, confidential interviews averaging 40 minutes were conducted by phone in the spring of 2005. The interviews were recorded for transcription at WFSU, the local National Public Radio station. Missing the physical information of a face-to-face interview is unfortunate, but a telephone interview still allows more engagement than an email interview. Each editor was queried about his or her most recent Batchelder book, if there was more than one. (In some cases the editor's Batchelder book was not the one published by the house originally contacted, but by a house where the editor had formerly been employed.) The books were published from 1995-2004 by five different houses, and were written in four different languages (Dutch, German, Hebrew, and Turkish). Though the focus was on their Batchelder books, editors discussed their own and others' books. In order to share some of the examples presented, but still protect confidentiality, I wish to emphasise that mention of a book or author does not imply association with the editors interviewed. For example, author Cornelia Funke's name came up often because her books sell so well. That does not necessarily mean her editor was among the interviewees.

The interview guide covered:

- years of experience in children's publishing

- feelings about publishing translations

- the narrative of how the Batchelder book was acquired

- important business and personal factors in publishing the book

- troubling aspects of the process, including the role of controversial elements in the book

- perceived openness of US houses towards publishing translations now versus five years ago.

I saw the process as a sense-making exercise for the editors, who were reflecting on how they accomplished the difficult task of publishing translations. I therefore drew on Brenda Dervin's sense-making theory in designing the interview questions: '...Sense-Making assumes that people have gaps in situations, that they bridged these gaps, and that they put their new sense to work in guiding their behavior.' (Dervin, Foreman-Wernet, & Lauterbach, 2003: 256)

Findings

I will discuss the major themes that emerged from the analysis under the headings of motivations, problems, resources, information channels, and publication climate. I will then discuss the implications of these themes for the research question. Finally, I will provide a conclusion about what might improve the state of translation for children in the US.

Using Adobe's PDF reader and Microsoft Word's search functions, the interviews were transcribed and organised into the following themes:

Motivations

In describing why they publish translations, the editors focused on their passion for their work, enriching readers, risk-taking, and hope for a bestseller even though the odds are against it.

Passion for story: the word 'passion' came up in every interview. These editors select stories that they are passionate about. They are all committed to publishing translations, and describe it as 'a labour of love.'

Enrich readers: they wish to share with children the rich literary and cultural experience they themselves gained from the book. Some editors expressed literary reasons to publish translations, some pedagogical, some both. They felt that introducing young readers in the US to wonderful writers from other countries would broaden their perspectives. They hope to promote tolerance and understanding through good stories. It is not unusual for them to publish the first English translation of an author who is wildly popular and prolific in his or her home country and widely translated outside of the US. Not surprisingly, US editors want their own English-language books to be translated so the exchange can go the other way as well.

Risk-taking: they are not cowed by the threat of challenges to their books. Some even seem to revel in their role of bringing controversial books to the market.

Hope for bestseller: they choose books that fit their house's publishing mandate and which will sell, at least moderately, though significant sales are not expected. However, German writer Cornelia Funke's success in English translation (*The Thief Lord, Inkheart*, etc.) has galvanised the industry. Even though editors know that for every successful author such as Funke, there are hundreds of translations that fail, they still hope to find the next big bestseller.

Problems

Editors face many obstacles to publishing translations. They can expect relatively low sales and must figure out how to market books that do not have a ready audience and may not have excited much interest. They must rely on others for language skills they do not possess themselves, find appropriate translators, and deal with the complex process of translation, which requires much time but allows less editorial input. Finally, they must decide if potentially controversial elements are worth bad reviews, which will limit sales.

Poor sales: winning a major US children's book award such as the Newbery or Caldecott ensures strong sales and broad readership. Winning the Batchelder, the editors agree, is a very welcome recognition, but the resulting boost to sales is not substantial. Even winning this prestigious award is not enough to offset the high production costs and typically poor sales. In fact, a non-Batchelder book may sell more copies than a Batchelder book. Income from rights sales is minimal. This situation is not limited to children's book publishing; with few exceptions, literary translations published for adults are also a hard sell.

Marketing: the strong interest in multicultural education (sensitising children to diversity) would seem to provide an obvious market for translations. However, multicultural education focuses on the US experience, i.e. immigration narratives, not on the lives of people in other countries. In other words, we tend to celebrate diversity at home but ignore it abroad. Translations do not necessarily get a special marketing plan, and must fend for themselves in the marketplace. Editors expressed a range of opinion as to how comfortable their sales forces felt selling translations; some welcomed the books while others were wary.

Lack of user interest: if translations are hard to sell, there cannot be sufficient interest in them from possible buyers. Editors reported that in the past, some librarians had a tendency to treat Batchelder books as 'worthy', like medicine, rather than as exciting books in their own right. This happens less frequently now.

Reliance on others with language skills: language is a big problem. All of the editors talked about how they had to rely more than usual on readers' reports and the opinions of trusted others because they could not read the original. Though they may read somewhat in another language, or speak a little, all five editors expressed dismay at not being fluent enough to read and assess the original for themselves. As one pointed out, this is the only instance in which an editor will buy a book he or she has not personally read.

Translators and translation: locating an appropriate translator can be very difficult. Not only must the translator be adept at literary translation, he or she must understand and be in sympathy with the tenor of the book. A poorly translated sample chapter could kill a book's chances. If the editor is lucky enough to find and engage a good translator, there is then the danger that the translator may wish to adapt or even censor material to protect the young reader. (Only one of the five editors mentioned the translator-as-editor scenario.) The goal is to translate the reading experience: too literal a translation may not read well in English, but too smooth a translation may not convey the otherness of the original. This is a very complex undertaking because there are so many individuals, each with his or her own filter, between the reader and the text.

More work but less editorial input: for an editor who is used to working closely with the text, translations require extra effort but not so much editorial input. The original is a finished book and may have already been published in several countries. The editor will work with the translator and, if he or she is available, the author, but there is not as much room to make significant changes as when a book is being written for the first time. In the absence of an author, the editor may be reduced to working with the foreign rights department of the originating publisher.

Reviews and controversy: the editors did not think many reviewers trusted young readers to understand potentially controversial or simply different concepts. For example, they mentioned a brief review of Susie Morgenstern's book, *Secret Letters from 0 to 10*, which said the book's French school system setting would confuse the US reader. The reviewer does not give that reader credit for being able to figure it out or being curious enough to find out more. Such a review offers another excuse not to buy the book, when there is already so much resistance. Controversial topics such as sexuality and violence appear to be treated no differently by editors dealing with translations than with US books. An editor will alert the author to a particular scene or detail sure to be flagged in reviews, and ask if it could be written differently while maintaining the integrity of the story. Sometimes the author does not realise that a certain scene, innocuous enough in his or her own country, will be controversial in the US and does not mind making the change. If the author insists that the scene is integral to the story, the editor will accept it and expect it to be flagged by reviews, which will likely hurt sales. As noted above, the book may already exist in a number of different translations, so in fact this sort of scene change is seldom made. The editors did not describe it as self-censoring to improve critical reception, but it could certainly be seen in this light. Editors distinguish between content that may be shocking but is appropriate (such as earthy descriptions in a novel of village life), and what they find genuinely offensive (such as gratuitous cursing). Children may be upset, for example, by the violence and horror of a Holocaust story, but also inspired by characters' strength and endurance. One editor assumed the presence of parents, teachers, or other interested adults to whom the readers can turn for comfort or more information.

Resources

Ideally, editors will have acquired clout and experience, but training and mentoring are also important to creating the infrastructure necessary to publish translations. The influence of a conglomerate was considered more harmful than beneficial.

Editorial clout and experience: these editors have been in the business for a long time. They have honed their tastes, earned the respect of their peers, and have an enviable 'track record'. They enjoy the confidence of their employers, if they are not themselves the 'boss'. This gives them the freedom to develop a riskier list.

Training and mentoring: several editors talked about how difficult it was to figure out how to publish translations on their own, since there is no tradition of publishing translations in the US as there is in continental Europe. There was no one to mentor them at the time, though they are now in the position of being able to mentor others. An infrastructure must be built up in the firm over time so that a stable of authors, translators, etc. is available. In particular, it was important to have staff who speak other languages fluently. It was reported that at one house several fine Danish books were published because there was a Danish-speaking employee who could recognise the quality of the originals. Another frequently heard comment was that editors publish authors, not books, and here, too, time is required to develop the relationship.

Influence of conglomerates: the prevailing opinion agreed with Pullman (2005): the big multi-national corporations are only interested in the bottom line and stifle the editor's independence. Since translations are not lucrative, they are not likely to get published. However, one editor suggested that being part of a conglomerate could help, in that one has access to greater resources, including foreign imprints that might be a source for translations. However, smaller houses or imprints were seen as more likely to publish translations.

Information Channels

Editors benefit from personal connections and serendipity in trying to locate books to translate. Co-publishing arrangements facilitate this process. The Bologna Children's Book Fair offers many opportunities, including the White Ravens display at the International Youth Library (IYL) booth, and the chance to consult funding agencies representing national groups of children's publishers.

Personal connections: long-term relationships with foreign authors, illustrators, translators, editors or agents are the most likely path to locating books to translate and publish. These business connections may also be friendships. Serendipity is a factor.

Co-publishing: official or unofficial co-publishing arrangements with foreign houses lead to translations, especially if the two houses have similar lists. This could involve a simple first chance to look over the list or a more formal arrangement.

Bologna Children's Book Fair: publishers can buy and sell rights to books at various book fairs, but Bologna, held every year in early April, is the most important venue for children's publishers.

The White Ravens: this recommended annual list of quality children's books suitable for translation is prepared by the IYL in Munich. A display of the books is brought to Bologna, so editors may examine them and make appointments with the originating publisher. The list is also posted to the IYL website (IYL, 2005). Though they knew of the service, none of the editors interviewed made use of this resource, relying instead on their own well-developed channels. I understand from the IYL that many other publishers do, in fact, use The White Ravens.

Funding agencies: there are organisations that promote and subsidise the translation of titles from a national group of publishers: for example, the German Book Office in New York, a similar group for Scandinavian publishers, and another for Israeli publishers. They only fund half the cost of a children's translation, though, which, according to the editors, reflects the low esteem in which children's literature is generally held. Reactions from the editors to these agencies ranged from tremendous enthusiasm, to moderate interest, to no knowledge of them.

Publication Climate

Editors commented on the current publication climate and how it has improved.

Perceived openness of US houses to translations: all but one of the editors said that US houses are more open to publishing translations today than they were five years ago. The fifth editor's response was neutral. Everyone agreed that the US market is gradually becoming more accepting of at least the illustration styles of foreign books, the Internet having made the world smaller and more connected. Though competitive, they all welcomed the prospect of more translations being published by other houses.

Discussion of Findings and Implications

I discuss the editors' motivations, problems, resources, information channels, and perception of the publication climate below, with reference to the research question: how do editors select books for translation?

Motivations

Since editors are not expecting significant sales, it seems reasonable that other strong motivations, such as passion for the story, must be present. Finding exciting books from different parts of the world to introduce to children must be personally rewarding. Of course editors would like to see bigger sales, and bestseller Cornelia Funke gives them hope.

Problems

Multicultural and international books (including translations) clearly have qualities in common. I use here the Cooperative Children's Book Center definition of multicultural books as literature 'by and about people of color' (Horning et al., 2005:17) and limit it to books originating in the US Translations (such as those eligible for the Batchelder Award) are first published in a foreign language outside of the US Both provide an insider's look at culture, and may well exist side-by-side on a publisher's list. The two categories are even conflated in the literature; looking for one will regularly bring up articles about the other. However, they seem not to have the same market.

Are poor sales inevitable? Jobe (1996) suggests this may be a self-fulfilling prophecy on the part of publishers. If there were more of a demand, sales would increase. If teachers and librarians can be convinced that this is a valuable type of publishing for children, they should be willing to support the publishers. Buyers for the chain bookstores are also gatekeepers. They are willing to stock high-profile translations, such as Cornelia Funke's books; perhaps they could be persuaded that, given the chance, other translations would sell too.

Despite the risk-taking nature of these elite editors and their denial of self-censorship, they do, with their eye to the bottom line, discuss with authors possible detriments to sales. There is a fine line between censorship and good business practice. They were ready to reject books they did not like or did not think would have a market, as any editor would, and willing to go to considerable trouble to preserve and protect the integrity of a translated text that they loved. This seems not to differ from how editors treat their US books. Of course sometimes even bad publicity increases sales. This is where the 'experience and clout' come in. Established editors can afford to champion books, while a junior editor may not have that luxury.

For book reviewers writing for educational and library journals, reviewing a book from another country, translated from another language, takes more work. Ideally the reviewer would also be able to read the original, but this does not happen very often. Usually reviewers have a short deadline and are limited to a paragraph for plot summary and evaluation. In so brief a space, any negative comment tends to take on exaggerated importance. Of course reviewers should feel free to make such comments, but they should be substantive, not trivial, if they genuinely wish to recommend purchase of the book.

The language issue was somewhat of a surprise. Coming from Canada, an officially bilingual (French and English) country, I expected some of the US editors to speak Spanish, at least. In arguing for internationalism in children's literature, Joels (1999) notes that Americans are hampered because they seldom learn a foreign language. My sample of five was small but representative. It was clear that just having a staff member able to translate a submission letter, let alone evaluate a book in the original language, would be a great asset. Any outside help, such as literary scouts, would be welcome as well. The importance of finding not just a good translator, but the right translator, came up a number of times.

Resources

There is great need for infrastructure, training, and mentoring. Perhaps publishing schools could include working with translations as an integral part of their children's publishing programs. In addition, continuing education courses and conference workshops could be offered for booksellers, teachers, and librarians by their professional associations.

Information Channels

Overall these findings confirm the anecdotal information about publishing translations and conclusions from related research. The importance of personal connections is a case in point. This was emphasised by author, translator, and critic Virginia Allen Jensen in her as-yet-unpublished Dorothy Briley lecture delivered at the United States Board on Books for Young People (USBBY) conference on 30 October 2005. White and Cox (2004), in their longitudinal study of recommended translations, state that in the case of particular languages (notably German, Swedish, Dutch, and Italian), the most important single factor in the publication of translations is a pre-existing relationship between foreign and US publishers. Though existing contacts are the information channels of choice for experienced editors, resources such as the funding agencies and the White Ravens list are available to neophytes.

Publication Climate

Coming after the litany of problems editors face in publishing translations, the consensus that US houses are more open to translations now than five years ago was a surprise. One explanation is a shift in national taste. USBBY and the Children's Book Council (CBC), the association of US children's book publishers, jointly launched an annual list, 'Outstanding

International Books', in the February 2006 issue of *School Library Journal*. (Isaacs, 2006) The list includes translations. An accompanying article describes many of the difficulties publishers face in publishing translations, and advocates for more translations to give children greater diversity and richness in their reading choices. (Lindsay, 2006) However, this activity contradicts the problematic general 'lack of interest' editors see around them. Both the flowering of interest and the resistance co-exist. Perhaps the movement towards more openness from publishing houses will help encourage this trend so that one day there will be enough translations to make possible a list of 'Outstanding Translations.' Similarly, more translations would mean the Batchelder Committee had a wider field from which to select their winners. It would also be desirable to have more books from South America, Africa, and Asia. However, the editors' contacts were predominantly Western European, which is typical of which books are most plentiful and get translated. (White & Cox, 2004) As Jobe (1996:528) says, 'All of us who labour on the promotion of quality children's literature must stand up and support the increased availability of expert translations.'

Conclusion

Pullman (2005) describes the circular conundrum that keeps literary translations from becoming financially viable. This qualitative, exploratory study substantiates his opinion, and considers how the circle may be broken in the US I examined the process by which five experienced acquisitions editors locate and choose children's books from other countries to translate and publish for the US market. Their motivations, problems, resources, information channels, and perceptions of the current publication climate are identified and discussed with an eye to demonstrating what works well and what does not. In a 'bottom-line' publishing environment, the possibility of poor sales deters many houses from attempting translations. Those who do take the risk need support and encouragement beyond the Batchelder, valuable though it is: they need better sales. Improved and more widespread reviewing will help expand the market. Acceptance and promotion by booksellers, especially chain booksellers, could add to both sales and demand. Once parents and children get the opportunity actually to read translations, if they like them, they will create their own 'buzz.' The trend towards greater openness from US houses towards publishing translations brings children a step closer to their literary window to the world.

Bibliography

Bean, J (2003) 'A View from Overseas' *Publishers Weekly*, Vol. 250, no. 42, 20 Oct, pp24-26

Dervin, B, Foreman-Wernet, L, & Lauterbach, E (eds.) (2003). *Sense-making Methodology Reader: Selected Writings of Brenda Dervin*, Cresskill, NJ: Hampton Press

Fontana, A, & Frey, J H (1994) 'Interviewing: The Art of Science' in Denzin, N K, & Lincoln, Y S (eds.), *Handbook of Qualitative Research*, Thousand Oaks, California, US: Sage, pp361-376

Freeman, E B, & Lehman, B A (2001) *Global Perspectives in Children's Literature*, Boston: Allyn and Bacon

Horning, K T, Lindgren, M V, Rudiger, H, & Schliesman, M (2005) 'Observations on Publishing in 2004' in Horning, K T, Lindgren, M V, Rudiger, H, & Schliesman, M, with Elias, T (eds.) *CCBC Choices 2005*, Madison: Cooperative Children's Book Center, School of Education, University of Wisconsin-Madison, pp10-20

Isaacs, K (2006) 'It's a Big World after All', *School Library Journal*, Vol. 52, no. 2, Feb, pp40-44

Jobe, R (1996) 'Translation' in Hunt, P (ed.) *International Companion Encyclopedia of Children's Literature*, London: Routledge, pp519-529

Jobe, R (2001) 'Translation' in Cullinan, B, & Person, D G (eds.) *Continuum Encyclopedia of Children's Literature*, New York: Continuum, pp781-783

Joels, R W (1999) 'Weaving World Understanding: The Importance of Translations in International Children's Literature', *Children's Literature in Education*, Vol. 30, no. 1, pp65-83

Lepman, J (2002) *A Bridge of Children's Books*, Dublin: O'Brien

Lindsay, N (2006) 'Bringing Home the World: A Librarian Puts Forth a Shopping List for International Literature', *School Library Journal*, Vol. 52, no. 2, Feb, pp36-37

Lo, D E (2001) 'Borrowed Voices: Using Literature to Teach Global Perspectives to Middle School Students', *The Clearing House*, Vol. 75, no. 2, pp85-87

Marshall, C, & Rossman, G B (1995) *Designing Qualitative Research*, 2nd edn, Thousand Oaks, California, US: Sage

Pullman, P (2005) 'Still Lost in Translation', *Times Educational Supplement*, 24 Sept, p23

Roxburgh, S (2004) 'The Myopic American', *School Library Journal*, Vol. 50, no. 1, Jan, pp48-50

Stan, S (ed.) (2002) *The World through Children's Books*, Lanham, Maryland, US: Scarecrow

Tomlinson, C M (ed.) (1998) *Children's Books from Other Countries*. Lanham, Maryland, US: Scarecrow

Tomlinson, C M (2002) 'An Overview of International Children's Literature', in Stan, S (ed.) *The World through Children's Books*. Lanham, Maryland, US: Scarecrow, pp3-26

White, M & Cox, R (2004) 'A Longitudinal Study of Recommended Translated Children's Books Published in the United States between 1990 and 2000', *Teacher Librarian,* Vol. 31, no. 4, Apr, pp25-29

Websites

ALA (2006). Mildred L. Batchelder Award
www.ala.org/ala/alsc/awardsscholarships/literaryawds/batchelderaward/batc helderaward.htm
Accessed 13 April 2006

IYL (2005) White Ravens
http://www.ijb.de/whiteravens2.htm
Accessed 13 April 2006

Further Perspectives on Publishing Books from Abroad

Patricia Billings & Neal Hoskins

Expanding Textual and Visual Vocabularies with Children's Picture Books in Translation, and Expanding the Market

Patricia Billings

The decoding skills that children use to understand picture books are adaptable and expandable; children are eminently able to interpret and enjoy translated texts as much as 'native' texts. Translated picture books offer children rich opportunities for expanding their textual and visual vocabularies, which can enhance their reading and perception skills in general. Translated picture books present a unique case of translated text, in that their component text and illustrations are so deeply and crucially linked. In effect, the reader is 'translating' both the text and the images, and the overall concept of the book. This presents a paradox: the translation is at the same time more difficult (the translated text must relate accurately to the pictures on the page) and easier (the pictures on the page are visual cues to the meanings of the words).

At Milet, when we select a picture book for translation, we do not look so much at what the book may say about the culture from which it derives as about the way in which it employs and enlarges a range of visual vocabularies, how it presents new ways of representing and seeing, and the benefits of this for children reading in English. We are most interested in books that enable children to expand their visual and textual vocabularies, and thus open up pathways to understanding a wider range of books and art forms, as well as building overall cognitive skills. Four picture books by French author/illustrator Hervé Tullet published in English by Milet (*Night & Day*, *Pink Lemon*, *Yellow & Round*, *Blue & Square*) present a good example of the opportunities for children offered by translated books. With their vibrant, often abstract illustration style and their clever, philosophical plays on words, Tullet's books present British children with different and expanded ways of reading and representing.

Tullet's first translated title, *Night & Day*, met with opposition from some bookshops buyers for its perceived 'Frenchness', yet this same Frenchness was celebrated in reviews of *Night & Day* and of the other Tullet titles. How can publishers tackle the conservatism and fear of difference in the market, to allow children access to the widest range of reading and visual pleasures? In Milet's experience, it is neither the readers – the children, parents and teachers – nor the reviewers who are resistant to translated books. Rather, it is the bookshop buyers who are the 'gatekeepers', and who, in their decisions on which books will appear on the shelves and which ones will not, can act as a barrier between the books and their potential and willing readers. As publishers of translated books, this is perhaps our biggest challenge: to influence buyers so that children are allowed access to 'foreign' stories and styles, which they are eminently able to understand, interpret, appreciate and love.

Milet's bilingual books, particularly those in community languages, may appear more difficult to market and sell than books translated into English. Yet the buyers for these books, in the educational sector but also increasingly in the trade, seem not the least bit daunted by their 'strangeness' and do not raise the same barriers. This proves that there is a 'way in' to the trade, which we can work to widen.

Bringing the Best of Translated Children's Books to the UK

Neal Hoskins

Only three percent of books published in the UK are translations, and of these, only around ten translated picture books for children are printed. Starting with these facts, before WingedChariot set up its new imprint, we tried to find out the reasons for this situation. The answers we found included: a perceived lack of interest from the general public; the fact that translated books were costlier to make; the difficulty of knowing from a UK perspective whether a book will do well; the abundance of good UK illustrators; and, most important, a lack of real interest on the part of bookshops in stocking them. Despite this, WingedChariot took the view that there are so many gems published abroad that there is space for a well-honed list of fine books. Working with the authors and translators who are sometimes themselves writers, we produced four titles in 2005.

Alongside the books and very much at the forefront of our work, we also produced support documents telling readers more about the authors, country of origin and other aspects of the books. We also recorded the stories in the original languages and put all these files on line at wingedchariot.com. This was a first from a UK publisher. We have just begun and know we need to fight hard to make our niche in the market place, but we think the books stand out. With the support of word-of-mouth recommendations from enthusiasts, we hope to bring to UK readers a new and vibrant collection of stories and pictures from other countries and cultures. Indeed we have found our collaboration with various European literature foundations to be very fruitful and helpful to our endeavours.

Approaches to Translation:

Domestication and Foreignisation

Approaches to Translation: Domestication and Foreignisation

The main question which is confronted in the papers in this section is the extent to which translators should help their young readers over the potential difficulties they may experience in books from other languages and cultures by 'domesticating' the exotic elements. Alternatively, should they encourage in their readers a sense of the attraction of the unfamiliar, in the hope of raising their enthusiasm for 'far-away places with strange sounding names,' as a once popular song put it. There is clearly no single 'right' answer to this conundrum – to some extent policy may depend on the age and background of the target audience, not to mention the growth of a global audience for certain stories in which the characters, partly because of commercialisation, have become universally recognised under their original names.

The theoretical issues are fully spelt out in the papers which follow by Margherita Ippolito, who looks at the differing approaches to the work of Beatrix Potter taken by two Italian translators, and Michal Borodo, who gives particular attention to the impact of global media on the translation into Polish of a range of children's texts. Marta Minier shows how similar issues have faced the Hungarian translator of the Harry Potter books. In all these instances, it appears that a good deal depends on the reputation of the translator; there is it would appear an increasing trend for the translator to become less 'invisible' and consequently to have the confidence to impart some distinctive touches to the resulting text. Darja Mazi-Leskovar focuses on various translations into Slovenian of American classics such as *Uncle Tom's Cabin* and *The Last of the Mohicans*, relating some of the differences over time to changes in the cultural climate in the target language.

A rather different focus is taken by Belén González Cascallana, in that the Spanish translations she is scrutinising, of the novels of Deborah Phillips, are themselves texts which are already bringing the 'exotic' of Afghanistan to the English-speaking reader. She gives a wide range of examples presenting both the similarities and the differences between the approaches employed.

Translation of Culture-Specific Items in Children's Literature: The Case of Beatrix Potter

Margherita Ippolito

Some Theoretical Issues

Interlingual translation is a process which implies more than the simple conversion of one language into another; it requires a complex operation of intercultural transfer, involving two different cultural contexts and unique universes of discourse. A source text emerges from specific historical and social conditions, and conveys the values, habits, dreams and experiences of a particular social group. Translating means decoding and interpreting the text, while keeping in view its situational and cultural contexts, in order to recode it through the features of another language and of another culture. Translating, therefore, requires more than the knowledge of the entries of bilingual or monolingual dictionaries, because these are inadequate to describe culture. Culture may be defined as a map of the world shared by the same group of people, which is made up of 'a system of congruent and interrelated beliefs, values, strategies and cognitive environments which guide the shared basis of behaviour' (Katan, 1999: 17).

The present paper concerns the translation of culture-specific items (CSIs), which are among the most visible expressions of culture. These lexical items relate to a deeply rooted cultural background and pose crucial translation problems due to the lack, in the target culture, of lexical items with the same semantic value as the source text lemma:

> ... in translation a CSI does not exist of itself, but as the result of a conflict arising from any linguistically represented reference in a source text, which, when transferred to a target language, poses a translation problem due to the non-existence or to the different value (whether determined by ideology, usage, frequency, etc.) of the given item in the target language culture. (Aixelá, 1996: 57)

According to Göte Klingberg, culture-bound data belong to certain specific categories:

- literary references

- foreign languages in the source text

- references to mythology and popular belief

- historical, religious and political background

- building and home furnishing, food

- customs, play and games

- flora and fauna

- personal names, titles, names of domestic animals, names of objects

- geographical names

- weights and measures (Klingberg, 1986: 17-18)

The translation problem raised by these groups of culture-bound elements depends on the pair of languages in use, and on the age, the cultural level and the linguistic competence of the translation receiver. For instance, the phrase 'as white as snow' does not constitute a culture-specific reference in a translation from English into Italian, but it poses a translation problem if this image has to be translated into languages in whose geographical and cultural context snow is unknown, as in some regions of central America (Nida, 1959: 29). Similarly, a linguistic item is culture-specific when it is perceived as strange, obscure and unknown by the potential addressee of the target text. Terms such as 'fair play,' 'politically correct' and 'briefing' can appear as loans in the Italian language; though they may not be understood by the average reader of an Italian tabloid, they are perfectly intelligible to everyone who reads the political page of an Italian quality paper.

When children are the audience of a text, the treatment of culture-specific items in translation will depend on the personal image of the child that translators have. Translators may assume two different positions and on this basis they will employ a specific translation strategy. On the one hand they may think that reading a book rich in culture-specific elements enables children to learn and enlarge their knowledge of the world, or on the other they may believe that children cannot deal with a foreign culture because they do not yet possess adequate interpretative and cognitive capacities. If translators suppose that cultural-bound elements promote children's cultural exchange and develop their world view, they will preserve new lexical items as far as possible. If however they think that the cultural datum might disturb the children's reading, resulting in incomprehensibility and strangeness, they will tend towards the adaptation of the new element into the familiar target culture.

The scholars Riitta Oittinen and Göte Klingberg sum up these different approaches to the translation of children's literature. Oittinen considers the translation of children's literature to be an adaptation of the source cultural system to the specific features of the target culture. Adapting does not imply a betrayal of the source text, but is rather an act of great fidelity to the real spirit of the original. To the extent that a story for children is pleasant, involving and amusing, these effects must be reproduced in the translation, so as to arouse in the target text reader the same impressions and emotions as felt by the source text reader. The whole setting, the characters' names, historical events, religious and cultural references need to be manipulated, since children cannot identify with characters endowed with strange and unpronounceable names or who eat unfamiliar dishes; they cannot feel close to events told in a language full of incomprehensible words: 'Translating for children ... refers to translating for a certain audience and respecting this audience through taking the audience's will and abilities into consideration' (Oittinin, 2000: 69).

Klingberg, on the other hand, maintains that a translation should preserve the cultural values expressed by the original text, because these will promote mutual respect, friendship and dialogue, widen their knowledge of the world and open their minds to new and original ideas:
Another aim of translating children's books is to further the international outlook and understanding of the young readers. This aim will lead to the same adherence to the original. Removal of peculiarities of the foreign culture or change of cultural elements for such elements which belong to the culture of the target language will not further readers' knowledge of and interest in the foreign culture. (Klingberg, 1986: 10)

Many translation procedures stem from conservative and substitutive strategies. They are gathered into a taxonomy which goes from a lesser to a greater degree of intercultural manipulation. At the top of the scale are procedures which adhere as far as possible to the target text culture-bound element, whereas at the other end are procedures which transform the original reference in a substantial way:

- **loan:** the translator rewrites verbatim the culture-bound item

- **literal translation:** the translation is close to the meaning and form of the source text

- **intratextual explanation:** the translator preserves the foreign element adding a short explanation

- **exratextual explanation:** the explanation is given in the form of a footnote, of a preface, etc.

- **simplification:** the cultural datum is replaced by another cultural element which belongs to the source culture but which is also accepted and known by the target culture

- **substitution:** the foreign element can be substituted by a superordinate (i.e. plum-pudding → cake)

- **omission:** words, sentences, paragraphs are deleted

- **localisation:** the cultural setting of the source text is transferred into a more familiar context.

These translation procedures may be combined together, so that in the same translation, culture-bound elements can be omitted or copied in their original form. However these modalities should never be mixed irrationally, and an unnatural mixture of foreign and familiar elements which would undermine the inner coherence of the text should be avoided. That is why every good translation presents a tendency towards either preservation or adaptation.

Beatrix Potter's *Tales*

The *Tales* of Beatrix Potter were translated into Italian for the first time in Italy in 1981 by Giulia Niccolai, and then in 1988 they were retranslated by Donatella Ziliotto, whose translations are still in print.[1] Victorian and Edwardian England constitutes the stage on which Potter's creatures move. There are numerous unmistakeably English elements: the furniture (the four-poster bed for instance); the clothes (such as the bonnets, pinafores and tuckers worn by her characters); the landscape (the Lake District, the picturesque setting of many of her tales); the traditional nursery rhymes, limericks and riddles which embellish her narrative scenario; and her subtle and penetrating irony. As Carpenter and Prichard (1984) comment:

> Many of Beatrix Potter's books have been translated into French, Dutch, German, Japanese, and Welsh, and some titles have appeared in other languages, but her view of the world is too essentially English to be transposed easily from that language. (1984: 424)

In *The Tale of Jeremy Fisher*, the eponymous frog invites two friends to dinner. These friends are very important people, as their names and titles witness: they are Mr. Alderman Ptolemy Tortoise and Sir Isaac Newton. Beyond the difficulty of rendering the irony implied in these proper names given respectively to an awkward tortoise and a newt, the translator has to find a solution for the translation of the titles 'Alderman' and 'Sir' which have no similar semantic equivalent in the Italian language. Parallel passages indicate the strategies used in the Italian versions:

> If I catch more than five fish, I will invite my friends Mr. **Alderman Ptolemy Tortoise** and **Sir Isaac Newton**. (Beatrix Potter: 121)

> Se prenderò più di cinque pesci, inviterò i miei amici, il Signor **Alderman Ptolemy Tartaruga** e **Sir Isaac Newton**. (Donatella Ziliotto: 121)

(If I catch more than five fish, I will invite my friends, Mr. **Alderman Ptolemy Tartaruga** and **Sir Isaac Newton**. [My re-translation])

Se pesco più di cinque pesci inviterò i miei amici: il Signor **Notabile Tolomeo Tartaruga** e il tritone, **Sir Isaac Newton**. (Giulia Niccolai: 9)
(If I catch more than five fish I will invite my friends: the **Notable Tolomeo Tartaruga** and the newt, **Sir Isaac Newton**. [My re-translation])

Both Ziliotto and Niccolai retain the noble title 'Sir', which can be accepted by the Italian child reader as it is familiar from other well-known texts for children; Sir Biss ('Sir Hiss' in the source language version), for instance, is King John's adviser in the adaptation of *Robin Hood* produced by Walt Disney. 'Alderman', however, is completely unfamiliar to an Italian child. Ziliotto uses the procedure of the *loan* and copies verbatim this title beside the character's name, which is reported exactly in its English graphic form, although the Italian equivalent is Tolomeo. Niccolai opts for a *substitution* and finds a superordinate of 'Alderman' which transmits the authority and the distinction of this post. She chooses 'Notabile', meaning 'notable', an epithet which can be applied to doctors, lawyers, professors, mayors, barons or the like. Moreover, she transcribes 'Ptolemy' into Italian ('Tolomeo'). The name of the famous scientist, Isaac Newton, is retained by both translators because in Italy he is known with that name, even though it is pronounced slightly differently: [isak].

In *The Tale of Benjamin Bunny* two cousins, Peter Rabbit and Benjamin Bunny, sneak furtively into Mr. McGregor's garden to recover the clothes lost by Peter during a previous excursion, which have subsequently been used to dress a scarecrow. The bunnies immediately notice the scarecrow:

Peter's coat and shoes were plainly to be seen upon the scarecrow, topped with an old **tam-o-shanter** of Mr. McGregor. (Beatrix Potter: 59)

The culture-specific item, the 'tam-o-shanter', does not exist in the Italian language. It is a characteristically Scottish woollen hat, worn pulled down on one side, as one illustration of Benjamin Bunny with the tam-o-shanter shows. The Italian translations are:

La giacca e le scarpe di Peter erano chiaramente visibili addosso allo spaventapasseri, con l'aggiunta di un frusto **berretto scozzese** del Signor McGregor. (Donatella Ziliotto: 59)

(Peter's coat and shoes were plainly to be seen upon the scarecrow, topped with a worn-out **Scottish hat** of Mr. McGregor. [My re-translation])

La giacca e le scarpe di Ludovico erano visibilissime sullo spaventapasseri sormontato da un **berretto** del Signor McGregor. (Giulia Niccolai: 22)
(Ludovico's coat and shoes were plainly to be seen upon the scarecrow, topped with a **hat** of Mr. McGregor. [My re-translation])

Ziliotto employs the procedure of *substitution* because she replaces the culture-specific datum with an explanation, although she does not renounce restoring the flavour of foreign culture as she explains that the hat worn by the scarecrow is Scottish. Niccolai opts for the procedure of *substitution* by using the generic superordinate 'hat', but doing so she deletes the cultural reference to Scotland. Moreover, Niccolai replaces the English name of the rabbit (Peter) with the Italian name 'Ludovico', removing once again the reference to a foreign country.

In the *Tale of Squirrel Nutkin* a characteristically British Christmas sweet course is mentioned: the 'plum-pudding':

On the fourth day the squirrels brought a present of six fat beetles, which were as good as plums in *plum-pudding* for Old Brown. (Beatrix Potter: 30)

Il quarto giorno gli scoiattoli portarono sei grassi scarafaggi, che il vecchio Brown trovò squisiti come prugne in un *plum-cake*. (Donatella Ziliotto: 30)
(On the fourth day the squirrels brought six fat beetles, which Old Brown found as good as plums in a *plum-cake*. [My re-translation])

Il quarto giorno gli scoiattoli portarono in regalo sei grassi insetti che al Signor Bigio dovevano piacere come a noi piacciono le prugne nel *plum-pudding*. (Giulia Niccolai: 34)
(On the fourth day the squirrels brought a present of six fat insects, which Mr Grey liked as we like plums in *plum-pudding*. [My re-translation])

Giulia Niccolai preserves the cultural-bound datum, although Italian children would not be able to imagine the taste and appearance of this famous Christmas dish, because it does not appear in the Italian culinary tradition. Donatella Ziliotto prefers the procedure of *simplification*, by replacing the source text cultural datum ('plum-pudding') with another cultural element

112

('plum-cake'), which is shared by both English and Italian culture, although having different meanings. The plum-cake is known to an Italian child because it is now part of the Italian cookery and because it is the name of a very popular snack. This translation choice, moreover, by preserving a slightly foreignising effect due to the spelling of the word, is consistent with the translation strategy preferred by Ziliotto throughout her translation of Potter's *Tales*, which is oriented to the source text.

Giulia Niccolai's translation of *The Tale of Squirrel Nutkin* offers an interesting example of *localisation*. The translator moves the setting from England to Italy. She renders all characters' names semantically transparent in order to be faithful to the author's intentions. Beatrix Potter had coined some signifying names for her characters, two squirrels and an owl, which connote and characterise them: 'Nutkin', 'Twinkleberry' and 'Old Brown'. The translator transforms 'Nutkin', a 'transparent composite name' (Manini, 1996: 165), which is composed of two lemma - 'nut' and the diminutive 'kin'- into the agglutinative diminutive of the first lemma 'Nocciolina' (Little Nut); she also creates the neologism 'Squirallo', to translate the name 'Twinkleberry.' This invented name both preserves the phonosymbolic aspect of the original name which suggests something which rings happily, and reproduces the onomatopoeic sound of the word 'squirrel', often repeated in the original tale. Finally, she translates literally the first part of the owl's name, 'Old' which becomes 'Vecchio', but replaces the colour 'Brown' with 'Bigio', which means grey. There is a little inconsistency, however, because the illustration, which is integral to the text, shows a brown owl, with no grey feathers.

The translation procedure of *localisation* requires strong coherence in the treatment of all other culture-specific elements of the source text. It would be puzzling if readers found Italian names side by side with foreign cultural items. In the translation by Giulia Niccolai, however, different cultural elements appear, such as 'plum-pudding' and 'Humpty Dumpty'. They are not translated, thus the inner logic and coherence of the text is undermined. Donatella Ziliotto behaves differently. She does not translate the proper names of the squirrels and only partially translates the name of the owl, which becomes 'Vecchio Brown' ('Old Brown'). Ziliotto's translation does not show any inner inconsistency, though young readers will not be able to grasp the meaning of these descriptive names, and will have serious difficulties in pronouncing them, because they include some letters (w, k, y) which are not part of the Italian alphabet.

An example of *literal translation* is provided by Niccolai's translation of the

113

name of the farm where Lucie, the little protagonist of the *Tale of Mrs. Tiggy-winkle*, lives:

Once upon a time there was a little girl called Lucie, who lived at a farm called **Little-town**. (Beatrix Potter: 87)

C'era una volta una bambina chiamata Lucie, che viveva in una fattoria chiamata **Little-town**. (Donatella Ziliotto: 87)
(Once upon a time there was a little girl called Lucie, who lived at a farm called **Little-town**. [My re-translation])

C'era una volta una bambina di nome Lucie che viveva in una fattoria chiamata la *Cittadella*. (Giulia Niccolai: 9)
(Once upon a time there was a little girl called Lucie, who lived at a farm called *Cittadella*. [My re-translation])

Ziliotto preserves the English name of the farm while Niccolai translates 'Little-town' literally into 'Cittadella'. After a few pages the name of this farm appears again near other two farms: Skelghyl and Gatesgarth.

Those are woolly coats belonging to the little lambs at **Skelghyl** ... And here's one marked for **Gatesgarth,** and three that come from **Little-town**. (Beatrix Potter: 96)

Sono le giacche di lana degli agnellini di **Skelghyl** ... Guarda le cifre sulle spalle: ce n'è uno che viene da **Gatesgarth** e tre da **Littletown**. (Donatella Ziliotto: 96)
(They are the woolly jackets of some little lambs at **Skelghyl** ... Look at the numbers on the shoulders: there is one coming from **Gatesgarth** and three from **Littletown**. [My re-translation])

Questi sono soprabitini di lana degli agnellini di **Skelghyl** ... E qui ce n'è uno marchiato **Gatesgarth**, e qui altri tre che vengono dalla **Cittadella**. (Giulia Niccolai: 42)
(Those are little woolly coats of some little lambs at **Skelghyl** ... And here's one marked **Gatesgarth**, and here are three more that come from **Cittadella**. [My re-translation])

Both translators maintain these English proper names, but if Ziliotto is always coherent in her choices, Niccolai cannot avoid another inconsistency, because 'Cittadella', close to two foreign names, constitutes an evident contradiction inside its linguistic co-text and its cultural context.

Although only a few examples of the translation procedures used by Ziliotto and Niccolai have been presented here, it is possible from this descriptive comparison to propose certain generalisations concerning the strategies chosen: Giulia Niccolai adopts a target-text-oriented translation strategy because she tends to remove the foreign atmosphere; Donatella Ziliotto adopts a much more conservative strategy, even when this means that young readers will encounter pronunciation problems and will not understand the meaning or the allusion. Both translators, however, contribute to different degrees to the evocation of a typically British background.

The volume of data studied here is certainly too small to allow any global conclusion about the translation norms of children's literature in Italy, however this analysis shows that the country accepts the language and culture of the English-speaking world. This thesis is strengthened further both by the large amount of translations from English for young readers currently available (according to the Italian Statistics Institute, ISTAT, in 2003 48.3% of children's books published were translations and 33.4% were translations from English[2]), and by the particular attention that the Italian school system pays to the teaching of the English language (the new reform of elementary education makes the teaching of English compulsory from the first class of primary school, when children are 5 years old[3]).

Thus, the translation of Beatrix Potter's *Tales*, and in particular the treatment of culture-specific items, demonstrates how Italian children, even at the age of five and six, come into contact with British culture and understand that there are remote and fascinating worlds to be discovered. 'Since children's perceptions of other cultures are formed – at least in part – by the books they read, children's literature is a potential site for linguistic and cultural exchange' (Lathey, 2001: 296).

Notes

1. The Tales and the translations considered are: Beatrix Potter, The Tale of Jeremy Fisher, The Tale of Benjamin Bunny, The Tale of Squirrel Nutkin, The Tale of Mrs. Tiggy-winkle, Frederick Warne, London, 2002; La Favola del Signor Geremia Pescatore, La Favola di Costantino Coniglietto, La Favola dello Scoiattolo Nocciolina, La Favola della Signora Riccio Rotolò, translated by Giulia Niccolai, Emme Edizioni, Milano, 1981; La Storia del Signor Jeremy Pescatore, La Storia di Benjamin Coniglio, La Storia di Nutkin Scoiattolo, La Storia della Signora Trovatutto, translated by Donatella Ziliotto, Sperling & Kupfer, Milano, 1988.

2. www.culturaincifre.istat.it

3. Indicazioni Nazionali per i Piani di Studio Personalizzati nella Scuola Primaria, Decreto Legislativo n. 59, 2004

Bibliography

Primary sources

Potter, B (2002; 1904) *The Tale of Benjamin Bunny,* London: F Warne & Co.

Potter, B (2002; 1905) *The Tale of Mrs. Tiggy-winkle,* London: F Warne & Co.

Potter, B (2002; 1906) *The Tale of Squirrel Nutkin*, London: F Warne & Co.

Potter, B (2002; 1906) *The Tale of Mr. Jeremy Fisher,* London: F. Warne & Co.

Potter, B (1981) *La Favola di Costantino Coniglietto,* Milano: Emme Edizioni translated by G Niccolai

Potter, B (1981) *La Fvola della Signora Riccio Rotolò,* Milano: Emme Edizioni translated by G Niccolai

Potter, B (1981) *La Favola dello Scoiattolo Nocciolina,* Milano: Emme Edizioni translated by G Niccolai

Potter, B (1981) *La Favola del Signor Geremia Pescatore,* Milano: Emme Edizioni translated by G Niccolai

Potter, B (1988) *La Storia di Benjamin Coniglio,* Milano: Sperling & Kupfer translated by D Ziliotto

Potter, B (1988) *La Storia della Signora Trovatutto,* Milano: Sperling & Kupfer translated by D Ziliotto

Potter, B (1988) *La Storia di Nutkin Scoiattolo*, Milano: Sperling & Kupfer translated by D Ziliotto

Potter, B (1988) *La Storia del Signor Jeremy Pescatore,* Milano: Sperling & Kupfer translated by D Ziliotto

Secondary Sources

Aixelá Javier Franco (1996) 'Culture-specific Items in Translation', in Román Álvarez, Roman & Carmen-África Vidal, M (eds.), *Translation, Power, Subversion*, Clevedon, Philadelphia, Adelaide, Multilingual Matters, 1996, pp52-78

Bassnett, S (1991) *Translation Studies*, London and New York: Routledge

Bassnett, S and Lefevere, A (1990) *Translation, History and Culture,* London and New York: Pinter

Bell, A (1985) 'Translator's Notebook: The Naming of Names', *Signal,* 46, 1985, pp3-11

Beuchat, C & Valdevieso, C (1992) 'Translation of Children's Literature: Intercultural Communication', *Bookbird,* 30 (1), 1992, pp9-14

Carpenter, H & Prichard, M (1984) *The Oxford Companion to Children's Literature,* Oxford and New York: Oxford University Press

Davies, E (2003) 'A Goblin or a Dirty Nose? The Treatment of Culture-Specific References in Translation of the Harry Potter Books', in *The Translator,* 9 (1), 2003, pp65-100

Eco, U (2003) *Dire Quasi la Stessa Cosa: Esperienze di Traduzione,* Milano: RCS Libri

Holmes, J S (1988) *Translated! Papers on Literary Translation and Translation Studies,* Amsterdam: Rodopi

Indicazioni Nazionali per i Piani di Studio Personalizzati nella Scuola Primaria, Decreto Legislativo n. 59, 2004

Katan, D (1999) *Translating Cultures. An Introduction for Translators, Interpreters and Mediators,* Manchester: St. Jerome Publishing

Klingberg, G (1986) *Children's Fiction in the Hands of the Translators,* Lund: CWK Gleerup

Lathey, G (2001) 'Where Britain Meets 'the Continent': Language and Cultural Exchange in Children's Fiction,' *Children's Literature in Education,* 32 (4), 2001, pp295-303

Lindgren, A (1969) 'Traduire des Livres d'Enfants – est-ce Possibile?', in *Babel,* 15 (2), 1969, pp98-100

López, M F (2000) 'Translation Studies in Contemporary Children's Literature: A Comparison of Intercultural Ideological Factors', *Children's Literature Association Quarterly,* 2000, pp29-37

Mackey, M (ed.) (2002) *Beatrix Potter's Peter Rabbit. A Children's Classic at 100,* Lanham, Maryland: Scarecrow Press

Manini, L (1996) 'Meaningful Literary Names: Their Forms and Functions, and their Translation', in *The Translator*, 2 (2), 1996, pp161-178

Newmark, P (1981) *Approaches to Translation*, Oxford: Pergamon Press

Nida, E. (1959) 'Principles of Translation as exemplified by Bible Translating', in R. Brower (ed.), *On Translation*, Cambridge, Massachusetts, Harvard University Press, 1959, p. 11-31

Oittinen, R (2000) *Translating for Children*, New York & London: Garland Publishing

Tabbert, R (2002) 'Approaches to the Translation of Children's Literature', *Target*, 14 (2), 2002, pp304-351

Taylor, J, Whalley, J, Stevenson Hobbs, A & Battick, E (1987) *Beatrix Potter 1866-1943. The Artist and her World*, London: Warne

Wall, B (1991) *The Narrator's Voice: The Dilemma of Children's Fiction*, London: Macmillan

Webb Joels, R, (1999) 'Weaving World Understanding: The Importance of Translations in International Children's Literature', in *Children's Literature in Education*, 30 (1), 1999, pp65-83

White, M (1992) 'Children's Books from Other Languages: A Study of Successful Translations', *Journal of Youth Services in Libraries*, 5 (3), 1992, pp261-275

Yamazaki, A (2002) 'Why Change Names? On the Translation of Children's Books', *Children's Literature in Education*, 33 (1), 2002, pp53-62

Website

www.culturaincifre.istat.it

Linguistic Inventions, Culture-specific Terms and Intertexts in the Hungarian Translations of *Harry Potter*

Márta Minier

Introduction

The tradition of the translation of children's literature in Hungary has been a distinguished one, with reputed writers and translators trying their hands at creative translations – or rather rewrites – of children's classics, including *Winnie-the-Pooh*, *Alice in Wonderland* and *The Jungle Book*, all addressing a 'kiddult' readership. In this article, however, I will look at the *Harry Potter* series in Hungarian translation, with a special emphasis on terms coined by Rowling, culturally marked elements, the underlying concept of Britishness, and intertexts.[1] In Hungary the series has been published by a fairly unknown publishing house called Animus Kiadó, which, emboldened by the success of the *Potter* books, went on to publish a few translations of children's bestsellers by Louis Sachar.

The 'Harry Potter' series has been a breakthrough for the translator, who now provides an exception to the general tendency of translators to remain 'invisible'. This attribute has become a contentious term in Translation Studies after Lawrence Venuti's work, *The Translator's Invisibility: A History of Translation*, which refers to the almost perennial low status of the translator in the literary establishment. The translations of J K Rowling's series have been undertaken by Boldizsár Tamás Tóth, who previously specialised in film translation, predominantly American blockbusters. He is the Hungarian translator of *Hannibal*, for instance, and a wide range of Disney productions for children. His experience in translating films has left its traces on his *Harry Potter* idiom. Small wonder that Tóth is also the translator of the films based on the first few volumes. In this present article I intend to demonstrate that this translator neither unquestionably domesticates, nor foreignises the texts. The analysis will include comparisons of names of persons, places, magical objects, school subjects, and so on, in the 'original' and in the Hungarian translation.[2] I will use the terms 'source text' and 'original' in inverted commas only, since the intertextual notion of translation problematises the feasibility of these concepts. The terms 'rendition' and 'equivalent' will be handled similarly, since full equivalence is an illusory ideal. According to the Sapir-Whorf hypothesis, every language shapes or forges 'reality' in its own manner (cf. O'Grady, 993: 242–4, 595). On the understanding that creative and academic work are not so clearly distinguishable under the aegis of the postmodern, I will also point out in what respects Tóth's translation strategies could be more daring or subversive. This is not at all to express any personal preferences but to shed more light on the theoretical concepts to be discussed.

Before discussing individual cases or types of 'rendition', a theoretical context needs to be outlined for the study of translations with respect to appropriation as well as to the circulation and relocation of cultural knowledge.[3] 'Regarding the manner of the translation, the conflict seems to be between making the outcome of the translation process a visibly borrowed text, or rather a familiar sounding one which could have been originally conceived in the receiving language' (Minier, 2002:102). Friedrich Schleiermacher states, 'Either the translator leaves the writer alone as much as possible and moves the reader toward the writer, or he leaves the reader alone as much as possible and moves the writer toward the reader' (1992: 42). Under Schleiermacher's influence, Lawrence Venuti divides translation strategies into foreignising and domesticating ones (1995: 17-27). A domesticating translation adjusts the text to the taste of the receiving community. In this approach, local expectations are taken into account to a greater extent. Foreignising practices are supposed to retain the otherness experienced in the original. Wilhelm von Humboldt argues that the reader of a translation should be facilitated to feel the foreign but not foreignness itself (1992: 58). In my view, foreignisation and domestication are the two poles of a fluctuating process, and it is rare for a translation to be exclusively either foreignising or domesticating.[4] As Venuti himself later attests, '...the very function of translating is assimilation, the inscription of a foreign text with domestic intelligibilities and interests' (1998: 11). Paloposki and Oittinen even go so far as to say that 'Maybe foreignizing is an illusion which does not really exist. Perhaps we should only speak of different levels and dimensions of domestication' (2000: 386).

Lawrence Venuti puts forward foreignisation as the politically correct tendency of our day. However, it is truer to say that foreignness is re-conceived, and thus is constructed rather than retained. A translation as a metatext will speak about how an individual culture (and translator) perceives and constructs within its own boundaries the foreignness of another culture; hence, it is determined to reveal a great deal about contemporaneous discourses in a receiving community.

Names in the 'Harry Potter' Series

Overtly telling names in the series, such as those of some of the teachers, the officials, and the journalist, together with terms containing some kind of wordplay, are usually very innovatively transplanted into Hungarian. For instance, the Hungarian counterpart of Professor Snape is called *Piton* (the Hungarian for 'python'). The herbology tutor, Professor Sprout reincarnates as *Bimba professzor* (cf. *bimbó*, the Hungarian for 'sprouts' and possibly the adjective *bamba*, meaning 'oafish' and 'absent-minded'). The humour here,

120

just as in the English name, addresses the character's profession. *Mógus professzor* is the Hungarian counterpart for Professor Quirrel, where *mógus* is a free association with *mókus* (by way of changing a single consonant), the Hungarian for 'squirrel', a word that the name Quirrel resembles. It is also a distorted version of the Hungarian word *mágus* [magician, magus], suggesting that the professor does not always live up to expectations as a magician. The name of the uninhibited journalist, Rita Skeeter, is put across as *Rita Vitrol*. The Hungarian noun *vitriol* [sharp, cutting wit], of which the surname is a distortion, is most often used when describing the style of a daring and provocative journalist, much like its English counterpart, although it may be slightly milder in tone. Bartemius Crouch's surname is turned into *Kupor*, which is not an existing word as such, yet comes across as a stem related to two verbs: *kuporog* [crouch, squat] and *kuporgat* [put away in a very sparing manner]. Thus, another semantic field, that of thrift and meanness, is also at play in Tóth's version.

In a list of authors of textbooks, *'Bircsók, Bathilda'* is used for 'Bagshot, Bathilda'. Apart from being a similarly alliterating name, Bircsók recalls the word *bibircsók*, a noun for 'wart (particularly on the nose)', associated with wicked witches in Hungarian fairytales. On the same list of required readings *Dabrak* stands for Goshawk, invoking the well-known spell *abrakadabra* [abracadabra]; although it is difficult to link this word to any specific children's story or television programme, it is a phrase strongly rooted in Hungarian cultural memory and is probably the first magic spell Hungarian children come across. This is an instance of foregrounding the domestic cultural knowledge in the appropriation: children will recognise it as something familiar, and probably be unaware that the term exists in other languages too.

In like vein, a witty solution for Flourish and Blotts is offered in the form of *Czikornyai és Pacza*, imitating the spelling of traditional and prestigious Hungarian family names by using the obsolete letter combination *cz* instead of the common and codified *c*. This naming is jocose enough because *cikornya* means 'bombast' or 'flourish', and *paca* stands for 'an undesirable blot of ink on the paper.' The pocket sneakoscope is innovatively turned into *zsebgyanuszkóp* [pocket + suspicion + 'scope']. The ending *szkóp* is associated with (semi-)scientific jargon in Hungarian, so that a connotation similar to that of the original is carried by the Hungarian word.

Professor McGonagall's name becomes *McGalagony*; this, besides being easier to utter and more euphonious (Boldizsár, 2001: 546), also rings potentially even more 'English' to the Hungarian ear than the original name. As Elizabeth D Schafer notes, 'Her Scottish last name hints that she is both bold and bitter' (2000: 58). An average Hungarian reader, however, would not notice that McGonagall is a Scottish-sounding rather than an English-sounding surname; it would most probably fall into the category of 'English' names. At the same time, the name *McGalagony* loosely conjures up the sound of the word *galagonya*, the Hungarian for 'hawthorn', which appears in a famous poem for children by the acclaimed Modernist poet Sándor Weöres (a text also turned into a song). As a result, in this name familiarity and foreignness are both at play. The professor's first name, Minerva, is an allusion to the wise goddess, Athena, which, as part of the European cultural heritage, also works for Hungarian readers.

The 'rendition' for Gryffindor is *Griffendél*; this name rhymes with Chip and Dale, for instance (from a children's animated series), and with other words ending in *-ale* which are already familiar to young Hungarian viewers of American cartoons. This is again closer to the stereotypical Hungarian notion of an 'English' name than Gryffindor is. (As noted above, Tóth is also a translator of Disney movies.)

Foreign Terms

Another characteristic treatment of foreignness is when the alien expression is foreignised in the translation not by retaining the foreign phrases in Rowling's text but by finding terms that are foreign-sounding to the Hungarian ear. Expressions from the Latin (such as Dumbledore's first name, Albus) or imitating Latin terms qualify for such purposes very well, since educated Hungarian readers are used to coming across Latin expressions in their reading. Ildikó Boldizsár emphasises in a review how easily the translator handles Latin (2001: 546). In this respect, too, it is the foreign-as-familiar that is encountered, as opposed to the purely foreign or purely domestic. Some of the spells serve as elucidating examples here; for instance, the summoning charm 'Accio!' becomes '*Invito!*' The translator is respectful towards the 'original' as he identifies an intention in it and tries to follow the same principle, here by invoking a foreign/highbrow atmosphere in his translation. He cleverly keeps in mind that the same term will not necessarily conjure up notions of otherness for readers in the receiving language as it does in the 'source' language.

Another gesture of foreignising the familiar occurs when Tóth translates Cornelius Fudge's surname as *Caramel*, giving a Latinate spelling of *karamell*, the Hungarian for 'fudge'. This strategy is further clarified by the translation of the Mirror of Erised, which is transformed into the more Latin-sounding and pronounceable *Edevis tükre* [the mirror of Edevis]. The inscription on the frame of the mirror is 'Edevis amen ahze erkyt docr amen' (1999: 195), while the original foreign text reads 'Erised stra ehru oyt ube cafru oyt on wohsi' (1997: 225). Thus, the title of Chapter Twelve of the first volume needed to be changed accordingly and became 'Edevis tükre' [The Mirror of Edevis]. In a similar manner to that of the 'original', Tóth's solution reads backwards as 'nem arcod tükre ez, hanem a szívedé' [it is not the mirror of your face but that of your heart].

A peculiar and related case in point is Hogwarts School of Witchcraft and Wizardry. The Hungarian version for this is *Roxfort*, which, sounding so similar to Oxford, has a whiff of humorous criticism about it, especially for the adult readers. Consistently, Hogsmeade, the name of the village adjacent to Hogwarts, is translated as *Roxmorts*. This is to do with listing or 'storing' Oxford as a custodian of quintessential Britishness in an (imaginary) Hungarian cultural lexicon. The result is a 'more (typically) British' name than Hogwarts, the original. This occurrence of emulation in the translations is not unique; there are a few more scattered examples of the phenomenon, though they are less conspicuous.

There are cases where the whole idiom of a character sounds foreign or ethnically marked to the British reader. The head of the visiting French school, Madame Maxime, and her student, Fleur, speak a Frenchified English in *Harry Potter and the Goblet of Fire*. Their 'Hungarian' is similarly French-sounding. Oddly enough, the other visiting professor, the Eastern European Karkaroff, speaks fluent English (and Hungarian). Small wonder that nothing regional comes across in the Hungarian translations from Hagrid's Scottish accent or Seamus Finnigan's Irish brogue, either.

In some cases, the onomatopoeic sound of the terms has provided guidance for the translator. Hufflepuff is 'rendered' as *Hugrabug* (a playful take on the slightly onomatopoeic verb for 'jump': *ugrabugrál*). Slytherin is inventively translated as *Mardekár* [Bites-what-a-pity]; apart from the reference to snakes, the dark-sounding word (with a few low vowels in it) has a strong associative power. Snitch is Hungarianised with the slightly onomatopoeic *cikesz* (a word made up by the translator, inspired by the verb *cikázik*, meaning 'flash' or 'zigzag').

A word puzzling and innovative in the original, 'undursleyish', is translated as *legdursleyszerűtlenebb* [most undursleyish]. The Hungarian language allows for even more freedom in bending the word endings: playing with suffixes, conjugation and declension. The Sorting Hat becomes *Teszlek süveg*, which would translate back into English as "I-place-you'-stovepipe-hat'. As an agglutinating language, Hungarian is capable of expressing a phrase such as 'I place you' in one single word.

Diagon Alley is turned into *Abszol út*, a pun on the word *abszolút*, the Hungarian 'equivalent' of absolute (just as Rowling's English term can be read as the deviation of the word 'diagonally'). *Út* is the Hungarian for 'road', so that the translation is somewhat of a structural *calque* of the original phrase, which contains the word *alley*. In such cases the translator engages in a quasi-etymological game, trying to make up words from existing lexical items, replenishing them with new potential connotations. This is akin to how the author herself was working. As Jack Zipes admits, 'Rowling likes to play with names using foreign associations and phonetics to induce associations. Volde evokes some German or Scandinavian names' (2000: 181). Voldemort can also be read as a name referring to death (cf. the French *mort*, meaning 'death'). Translations in other languages abound in similar ludic solutions. The following anecdotal example recounted by Rowling herself illustrates an instance where this process does not work so effectively:

> In the Italian translation, Professor Dumbledore has been translated into Professore Silencio. The translator has taken the 'dumb' from the name and based the translation on that. In fact 'dumbledore' is the old English word for bumblebee. I chose it because my image is of this benign wizard, always on the move, humming to himself, and I loved the sound of the word too. For me 'Silencio' is a complete contradiction. (2000: 33)

There are, however, a number of cases where the Hungarian translator has made hardly any visible change. Ravenclaw is analogically translated as alliterating *Hollóhát* [Ravenback]. Madam Pomfrey's and Ollivander's names stay the same, so does that of Mrs Norris, the cat. The telling name of the librarian, Madam Pince, is turned into *Madam Cvikker* [Madam Pince-nez]. *Kövér Dáma* [Fat Dame] is introduced instead of Fat Lady. This is clever because it recalls the name of one of the images of playing cards, which is called *dáma* [dame] in Hungarian. *Disznóorr* [Pig's Nose] is used for Snout, rather accurately. Norbert the Norwegian ridgeback becomes *Norbert, a tarajos norvég* [Norbert, the combed Norwegian]. The *Daily Prophet* newspaper is replaced by *Reggeli Próféta* [Morning Prophet], and Chocolate Frogs by *csokibéka* [chock frogs]. Prefect is literally translated as *Prefektus*, even the nickname *prefi* is used (the ending *i* is indicative of a nickname). Bertie Bott's Every-Flavour Beans are distributed as *Bagoly Berti-féle Mindenízű Drazsé* (the Hungarian for 'owl' is used for Bott].[5] He Who Must Not Be Named is introduced as *Ő, Akit Nem Nevezünk Nevén* [He Whom We Don't Call By The Name]. The term for Invisibility Cloak - *láthatatlanná tevő/tévő köpönyeg* [a cloak making you invisible] - is less compact than the English term, although it expresses the notion appropriately, and it alludes to the name of a similar 'magic gadget' in Hungarian folk tales.

Some Foreignising Translations

Some phrases that are merely transliterated in a more crudely foreignising fashion. The special terms describing different aspects of the wizard world (such as currency) are put across via the adoption of these terms: *mugli* is introduced for Muggle, *kviddics* for Quidditch, *knút* for Knut.[6] The term *dementor* is left as it is, foreign-sounding, and in a sense, still familiar-sounding due to the Latinate ending well-known from loanwords such as *mentor*. It is also notable that most of the central child characters have relatively realistic names, which helps children believe that Harry and his mates are like everyday kids. In her review the poet and critic Eszter Babarczy praises this balancing attitude of the translator:

> The book is good, witty, and well crafted; it carries away the reader, and this applies to the Hungarian edition too, which has found the feasible compromise between over-Hungarianising and a purposeless, direct borrowing of inventions that are already part of an international cult (Muggle: the goofy everyday world; Quidditsch [sic!]: the great international wizard sport). Let's just imagine that our child starts chatting with another young holidaymaker on the beach without knowing what Quidditsch [sic!] is or who Voldemart [sic!] is, because instead of Quidditsch [sic!] and Voldemart [sic!] something 'very Hungarian' is translated into the book.[7]

Terms Specific to Culture

What happens to culture-specific notions is of crucial importance from the perspective of translation studies. Some of these are replaced by Hungarian notions of similar connotative value in the text. Some of these are, rather unsurprisingly, food names. According to Karen Manners Smith, 'Besides game and sport, food might be the most important – almost obsessive – part of boarding school life and stories' (2002: 81). As she remarks, food at Hogwarts 'tastes exquisite, though it is, for the most part, recognizably British fare. English food is not a notable world cuisine, but it is cozy and familiar to Rowling's readers ...' (2002: 82). Sherbet lemon (a concept unknown in Hungary) is domesticated as *citromos italpor* [lemon juice powder], which can indeed be purchased in Hungarian supermarkets, even though it has not been very common in the last few years. Baked beans as such do not exist in Hungary either. This item is replaced by a rather rustic dish called *babfőzelék* [bean sauce], which is not exactly students' first pick from school canteen menus. Jacket potatoes, a culinary term for a dish which is clearly not part of Hungarian cuisine, is translated as *töltött krumpli* [stuffed potatoes], sounding much more exotic than its less distinguished British counterpart.

A reference to an interview with Tóth, the translator, will highlight the practical difficulty in translating instances of otherness. When the interviewer, Tímea Hungler, asks him about rendering culture-specific terms, he asserts the importance of measuring up whether the respective foreign notion is familiar enough in Hungary. If it is, it can be left in its original version. He comes up with an example from his experience of translating film. When translating *Almost Famous*, he 'rendered' groupie as *cápa* (the Hungarian for 'shark' as well as a slang term synonymous with the seventies' slang word groupie). Some friends of his, who have seen the film in Tóth's translation, insisted that the term *groupie* should have been retained, because 'everybody knows it.' This illustrates that the translator does not necessarily judge 'accurately', that is, he is not necessarily able to please all strata of the audience. Tóth's general comment relates very well to his take on the *Harry Potter* series:

> If a reference is very internal, such as an in-joke referring to a certain country or individual, I don't use the name of this person but look for a concise term to circumscribe the situation. In fact, I explain the name, I provide the text with a footnote.[8]

The above passage underlines the translator's activity as a critic, a commentator of the text s/he translates.

Cultural Translation within the Series

The next section will further focus on cultural translation *within* the *Potter* series (how the novels translate, i.e. mediate, summarise, footnote, distil western, mainly European culture) and *of* the *Potter* series (how this mediation may work in foreign-language translations), also drawing on the notion of reading as translation. Karl Vossler views translation as 'the most intensive form of reading, namely of a reading which becomes itself creative and productive again, via understanding, explanation, and criticism...' (quoted in Oittinen, 2000: 37). As demonstrated above, there are numerous elements of Rowling's novels that allude to a European cultural heritage that may be assumed to be shared, and these terms or references, such as the Cinderella prototype, translate smoothly into Hungarian, even though some of these allusions may only be identifiable to young adults or grown-ups.[9] However, several issues specific to the UK are not problematised by the Hungarian translations, due to a lack of shared knowledge between the implied reader of Rowling's text and the implied reader of Tóth's translation. Thus, certain references remain mute for the readers of the Hungarian (and probably most other) translations.

How intertexts come across in the translation may also be viewed as an issue of cultural relocation. Intertexts that may be easily recognisable for readers of 'the original' are not determined to be such obvious connections for readers of translations in different languages. For instance, the playful allusion to Shakespeare, latent in the name of Hermione (so convincingly identified by Miranda Johnston-Haddad) may not ring a bell for some foreign readers, even if the name is not domesticated but left as it is in the 'original'. *The Winter's Tale* (or *A Midsummer Night's Dream*) may not be so frequently read and staged outside of English-speaking cultures. References to *Titus Andronicus* and *Richard III* may be bypassed for the same reason: they do not necessarily rank among the most popular Shakespeare plays outside the UK. A thematic intertext that Johnston-Haddad identifies with *Titus* is the instance when Wormtail sacrifices his right hand in order for Voldemort to reappear in human form. This is reminiscent of Emperor Saturninus requesting Titus's hand for saving his sons' lives in Act III, Scene 1 (2003:165). Another shared element is the importance of family and parentage. Titus Andronicus stands up for his children, and Harry's intention is to avenge the wrongs done to his family (cf. Johnston-Haddad, 2003: 169). The scene revisited from *Richard III* is Act 5, Scene 3, where Henry Richmond (later Henry VII) and Richard go to bed the night before the battle of Bosworth, and the ghosts of Richard's victims appear (in the order they were killed), cursing Richard and encouraging Richmond. In *Harry Potter and the Chamber of Secrets*, during the battle between the wands of Voldemort and Harry, Voldemort's wand produces Voldemort's victims (starting with the most recent one) in connection with the spells the wand was used to perform. They support Harry and he cannot hear what they hiss to Voldemort (cf. Johnston-Haddad, 2003: 167). The author of the article also emphasises 'similar themes of kinship and vengeance' (2003: 163). Nevertheless, I tend to think that the reader's response in this respect is also informed by the stratification of the audience in terms of age and education, not only by ethnic origin or national identity.

Zipes also makes mention of several elusive intertexts (without using the term *intertext* itself), such as David, Tom Thumb, Jack the Giant Killer, Aladdin, and Horatio Alger (2000: 175). Andrew Blake emphasises that the *Potter* books also revisit the Arthurian legends (2002: 17). Such allusions are not easy to mediate, and much depends on the readers' knowledge and the translator-as-reader's reading experience and general erudition. Again, it should be emphasised that the *Harry Potter* books and the translations are meant for a very assorted, indeed kiddult, readership in terms of age and education.

The popular culture intertextual web, which is mapped out rather wryly by Jack Zipes, may be more in tune with children's cultural memory and reading taste than, for instance, the figure of Horatio Alger is. This is a more 'international' referential network of globalised culture in which the Potter books (and the film versions) can be read.

> Harry must play the role of a modern-day TV sleuth in each novel.
> ... He is the ultimate detective, and Ron, as in all buddy/cop films,
> is always at his side ... He is a perfect model for boys because he
> excels in almost everything he undertakes. But this is also his
> difficulty as a literary character: he is too flawless and almost a
> caricature of various protagonists from pop culture. Like young
> heroes today, Harry appeals to young readers (and adults)

because Rowling has endowed him with supernatural powers of the sort we can see in *The Power Rangers, X-Men, Star Wars, Buffy the Vampire Slayer,* and numerous other TV shows and films ... The scheme of things is very similar to the Disney Corporation's *The Lion King,* which celebrates male dominance and blood rule. (2000: 179-183)

Elizabeth D Schafer also enlists the *James Bond* films and *Sabrina the Teenage Witch* as possible parallels, and, like Zipes, she also mentions *Star Wars* (2000: 217 & 422-423). Regarding the stratification of the *Potter* readership alongside language and national identity, Schafer does not see the cultural relocation as too problematic. She trusts that a universal wizard kid, such as Harry, is supposed to find his way to everybody's heart:

Although the Muggle and wizard cultures in which Harry lives are quite different from other cultures, readers nonetheless recognize universal concepts. The exotic details to readers outside Britain enhance the series' fantastical nature. While British readers acknowledge aspects of their own culture and even feel nostalgic or sentimental about boarding schools, foreigners perceive the story as a glimpse through a magical window into another world. They may identify with the humanity of the characters and the universality of the themes, but the specifics of the story are reminiscent of watching a documentary with explanatory subtitles. (2000: 17)

In this semi-scholarly text we may witness the emergence of a literary cult. As she further argues:

Harry has enchanted people worldwide, and his magic connects people from different cultures with a common bond. Imagination, humor, and empathy are not confined by geographical borders, skin color, or language. Even though Harry is a British schoolboy, his fears and joys are familiar to most humans regardless of where they live. People understand the universal feelings of shyness and insecurity as well as the concepts of respect and justice. The name Harry Potter is recognizable to native speakers of languages ranging from Arabic to Chinese. (2000: 16-17)

As we have seen from the examples discussed, it is valid that the translations should communicate and recontextualise cultural knowledge for children (and adults). However, regarding *Harry Potter* as a fountain of knowledge of British culture would be misleading. This is not to say that the series does not contain a great deal about British culture and British perceptions of otherness (especially when it comes to the Triwizard

Tournament, dragons in Romania, Bertha Jorkins disappearing in Albania, Professor Quirrell also travelling there, the East European headmaster, Karkaroff, presented as a former supporter of Voldemort, and so on). Moreover, Andrew Blake lists Harry Potter amongst the three 'non-religious global cultural icons' that Britain has produced. After Sherlock Holmes and James Bond, he envisages Harry Potter as the latest distinctly British hero who has a universal appeal (2002: 91).

Nevertheless, the reading or critical activity (including the translator's task) will not be a sheer unpacking of meaning, since the cultural knowledge is not ossified in the book but open to continuous (ideological) critique. What Elizabeth D Schafer perceives as the strength of the series (universal values) is exactly what Jack Zipes dismisses about what he calls 'cute and ordinary' books (2000:175). Zipes styles Harry a 'postmodern whiz kid' as well as a Christian knight (2000:174), though Zipes appears far from pleased by this amalgamation:

> He is white, Anglo-Saxon, bright, athletic, and honest ... He is the classic Boy Scout, a little mischievous like Tom Sawyer or one of the Hardy boys. He does not curse; he speaks standard English grammatically, as do all his friends; he is respectful to his elders; and he has perfect manners. (2000: 178-179)

These are aspects that a translation negotiates instead of channeling exotic information about Britishness into foreign schoolchildren's heads. In Giselle Lisa Anatole's view, the *Potter* books do not break away decisively from British imperialism: 'Rowling seems to project a more traditional, nostalgic view of imperial Center and less-civilized Periphery in her Harry Potter series' (2002: 165):

> Magical Britain, and Hogwarts in particular, thus become the magical metropole, despite their initial resemblance to a foreign landscape of otherness. Everywhere else subsequently falls into the category of periphery. (2002: 164)

A radical translator might well go against the assertion of the Ruritania myth, a mystification of Eastern Europe and the Balkans (rather as a unified mass, though Romania, Bulgaria and Albania are mentioned explicitly), which is executed mainly by affirming the Gothic stereotypes about Transylvania and Albania.[10] An experimental translator or adaptor might talk back to this tradition, and have some of the Transylvanian dragons and Voldemort-related characters that are situated in the Balkans re-placed somewhere in 'the Occident'. This would be a *hyperbole*, a corrective translation or adaptation, but Tóth clearly does not intend to practise such politicised impertinence.[11] Another radical translation or adaptation strategy would be to substitute these elements for references to cultures that Hungarian culture (which, as such, is of course, ungraspable) may patronise, may feel superior to: cultures that may be Hungary's 'others'.

Certain references 'closer to home' will read very differently to the Hungarian readers than to English speakers, or indeed readers of other translations. A case in point is the 'beast' named Hungarian Horntail in Rowling's fourth book, and renamed as *Magyar Mennydörgős* [Hungarian Thunderbolt/ Thundery Hungarian] by Tóth. While Hungarian Horntail carries the potential of something exotic and dangerous to the British readers, the much more prestigious-sounding Magyar Mennydörgős certainly comes across as a domestic element of the Potter world (such a name can crop up in Hungarian tales or children's books), and it may even appeal to national pride; after all the Hungarian one is the most crafty, clever beast in the tournament, and thus, the most difficult one to defeat.

As opposed to the value system of culturally conservative Middle England, persuasively represented in the novels by the Dursleys, for example, Hogwarts is characterised by ethnic diversity.[12] A similar phenomenon is noticeable in the film versions. Again, some of the cultural negotiation that is apparent for readers of the 'original' (not only for British readers, and probably not for every individual British reader) may be mute for the foreign language reader and translator. For instance, the presence of a certain Parvati Patil at Hogwarts exemplifies political correctness on the part of the author. It could be seen as almost compulsory that a character with an Indian or Pakistani sounding name be included in a children's book that has at least some reference to the British educational system of the day, given the significant presence of Asian minority groups in the ethnic composition of the country. The surname of the Patil sisters sounds like a twisted version of the common Indian name, *Patel*, which would ring a bell for most British readers.[13] On the other hand, Elaine Ostry argues that all these characters are minor characters, and 'all the major players are Anglo-Saxon' (2002: 93). Schafer contends that characters such as (the presumably Chinese) Cho Chang, the Patil twins, Dean Thomas and Angelina Johnson, both supposedly black, and the Irish-sounding Seamus Finnigan 'provide ethnic diversity at Hogwarts' (2000: 63). The dreadlocked Lee Jordan, who may be identified as African-Caribbean, could be added to the list (Blake, 2002: 108). For the sake of topicality, an overtly domesticating translation would perhaps translate one of these characters into a Romany student in Hungary (and would probably address other ethnic minorities too). However, as we have seen, Tóth's translations avoid too much domestication and politicisation. Thus, it comes as no surprise that Parvati Patil et al. have the same names in the Hungarian edition; however, it is doubtful that the name offers similar connotations to most Hungarian readers.

130

Even though I find the previous example a sign of engagement with political correctness by Rowling, there have been readings of its opposite too. For Julia Park Rodrigues, who reviews the *Potter* books for a women writers' magazine, the Weasleys evoke the stereotypical poor Irish Catholic family. Commenting on the character of Ron and his family, the reviewer notes:

> He's red-haired and freckled, from a large family of wizards, and he's one of Harry's best friends. But he's also dirt-poor, stuck with hand-me-downs and too many siblings. The Weasleys' home is called 'The Burrow,' suggesting rabbits and their prolific breeding. In other words, the Weasleys are the perfect caricature of the poor Irish-Catholic family, as seen from Rowling's middle-class-Protestant-British view. Although most other Rowling characters have Dickensian names, comic-descriptive or onomatopoeic, the Weasleys' name seems like a slam; its associations are hardly charming. (2003)

In another article Julia Park also mentions Mrs Weasley's first name, Molly as a typical Irish name, and corned beef, disliked by Ron, as typical Irish food (2002: 186). Is Harry then an 'Everychild', or a 'magical' version of a British child?[14] As the ideological judgements of different readers attest, the texts do not prove to be ideologically as innocent as Shafer's cultic paradigm seems to suggest.

Referring back to Shafer's comment, it is also rather unwise, perhaps even ignorant, to disregard the fact that other cultures also have boarding school education, even if it is not Oxford, Cambridge or Ampleforth (the latter, a Benedictine school in North Yorkshire, has been regarded as a source of inspiration for Rowling's invention, Hogwarts).[15] Some Hungarian students can relate to their own boarding school memories or experiences when reading the books. However, the division of the school population into 'houses' or smaller communities will be unusual. Foreign readers may also be very familiar with the British public school system from their studies, and other reading or viewing experiences, and may be able to read the book as a parody of this system.

Conclusion

André Lefevere introduced the term *refraction* for texts 'processed for a certain audience (children, for example), or adapted to a certain poetics or a certain ideology' (quoted in Gentzler, 1993: 140). In order to exemplify the term, he offers an amusing example from the history of translating and adapting for children. Tóth's translations may be seen as refractions from the perspective of the cultural relocation of British children magic world. As Nancy K Jentsch asserts, 'the translator of the Harry Potter series has a unique challenge in the genre [translation], that is, to portray a setting and its people that are a world apart from ours, and at the same time located due north of London' (2002: 285). Many of Rowling's European references do come across in the Hungarian translations, which also map out a 'wizard Europe', as do the *Potter* books in their original, yet the polarisation and occasional stereotyping may be more apparent when the Hungarian translations are read, as a result of the differences in audiences, including the translator-as-reader.

Tóth respects the otherness of the 'original', and, in the main, does not relocate the wizard world in Hungary. On the contrary, his translations seem to be intended to reconceive the foreignness the translator may have encountered in his own reading of the 'originals', most of which would ring as familiar to the British audience. This activity is hampered when it comes to the *Potter* books mapping out a 'wizard Britain (or UK?)', for instance, by regional dialects, accents and numerous other markers of ethnic belonging, including non-English ethnicity (such as the Patil sisters). As Blake asserts, 'However you localise the translation, Harry is very English, and goes to a very English-style school' (2002: 89). The abovementioned referential system would be largely unnoticeable to the Hungarian reader (and indeed, impossible to mediate, unless via domesticating localisation), and Tóth's translations compensate for that by mapping out an alternative 'wizard Britain', which, in certain aspects, comes across as more British or, at times, (for Hungarians) more exotic or mysterious than Rowling's. Roxfort, for example, gives the impression of Oxford's counterpart in the British 'wizard establishment.' Stuffed potatoes come across as something unfamiliar and exotic, in contrast with the familiarity of jacket potatoes to a British audience. Due to the semantic fluidity of the process of translation as such, and the traits of these particular translations, Harry Potter in Hungarian, and the fictitious world around him, carry British, Hungarian and Western connotations almost coterminously.

Tóth's translations appeal both to children and adults. Being *kiddult* texts, they address the cultural memories of both children and adult groups, including potential references and intertexts for both. The translations play with what is familiar and what is foreign, disguising these in one another, and thus opening up avenues for cultural critique. This case study is intended to facilitate moving beyond the clever but somewhat straitjacket-like binary opposition of foreignisation and domestication, highlighting that it is rather the foreign-as-familiar and the familiar-as-foreign that feature in these reworkings.[16]

Notes

1. The present article is a revised version of an essay I published in *The Anachronist* under the title 'Beyond Domestication and Foreignisation: Harry Potter in Hungarian Translation' (2004:153-174).

132

2. My approximate translations of Hungarian terms and quotations will be indicated in square brackets.

3. Chantal Zabus in her *Tempests after Shakespeare* (2002:2) talks of rewrites reorienting the circulation of knowledge; this applies to translation 'proper' too. Other semi-technical terms such as 'foreign material' and 'cultural content' are also in use. For the former cf. Oittinen 2000: 90, and for the latter cf. Susan Stan quoted Oittinen 2000: 150. For a different aspect of knowledge in the Potter series see Hopkins 2002.

4. For thoroughgoing criticism of Venuti's polarisation of translation strategies cf. Oittinen 2000:73-74, and Paloposki and Oittinen 2000: 373-390.

5. `Rowling's pleasure in inventing food both delicious and disgusting is reminiscent of Roald Dahl's children's fiction' (Manners Smith, 2002:82). This creative take on food is followed rather imaginatively by the translator.

6. Interestingly, the Italian and Dutch translations domesticate the word Muggle. The Italian *babboni* derives from the word *babbioni* [idiots], and the Dutch *dreutzel* is made up from *dreutle* [clumsy]. See Blake 2002: 106. These terms thus go against the tradition of an international 'uniform' Potter lingo. However, the readers can probably relate to the terms very easily, and may link them to their own society. As Blake notes, these have become terms of abuse, just as much as their English counterpart has.

7. '[...] a könyv jó, szellemes, technikás, sodorja az olvasót, és ez elmondható a magyar kiadásról is, amely eltalálta a helyes középutat a máris nemzetközi kultusz tárgyát alkotó invenciók (Muggle: a tökfej normális világ, Quidditsch: a nagy nemzeti varázsló sport) túlzott magyarítása és elvtelen átvétele között. Képzeljük csak el, hogy gyermekünk szóba elegyedik a családi nyaralás során a szomszéd strandolóval, de nem tudja, mi a Quidditsch vagy ki Voldemart, mert kviddics és Voldemart helyett valami nagyon magyarosat fordítottak neki bele a könyvbe.' Spelling mistakes were in the source, the extract is translated by M M.

8. 'Ha túlzottan belterjes, az adott országra utaló egy poén, például egy bizonyos emberre vonatkozik, nem a nevet írom le, hanem egy frappáns, a helyzetet körülíró kifejezést keresek, gyakorlatilag megmagyarázom a nevet, lábjegyzetet készítek a szöveghez.' The extract is translated by M.M

9. For the Cinderella prototype see Blake 2002:17.

10. For the discussion of the myth of Ruritania see Goldsworthy 1998.

133

11. Douglas Robinson applies the term *hyperbole* for corrective translations where a chief concern is the improvement of the original (cf. Oittinen, p. 79).

12. For the notion of Middle England (what New Labour may see as the traditional, mainstream stratum of society in England) see Blake 2002: 25.

13. So much so that in a telling *lapsus calami* the name is indicated as *Patel* rather than *Patil* (Ostry 2002:94).

14. Roni Natov (2002) mentions the phrase 'Everychild' when she describes the typical trials and struggles Harry Potter as a questing hero goes through.

15. cf. *Ampleforth: My Teacher's a Monk*, broadcast on ITV, UK, 22:30 on 29 April 2003

16. My special thanks go to Penny Brown, who encouraged me to write up this material for publication, and to Anikó Szilágyi, for offering valuable comments on a previous version of the essay. The article is dedicated to my aunt Kati, who first presented me with the *Harry Potter* books in Hungarian.

Bibliography

Primary sources

Rowling, J K (1997) *Harry Potter and the Philosopher's Stone*, London: Bloomsbury

Rowling, J K (1999) *Harry Potter és a Bölcsek Köve*, Tóth, T B (trans.), Budapest: Animus

Rowling, J K (1998) *Harry Potter and the Chamber of Secrets*, London: Bloomsbury

Rowling, J K (2000) *Harry Potter és a Titkok Kamrája*, Tóth, T B (trans.), Budapest: Animus

Rowling, J K (1999) *Harry Potter and the Prisoner of Azkaban*, London: Bloomsbury
Rowling, J K (2000) *Harry Potter és az Azkabani Fogoly*, Tóth, T B (trans.), Budapest: Animus

Rowling, J K (2000) *Harry Potter and the Goblet of Fire*, London: Bloomsbury

Rowling, J K (2000) *Harry Potter és a Tűz Serlege*, Tóth, T B (trans.), Budapest: Animus

Rowling, J K (2003) *Harry Potter and the Order of the Phoenix*, London: Bloomsbury

Rowling, J K (2003) *Harry Potter és a Főnix Rendje*, Tóth, T B (trans.), Budapest: Animus

Secondary sources

Anatol, G L (2002) 'The Fallen Empire: Exploring Ethnic Otherness in the World of Harry Potter,' in *Reading Harry Potter*, Anatol, G L (ed.), Westport, Connecticut & London: Praeger

Babarczy, E 'Millenniumi Bűbáj. J K Rowling: Harry Potter és a Bölcsek Köve [Millenial Charm: J K Rowling: Harry Potter and the Philosopher's Stone],' in *Mancs*
http://www.mancs.hu/legfrissebb.tdp-azon=0002kritika7.htm
Accessed 16 September 2003

Blake, A (2002) *The Irresistible Rise of Harry Potter*, London and New York: Verso

Boldizsár, I (2001) 'A Gyerekirodalom első Akciókönyve. (J K Rowling Négy Harry Potter-könyve)' [The First 'Action Book' in Children's Literature (J K Rowling's Four *Harry Potter* Books)], in *Holmi*: 4

Fraser, L (2000) 'An Interview with J K Rowling', Mammoth

Gentzler, E (1993) *Contemporary Translation Theories*, London: Routledge

Goldsworthy, V (1998) *Inventing Ruritania: The Imperialism of the Imagination*, New Haven and London: Yale University Press

Hopkins, L (2002) 'Harry Potter and the Acquisition of Knowledge,' in *Reading Harry Potter*, Anatol, G L (ed.) Westport, Connecticut & London: Praeger

Humboldt, W (1992) 'From 'Introduction to His Translation of *Agamemnon*', Sloan, S (trans.) in *Theories of Translation*, Schulte, R & Biguenet, J (eds.) Chicago & London: University of Chicago Press

Johnston-Haddad, M (2003) 'Harry Potter and the Shakespearean Allusion,' in: *Reimagining Shakespeare for Children and Young Adults*, Miller, N J (ed.) New York & London: Routledge

135

Hungler, T 'Tóth Tamás Boldizsár: Bűn rossz szinkronok készülnek' ['Some Dreadful Dubbings Are Being Done']
http://www.magyar.film.hu
Accessed 5 May 2003

Jentsch, N K (2002) 'Harry Potter and the Tower of Babel,' in *The Ivory Tower and Harry Potter: Perspectives on a Literary Phenomenon*, Whited, L A (ed.) Columbia, US & London: University of Missouri Press

Manners Smith, K (2002) 'Harry Potter's Schooldays: J K Rowling and the British Boarding School Novel', in *Reading Harry Potter*, Anatol, G L (ed.) Westport, Connecticut & London: Praeger

Minier, M (2002) 'Krapp's Last Tape: The Problematics of Investigating Translation as Acculturation,' in *New Voices in Irish Criticism 3*, Vandevelde, K (ed.) Dublin: Four Courts Press

Natov, R (2002) 'Harry Potter and the Extraordinariness of the Ordinary', in *The Ivory Tower and Harry Potter*, Whited, L A (ed.), Columbia, US & London: University of Missouri Press

O' Grady et al. (eds.) (1993) *Contemporary Linguistics: An Introduction*, New York: St Martin's Press

Oittinen, R (2000) *Translating for Children*, New York and London: Garland Publishing, Inc.

Ostry, E (2002) 'Accepting Mudbloods: The Ambivalent Social Vision of J K Rowling's Fairy Tales,' in *Reading Harry Potter*, Anatol, G L (ed.) Westport, Connecticut and London: Praeger

Paloposki, O & Oittinen, R (2000) 'The Domesticated Foreign,' in *Translation in Context*, Chesterman, A, San Salvador, N G & Gambier, Y (eds.), Amsterdam/ Philadelphia: John Benjamins

Park, J (2002) 'Class and Socioeconomic Identity in Harry Potter's England,' in *Reading Harry Potter*, Anatol, G L (ed.) Westport, Connecticut & London: Praeger

Park Rodrigues, J 'There's Something about Harry (Potter): A Second Look at the International Children's Book Phenomenon'
http://www.womenwriters.net/bookreviews/harrypotter.htm
Accessed 17 September 2003

Schafer, E D (2000) *Exploring Harry Potter*, London: Ebury Press

Schleiermacher, F (1992) 'From 'On the Different Methods of Translating" Bartscht, W (trans.) in *Theories of Translation,* Schulte, R & Biguenet, J (eds.), Chicago and London: University of Chicago Press

Venuti, L (1995) *The Translator's Invisibility: A History of Translation,* London and New York: Routledge

Venuti, L (1998) *The Scandals of Translation: Towards an Ethics of Difference,* London and New York: Routledge

Zabus, C (2002) *Tempests after Shakespeare,* New York: Palgrave

Zipes, J (2000) 'The Phenomenon of Harry Potter, or Why All the Talk?', in *Sticks and Stones: The Troublesome Success of Children's Literature from Slovenly Peter to Harry Potter,* New York and London: Routledge

Between the Global and the Local: Child-Oriented Translation Today

Michał Borodo

Introduction

This paper examines the constraints and mechanisms governing the production of translations directed at children at the turn of the 20th century, with Poland as my primary focus, though many of the described mechanisms could equally well be applied to other corners of the globe. After introducing the methodological basis, I look at large-scale extratextual trends and a panorama of contemporary child-related translation phenomena. The focus of the final section is primarily on translators' treatment of the foreign. In order to encompass the visual, including the important area of film, I shall employ the term 'child-oriented translation,' rather than 'children's literature translation.'

Systems and Norms Paradigm

The present research is situated within a broad systems and norms paradigm, which, it is argued, is a fairly productive approach to analysing child-oriented translation; at the same time it seems that child-oriented translation itself may be conducive to the development of the paradigm as a whole, being potentially capable of revitalising and refocusing it. I see this as:

- helping to rehabilitate the idea of a system, which seems to have acquired negative connotations within translation studies as something limiting in-depth research

- offering a challenge to the traditional binary opposition of 'target' and 'source' (text, norms, culture, etc.)

- giving a boost to the concept of adaptation, largely neglected within translation studies.

The paradigm as a whole has gone through a number of stages, starting with structuralism, when translated texts were mainly analysed in polysystemic terms, through the prism of their central or marginal position within the polysystem. A representative text in the field of child-oriented translation is Zohar Shavit's *Poetics of Children's Literature*, which still seems to be a key text in the field; in the chapter devoted to translation, Shavit decides 'to examine the implications of the systemic status of children's literature to substantiate the claim that the behaviour of translation of children's literature is largely determined by the position of children's literature within the literary polysystem' (Shavit 1986:112). The following stage, which is still to some extent with us, is that of elaboration, involving a number of new models, drawing from systems and norms, but at the same time taking them in new directions; in the field of child-oriented translation a significant figure is Tiina Puurtinen (1995), who elaborates on the idea of systems and norms and investigates the acceptability of Finnish translations for children through readability and speakability tests. The poststructuralist stage, which rather than replacing the elaboration stage runs parallel to it, questions the notion of systems, criticising it for its claims to objectivity, its overemphasis on regularities of translation behaviour, and its failure to take into account the agency of individual translators (e.g. Venuti, 1998: 27-30, Pym, 1998: 111-124, Lefevere, 2001: 244). Riitta Oittinen (2000), foregrounding the agency and creativity of a human translator as opposed to 'dehumanising' systems, could perhaps be seen as a representative of this approach within child-oriented translation research, even without writing directly against the idea of systems and norms.

Global Systems

While in translation studies as a whole Michael Cronin's *Translation and Globalization* (2003) could be perceived as a proclamation of the advent of a new phase, this approach seems not yet to have gained much visibility within child-oriented translation research. Certain early attempts to approach translated children's literature from this angle, however, can be recognised in the 1978 volume by Klingberg, in which Becker refers to global translation exchange patterns (1978: 28-45), and Weinreich sketches a decisively negative picture of co-editing as a sort of supranational publishing system or network in itself (1978: 147-158).

The idea of large-scale systems has been dealt with more explicitly by such children's text researchers as Marsha Kinder, writing of a supersystem, that is 'a network of intertextuality constructed around a figure or group of figures from pop culture,' which 'must cut across several modes of image production; must appeal to diverse generations…must foster collectability through a proliferation of related products' (1991: 122). While Kinder writes of a supersystem, the term preferred by others is Product (with a capital P!). Thus Tom Engelhardt speaks of 'a full-blown commercial apparatus and an ever-larger cast of adults bent on selling Product to the child' (1991: 62) and Michał Zając (2000) coins the term Total Product to denote a network of Disney-licensed translations interconnected with films and other related products marketed in turn-of-the-century Poland. The expanding universe of *Peter Rabbit*, to give another example, is mapped by Margaret Mackey, while the growing influence of child-oriented 'culture industry' networks, which have now become increasingly global, has long been criticised by Jack Zipes.

Why should child-oriented translation research embrace the globalisation perspective? And how may it contribute to the paradigm as a whole? As an instance, the highly popular *W.I.T.C.H.* series was originally created in Italian, by Italians, in Disney Italy, and was later extended to include another sub-series, this time created by a Danish author for Disney and Egmont. It is now marketed in about 60 countries including the US, Russia, Turkey, China, United Arab Emirates and Chile, in the form of comic book magazines, short stories, calendars, diaries and other accompanying products. It has also been made into an animation (also broadcast globally), this time created in France by Disney in co-production with Jetix Europe and French SIP Animation company. Another instance is a book containing abridged versions of stories by Carroll, Andersen, and the brothers Grimm, originally produced in Belgium and published simultaneously in a dozen other countries. It would seem that a great deal of what is now translated for children could generally be better described as generated by and integrated into global publishing and marketing systems, as well as having a complex multi-source and a large-scale multi-target. The traditional source/target dichotomy has thus become in many ways inadequate. It also seems less accurate to speak of translations as 'facts of the target culture' (Toury, 1995: 29), a description which was once seen in translation studies as revolutionary, or even to see them as conditioned by source or target culture in the first place. Rather they are often shaped by interactions between the global and the local.

It might be added at this point that no attempt has been made here to differentiate between the overlapping concepts of system, network, or map (the latter two being the preferred terms of Cronin and Lambert respectively), or to suggest the superiority of one of these concepts over another. The aim is rather to suggest an approach reaching far beyond individual case studies, through focusing on large-scale translation phenomena and their underlying mechanisms and constraints. The employment of the term 'system', arguably the most universal within a broader range of like terms, has the advantage of relating the current research to certain well- established earlier systemic approaches, suggesting continuity and 'taking further' rather than replacement.

Child-oriented Translation and Norms

In child-oriented translation research, the concept of norms has, at least until recently, proceeded along somewhat different lines from translation studies as a whole, being closely connected to a specific type of addressee. Around the time when Toury proposed the most influential set of norms to date – divided into preliminary, initial and operational norms – a different set, partly related to Toury's operational and initial norms, was suggested by Stolt. In the context of children's literature translation, Stolt distinguishes between:

- the educational trend, which manifests itself in censoring unsuitable elements or introducing didacticism (1978: 134)

- a tendency to adjust the textual in congruence with assumptions about children's needs and capacity, for which the 'generally accepted and wide-spread custom of substituting names' (p136) may serve as an illustration

- a tendency to sentimentalise and prettify: 'the ambition of many a translator to make everything a bit more beautiful and more full of genuine feeling' (p137).

Stolt's first two norms are clearly analogous to the two constraints proposed by Shavit, who argues that translated texts for children are not supposed to violate what may be referred to as a comprehensibility as well as an educational constraint (1986: 113).

A more recent approach is to be found in Desmidt, who, investigating 52 German editions of Lagerlof's *Nils Holgersson's Wonderful Journey*, comes up with another norm typology, distinguishing between:

- preliminary

- literary and educational

- pedagogical

- business norms. (2003: 168)

Desmidt's preliminary norms, adopted after Toury, relate to the selection of texts and the directness of translation. Literary and educational norms, somewhat specific to the case study in focus, as *Nils* was originally designed as a geography textbook, decide whether 'literary entertainment' or 'the educational aspect' is prioritised (2003: 171). The working of pedagogical norms manifests itself in two ways: in the tendency to simplify the story for a children's audience, and in the modification of elements which are not congruent with the prevalent pedagogical values in the new cultural environment of the text (2003: 172). The fourth type in the typology is referred to as business norms, which relate to the role of the publisher and such issues as copyright or the interconnectedness of children's literature translations with films. This is illustrated with a new wave of German re-editions, as well as new adaptations of *Nils Holgersson* generated by a successful German-Japanese television serial (2003: 173). The inclusion of preliminary and business norms is a welcome advance in comparison with Stolt and Shavit, leading to further contextualisation and to the examination of certain large-scale translation phenomena.

The question of interest in the present paper is whether these large-scale translation phenomena are paralleled by any changes in the textual, especially in translators' treatment of the cultural other. Discussing contemporary children's book publishing, Fraustino perceives the following as its most characteristic features:

- 'It is global'

- 'It is controlled by a small number of huge conglomerates'

- It is 'Anglocentric'. (2004: 647)

While in 1978 Stolt speaks of a 'generally accepted and wide-spread custom of substituting names,' Aixela, commenting on the translation strategy of naturalisation, digresses to say that 'this strategy is infrequently used in literature (with the clear exception of children's literature, *where it is also beginning to decline*)' [emphasis mine] (1996: 63). It appears then that a different set of norms has emerged more recently in the context of translators' treatment of the foreign.

Traditionally, as evident from the first two sets of norms above, child-oriented translation has frequently been conditioned by a separate set of norms, being characterised by a specific addressee, often ascribed special needs by translators and a secondary position within the polysystem, or generally a lower cultural prestige. Traditionally, this area seems to have been open to more liberal treatment and domestication. It may be that due to the prestige of English and the economic influence of expanding Anglo-American culture, a gradual shift from domesticating towards foreignising has taken place in the realm of child-oriented translation. Since many contemporary texts for children have become so immensely visible and culturally central, being frequently directed at a dual audience, translation methods may have become less liberal in terms of translators' treatment of the cultural other. Alternatively, it may be that the reaction to the massive export of Anglo-American texts is increasing domestication and their localisation. Perhaps it largely depends on the agency of individual translators, perhaps on the type of the translated text: whether it is an animation, an adaptation, a full-length contemporary text or a classic. These issues will be returned to in the third part of this article.

Between the Global and the Local

As suggested above, children's literature translation can be fruitfully approached with the focus on global translation mechanisms and networks. Rather than through the target and source opposition, or system understood as a polysystem, it can be analysed on a scale between the global and the local: where the global would include translations from entertainment conglomerates simultaneously distributed globally, the local would relate to certain country-specific historically conditioned translation phenomena. A couple of other phenomena, such as different forms of localisation or non-global intermediary adaptations, lie somewhere in between the two poles. Let us begin with the global end of the scale.

In *Translation and Globalization,* Michael Cronin observes that 'the colonialism of the nineteenth century and its fear of the Double as the colonial subject who was too human for comfort gives way to what we might term the 'clonialism' of the twenty-first century' (2003: 128), with the disturbing double (triple? thousand? trillion?) this time being the clone, in the form of the popular culture product such as an omnipresent American sitcom or Disney production. Cronin goes on to say, 'Under clonialism everything turns out to be a replica, a simulacrum, a copy of a limited set of economically and culturally powerful originals' (2003: 129). This seems to be an accurate description of a bulk of what is translated for children at the turn of the century. A limited number of titles/brands, be it *Harry Potter, W.I.T.C.H., Pokemon, Teenage Mutant Ninja Turtles,* or Disney-licensed *Winnie the Pooh* dominate childhood spaces of developed countries globally, in the form of translated films, books, and a variety of gadgets and toys.

The clonised empire is not necessarily an arena of conformity and passive acceptance however. It does sometimes write back. In interaction with local markets, some child-oriented texts may undergo hybridisation, being made into localised versions. An instance of a partly localised book series is the *Horrible Histories* educational series, which was initially available in Polish translation. Into this, books on Polish history produced by Polish writers have later been included, with the design and all the formal characteristics of the original books being retained. Another example is Polish versions of popular Disney picture books, in which the accompanying text, usually a moderately creative retelling, is produced by a local celebrity whose name may attract more buyers. The most spectacular and culturally visible examples of localisation, to which I shall return in the third part of this article, are to be found in Polish translations of animated films such as *Shrek,* which exploit and multiply local references to an astonishing degree. Globalisation, rather than clonialism, may thus in some cases be a more accurate term to describe contemporary child-oriented translations.

Adaptation Revisited

Bastin suggests that, 'Generally speaking, historians and scholars of translation take a negative view of adaptation, dismissing the phenomenon as distortion, falsification or censorship, but it is rare to find clear definitions of the terminology used in discussing this controversial concept' (2001: 6). Adopting a non-negative stance towards adaptation and not necessarily aiming at providing any clear-cut definition of it, let us nevertheless revisit the

143

concept by positioning it between the global and the local and suggesting a new possible categorisation of adaptation phenomena. Traditionally, adaptation seems to have mainly been analysed within translation studies in textual terms, if indeed it has been analysed at all. The concept has at times been dealt with as a narrowly defined translation strategy, with Vinay and Darbelnet's 1958 definition as one of the better known. Alternatively, it has been employed in a broader sense, alongside the equally peripheral notions of free translation, rewriting, or abridgement, to denote texts produced according to other than mainstream accuracy standards. Nevertheless, the main focus seems to have generally been on the treatment of the textual and, again after Bassnett, 'Much time and ink has been wasted attempting to differentiate between *translations*, *versions*, *adaptations* and the establishment of a hierarchy of 'correctness' between these categories' (2003: 81) [Bassnett's emphasis].

In child-oriented translation research specifically, the pendulum has swung from very conservative approaches, such as Klingberg's, to much more liberal ones, such as Oittinen's. According to Klingberg, children's texts have already been adjusted to children's capacity by the writer of the original, a concept which is referred to as *a degree of adaptation*, and consequently there is no need of *context adaptation,* that is of adapting and simplifying the texts any further for another child reader in a different culture (1978: 86). According to Klingberg, such modifications ought to be kept to the minimum, the major task of the translator being to preserve *a degree of adaptation* and refrain from *context adaptation* (p86), as this may lead to 'a falsification' (1978: 87). Two decades later, Oittinen points to the active role of translators, who have every right to their own interpretations, stating that 'even tales by H C Andersen should be adapted to keep them readable; they must be adapted or die' (2000: 80).

In the present paper I argue that the various studies of translators' treatment of the textual, however inspiring, should be supplemented with the analyses of their production and dissemination, as one striking thing about adaptation today is that much of it has in recent years gone global.

A **global adaptation** is thus the first category proposed in the analysis. The category involves adaptations accompanying such animations as *The Lion King, Monsters Inc.,* or *Madagascar,* almost simultaneously available on a global scale and in a wide range of translated books. Each animation is usually accompanied by at least a few translated books, differing in size and price.

To the second category belong **intermediary adaptations**, which differ from the first category in that they are not necessarily available on a global scale; their primary characteristic is that they are produced in one country, translated and sold in another country, and contain adapted texts originally produced in another country still. As an example, Russian children's books available in Polish translation in 1999 were mainly Russian adaptations of Andersen and the brothers Grimm while, in the very same year, Russian tales were available to Polish readers through a translation from Italian (Socha, 2002: 210). According to Socha, most of the Italian titles for children available in Poland in the 1990s were adaptations of non-Italian western classics (p210). In 1996, to give another example, as many as forty titles were imported to Poland from New Zealand, all of them intermediary adaptations of children's classics (p211). Generally, the major imports of intermediary adaptations into Poland in the closing years of the century were from Spain, Belgium, and Italy, whereas the adaptations themselves were mainly based on tales originally produced by Perrault, the brothers Grimm, and Andersen (p212).

Moving towards the local end of the scale we encounter **local adaptations**, usually based on such classics as *Gulliver's Travels*, *Alice*, *Peter Pan*, or *The Jungle Book*, produced by local adaptors and for the local market. They are mostly of little literary and artistic value, lacking originality and sometimes imitating more successful adaptations such as Disney's. The less said about them the better!

Before introducing the fourth adaptation type it might be added that what is characteristic of some of the above adaptations (perhaps especially intermediary adaptations), is their functioning as almost anonymous texts, as the names of the adaptor or of the author on whose work the adaptation is based are not always mentioned. Socha maintains, for instance, that most Spanish adaptations translated into Polish in the nineties were anonymous texts (2002: 212) and mentions the same tendency in the context of some Winnie-the-Pooh adaptations (p208). An interesting question, in a country like Poland, where children's culture has in many ways become the culture of adaptation, is what effect this multitude of adaptations - originals condensed, fragmented, translated, and multiplied – may have, alongside their growing anonymity, on the perception of child readers of children's literature and of literature in general.

The fourth type may be referred to as a **hypertext adaptation**. The category covers certain locally produced software programs (so far mainly available from Aidem Media company) based on such classics as *The Jungle Book*, *Robin Hood*, *Robinson Crusoe* and *Peter Pan;* these normally contain an adaptation of the original story in the form of a short animation accompanied by the narrator's voice and a number of games, which can be selected from the main menu through interaction with the computer screen and the voice commenting on the decisions taken by the reader-player. Though still in its infancy in Poland, this may well become a dynamically developing type of adaptation in the future.

The above four categories are no more than an invitation to further analysis of adaptation within translation studies, and the rediscovery of the concept of an area between the global and the local.

Old Friends and New Arrivals

Exploring the local end of the scale may result in discovering certain country-specific, historically conditioned, translation phenomena. In Poland, one such turn-of-the-century phenomenon may be referred to as the recycling of excluded translations. Certain interwar translations of girls' stories by, among others, Angela Brazil, Kate Douglas Wiggin, and Jean Webster, which were all judged to be too sentimental in communist Poland, and such authors as E. Atkinson (*Greyfriars Bobby*) or the Catholic priest Francis Finn, regarded as too religious in communist Poland, have been published anew at the turn of the century. Old friends have become welcome again.

Some other old friends, present in Poland all along, have become, despite the passage of time, much younger. Released from the monopoly of a few state-owned publishers, such classic texts as *Tom Sawyer, The Secret Garden, Little Lord Fauntleroy* and *Lassie* have become available in three or four new translations in the nineties. The record-breaker appears to be *Lassie;* since 1956, for about forty years, it was available in numerous editions, all with the very same translation, but in the nineties it has multiplied into as many as six new translations from various publishers, large and small.

Finally, the turn of the century is also the time for welcoming new arrivals, some of which, like E B White's *Stuart Little* and *Charlotte's Web*, L I Wilder's *Little House* series, or Dr Seuss, had to wait for their turn for almost fifty years. Some others, such as Ethel Turner's *Seven Little Australians*, Walter De La Mare's *The Three Mulla-Mulgars*, or Beatrix Potter's *Peter Rabbit* series, have waited for as long as a century. Potter, only briefly available at the turn of the sixties in a decisively domesticated translation with Polish illustrations, was in the final decade of the century launched in two different translations, one of which was produced by a popular young adult fiction author, M Musierowicz.

Domestication Past its Prime?

The focus of the third part of this article is on translators' treatment of the cultural other. The question already posed in the first part is whether large-scale translation phenomena, which may be referred to as clonisation or globalisation, are in some way reflected in translators' treatment of the foreign. Is it true that there has been a gradual shift from domesticating

146

towards foreignising tendencies? A book-length study which asks a similar question in the Polish context is Piotr Kwieciński's *Disturbing Strangeness* (2001), in which the author investigates the treatment of the cultural other in contemporary Polish translations of American sitcoms and press articles; his analysis to a large extent confirms a significant proportion of the foreign in the texts he examines. How about child-oriented translations?

Some of the most obvious indicators in the field under investigation seem to be names and titles; a cursory look at much of what has been recently translated for children in Poland seems to confirm that very many of them expose rather than conceal the foreign. Take the very first sentence from the currently marketed translation of Dahl's *Charlie and the Chocolate Factory*:

> Tych dwoje staruszków to ojciec i matka pana **Bucket**: dziadek **Joe** i babcia **Josephine**. A tych dwoje staruszków to ojciec i matka pani **Bucket**: dziadek **George** i babcia **Georgina**. Oto pan **Bucket**. A oto pani **Bucket**. Państwo **Bucket** mają syna, który nazywa się **Charlie Bucket**. (Dahl, 2004: 9-10)

Similar use of non-Polish names is found on the opening page of Neil Gaiman's *Coraline*:

> Na parterze – panna **Spink** i panna **Forcible**. Obie były stare i okrągłe, i hodowały mnóstwo starzejących się szkockich terierów o imionach takich jak **Hamish, Andrew** i **Jock**. (Gaiman, 2003: 9)

There are hundreds of other Polish translations of children's books in which a similar tendency can be observed. 'Privet Drive,' 'Dursley', and 'Grunnings' are to be found, unchanged, in the first three sentences of the Polish translation of You-Know-What-Book. 'Peabody', 'Billy Little,' and 'Tommy Tittlebottom' are left untouched in the Polish translation of *Mr. Peabody's Apples*, and the names in Madonna's child-oriented global pop product, *The English Roses*, are Nicole, Amy, Charlotte, Grace and Binah – none of them made into a Polish name. The same is also true of another multiracial girl group of five, in the already mentioned *W.I.T.C.H.* series. Here, the trick is obviously that the name of the group is made up of the first letters of the characters' names: Will, Irma, Taranee, Cornelia, and Hay Lin, but it would not have been difficult to come up with an alternative set of Polish names the first letters of which would still form the same acronym. The names of other characters as well as of places, be it 'Hearthfield', 'Shrine auditorium,' 'Insytut Sheffield,' and 'Sheffield News' are similarly retained in their original form. A cursory glance at books for the youngest readers will also reveal that foreign-looking names like Bob, Franklin, or Noddy are left untouched, though the entirely domesticated series *Koala Brothers* seems to be an exception. In the past, some of the above titles and names would probably also have been domesticated. Today, many of them seem to be functioning as brands integrated into global media and publishing systems and being synchronised with many other products such as toys and games.

While there are few present-day examples of domesticated children's books, examples from the past are ample. Some of the most spectacular Polish domestications are translations of *The Rose and the Ring* from the beginning of the twentieth century, *Winnie-the-Pooh* from the 1930s, *My Friend Mr. Leakey* 1940s, *Alice's Adventures* from the 1950s, and *The Tailor of Gloucester* from the 1960s. In the very first Polish translation of *Mary Poppins* the eponymous heroine was not Mary Poppins, but ... Agnieszka. Would this be possible with Harry Potter? While this may appear unthinkable today, Donald Duck was introduced to Poland in the late thirties under a very different name: 'Kiwajko' (Disney, 1938a). Huckleberry was not Huckleberry either, but 'Traf' (Disney, 1938a), while Pluto was named 'Apsik' by the Polish translator (Disney, 1938b). Were they introduced to Poland in today's globalised world, they would now doubt bear their original names.

This is not to say that foreignisation is entirely bound to the present or that domestication is entirely a thing of the past; the most foreignising *Alice* translation, to give just one example, is neither the one produced in the 1990s nor that of the 1980s, but that of the 1970s. On the whole, however, a gradual shift from domesticating to foreignising tendencies does seem to have taken place in Poland. Though we could probably stop at this point, the picture would be somewhat incomplete.

The Strange Case of Dr Seuss and Mr. Hyde

Though foreignisation in many ways emerges as a central translation strategy in turn-of-the-century Poland, it is necessary to broaden the study in order to include various instances of domestication and to highlight such factors as individual translators' agency and certain text-specific translation strategies. An example of domesticated texts currently produced is that of Polish translations of Dr Seuss. The books, originally based on the idea of controlled vocabulary, received a very liberal treatment in Polish translation. Polish rhymes and the translator's own sense of humour were prioritised, names such as 'Sally' or 'Horton' substituted with the Polish 'Hania' and 'Konstanty' respectively, or, to give a more extreme example, the opening line of *Horton Hatches the Egg:* 'Sighed Mayzie, a lazy bird hatching an egg' (Seuss, 2003b: 57) was domesticated into 'Westchnął ptak Grzebielucha zwany też Podpuszczajką' (2003b: 3). Here and elsewhere the original idea of making use of a limited number of simple words has been abandoned altogether, as some of the Polish words in the translations, including 'ekwilibrysta', 'mamona', 'stentorowy', 'graca', or 'kopystka' (2003a: 26; 29; 43; 22 & 20) may well appear slightly foreign or incomprehensible to the Polish child-reader. Though on the one hand an instance of domestication, the translations are accompanied by CDs, each with a recording of the original text, which text is also provided in smaller print at the end of the translation. The books as a whole are thus hardly a straightforward example of domestication. The text was translated by one of the best known Polish translators, Stanisław Barańczak, a name big enough to make the publisher include a short biographical note and a photograph at the back cover next to that of Dr Seuss, and it may well have been the combination of the translator's agency as well as his cultural prestige that can account for the final shape of the liberally domesticated texts and their being accepted as such by the publisher.

The individual translator, stereotypically conceived of as Mr. Hyde, a shadowy presence behind the translation process, has recently become more central within translation studies (given a boost by, among others, Venuti, Pym or Oiittinen within child-oriented translation research), gradually emerging as another major meme, 'another idea that spreads', in the pool of memes proposed by Chesterman (2000). The approach based on systems and norms, it is argued, will greatly benefit from being supplemented by the investigation of the visibility of real human translators, thus avoiding simplification and abstraction.

Among other examples of partly domesticated texts is *Wielkomilud*, a brilliant Polish translation of Roald Dahl's *The BFG* produced in 1991 by another great translator, Michał Kłobukowski. Another instance is the Polish translation of Ian Whybrow's *The Bad Wolf's Book of Badness*. The book, the Polish title of which is *Księga Straszliwej Niegrzeczności, Napisał Wilczuś z Wielkiej Złości*, was also translated by a well known translator and poet, the Polish ambassador to Ireland, Ernest Bryll. The reason behind the translation strategy in the case of the above two texts is that the books, bustling with wordplay, in a way impose this liberal method on their translators, who can thus deal with the task more or less successfully; in the process they may treat the text more or less liberally, lest in some other way they may risk producing a hermetic and incomprehensible translation for children. The same applies to texts in which alliteration is decisively in the foreground. Examples are *Horrid Henry*, translated as *Koszmarny Karolek;* Perfect Peter becomes Doskonały Daminek and all the other characters follow suit. *Judy Moody* is translated into Polish as *Hania Humorek*. The principle applies to most but not all texts exploiting alliteration; thus, though it would be easy to come up with an appropriate Polish name, *Molly Moon* is left untouched in the Polish translation. Domestication thus often seems to be related firstly to the agency of individual translators, often names big enough to allow them to translate as they please, and secondly, to texts in which the use of wordplay is central.

Another category in which domestication appears to dominate is that of global animations, in the Polish translations of which the local is frequently exploited to an astonishing degree through introducing references to Polish culture as well as using colloquial and slangy Polish expressions. One of very many child-oriented animations in which this strategy is employed is *Robots*, a 20th Century Fox and Blue Sky Studios 2005 production. In its Polish translation, the characters' original names are changed into 'Radek Dekiel' (Rodney Copperbottom) or 'Spawalski' (Big Weld), while the place names, such as Robot City or Rivet Town, are domesticated into the Polish sounding 'Robotowice', 'Nitowo', or 'Śrubowo Dolne.' Certain culture-bound sayings, sometimes slightly modified, are introduced, including 'Nie płacz, kiedy odjadę', 'Nie będzie Brzeszczot pluł nam w twarz', 'Będzie się działo', along with a large number of all kinds of colloquialisms such as: 'full wypas', 'wypasiona biba', 'spoko wodza', 'dzienks Radek, jesteś wporzo'. One of the most frequently quoted examples of a polonised animation is *Shrek*, whose Polish translator, Bartosz Wierzbięta, is credited with introducing this translation strategy as a norm for Polish translations of global animation productions. The viewers soon started to expect animations to be translated this way and to perceive this as an almost essential ingredient of a successful translation. While Venuti (1995: 2) would claim that producing a domesticated text makes the translator invisible, it is, in this case, precisely the other way round – thanks to his domesticated translations, Wierzbięta became one of the most recognisable Polish translators.

As this final section began with a reference to a famous literary translator's agency, it will close with a quote from a famous animation translator. When asked about his treatment of culture-bound expressions in his translations, Wierzbięta replied, 'In my becoming a translator I began to realise that my freedom to translate the way I wanted increased and that I could allow myself more freedom still'[1]. The individual translator thus established a translation norm for the field as a whole, providing an example of how the systems and norms approach and the translator's agency perspective may complement rather than contradict each other.

Conclusion

Child-oriented translation, as the final example of a glocalised animation, seems to be indicating, is increasingly shaped by interactions between the global and the local. It can be investigated with the focus on global media and publishing systems, with a close look at norms governing treatment of the cultural other in translation, and without losing sight of translators, who are active agents capable of introducing and changing norms. It would be interesting to take the present study further: to conduct a detailed analysis of Polish translations of child-oriented animations; to supplement the present research with the analyses of translations of contemporary classics (do they reveal a larger proportion of the foreign than their predecessors?); or to conduct surveys directed at translators in order to learn more about the agents behind the translation process. With the focus on these issues, and so many other issues awaiting investigation, child-oriented translation research is bound to expand. Perhaps it is in process of moving away from the niche it now occupies to the avant-garde of translation studies.

Notes

1. 'Dojrzewanie mojego warsztatu tłumacza polegało na tym, że zdawałem sobie sprawę z tego, że mam coraz większą wolność i na coraz większą wolność mogę sobie pozwolić'.

Bibliography

Primary sources

Byng, G (2003) *Niezwykła Księga Hipnotyzmu Molly Moon*. Adelt, Krzysztof (trans.), Warszawa: Egmont

Dahl, R (1991) *Wielkomilud*. Kłobukowski, Michal (trans.), Warszawa: GiG

Dahl, R (2004) *Charlie i Fabryka Czekolady*. Łoziński, Jerzy (trans.), Poznań: Wydawnictwo Zysk i S-ka

Disney, W (1938a) *Miki Strażak*. Tuwim, Julian (trans.), Warszawa: Przeworski

Disney, W (1938b) *Miki Apsik i Pyzia*. Tuwim, Julian (trans.), Warszawa: Przeworski

Gaiman, N (2003) *Koralina*. Braiter, Pauline (trans.), Warszawa: Wydawnictwo Mag

Madonna (2003) *Angielskie Różyczki*. Łoziński, Jerzy (trans.), Poznań: Wydawnictwo Zysk i S-ka

Madonna (2003) *Jabłka Pana Peabody'ego*. Łoziński, Jerzy (trans.), Poznań: Wydawnictwo Zysk i S-ka

McDonald, M (2004) *Hania Humorek*. Aldona Możdżyńska, Aldona (trans.), Warszawa: Egmont

Potter, B (1969) *Krawiec i Iego Kot*. Wortman, Stefania (trans.), Warszawa: Nasza Księgarnia

Potter, B (1991) *Bajki dla Najmłodszych*, Czarnocka-Wojs, Miroslawa (trans.), Warszawa: Alfa

151

Potter, B (2000) *Powiastki Beatrix Potter,* Musierowicz, Malgorzata (trans.), Warszawa: Muza

Robots (2005) Chris Wedge, Carlos Saldanha, 20th Century Fox / Blue Sky Studios, USA, 92 mins

Rowling, J K (2000) *Harry Potter,* Polkowski, Andrzej (trans.), Poznań: Wydawnictwo Media Rodzina

Seuss, T G (2003a) *Kot Prot.* Barańczak, Stanislaw (trans.), Poznań: Wydawnictwo Media Rodzina

Seuss, T G (2003b) *Słoń, Który Wysiedział Jajko.* Barańczak, Stanislaw (trans.), Poznań: Wydawnictwo Media Rodzina

Simon, F (2005) *Koszmarny Karolek.* Makuch, Maria (trans.), Kraków: Wydawnictwo Znak

Travers, P L (1957) *Agnieszka.* Tuwim, Irena (trans.), Warszawa: Nasza Księgarnia

Whybrow, I (1997) *Księga Straszliwej Niegrzeczności.* Bryll, Ernest (trans.), Warszawa: Wydawnictwo Philip Wilson

Secondary sources

Aixela, J F (1996) 'Culture-Specific Items in Translation', in Alvarez, R & Vidal, M C A (eds.) *Translation, Power, Subversion,* Clevedon-Philadelphia-Adelaide: Multilingual Matters

Bassnett, S (2003) *Translation Studies,* London and New York: Routledge

Bastin, G L (2001) 'Adaptation', in Baker, M *Routledge Encyclopedia of Translation Studies.* London and New York: Routledge

Becker, J (1978) 'The Internationalism of Children's Books: Translations and their Ideological Deformations in the Federal Republic of Germany', in Klingberg, G (ed.) *Children's Books in Translation: The Situation and the Problems.* Stockholm: Almqvist & Wiksell International

Chesterman, A (1997) *Memes of Translation,* Amsterdam: John Benjamins

Cronin, M (2003) *Translation and Globalization,* London and New York: Routledge

Desmidt, I (2003) "Jetzt bist du in Deutschland, Daumling.' *Nils Holgersson on Foreign Soil – Subject to New Norms*'. *Meta* 48

Engelhardt (1991) 'Reading May Be Harmful to Your Kids', *Harper's Magazine*, June 1991

Fraustino, L R (2004) 'Children's Book Publishing', in Hunt, P (ed.) *International Companion Encyclopedia of Children's Literature*, London: Routledge

Kinder, M (1991) *Playing with Power in Movies, Television and Video Games: From Muppet Babies to Teenage Mutant Ninja Turtles*, Berkeley: University of California Press

Klingberg, G (1978) 'The Different Aspects of Research into the Translation of Children's Books and its Practical Application', in Klingberg, G (ed.) *Children's Books in Translation: The Situation and the Problems*. Stockholm: Almqvist & Wiksell International

Kwiecinski, P (2001) *Disturbing Strangeness*, Toruń: Wydawnictwo Edytor

Lefevere, A (2001) 'Mother Courage's Cucumbers', in Venuti, L. (ed.) *The Translation Studies Reader*, London and New York: Routledge

Mackey, M (1998) *The Case of Peter Rabbit*, New York and London: Garland Publishing

Oittinen, R (2000) *Translating for Children*, London & New York: Garland Publishing

Puurtinen, T (1995) *Linguistic Acceptability in Translated Children's Literature*, Joensuu, Finland: University of Joensuu.

Pym, A (1998) *A Method in Translation History*, Manchester: St. Jerome

Shavit, Z (1986) *Poetics of Children's Literature,* Athens and London: University of Georgia Press

Socha, I (2002) 'Polskie Przekłady dla Dzieci i Młodzieży w Latach 90.', in Papuzińska, J (ed.) *Kultura literacka dzieci i młodzieży u progu XXI stulecia*, Warszawa: Wydawnictwo CEBID

Stolt, B (1978) 'How Emil becomes Michel – on the Translation of Cchildren's Books', in Klingberg, G (ed.) *Children's Books in Translation: The Situation and the Problems*. Stockholm: Almqvist & Wiksell International

Toury, G (1995) *Descriptive Translation Studies and Beyond,* Amsterdam: Benjamins

Weinrechert, T (1978) 'International Book Production for Children Related to Children's Local Experiences and Local Consciousness', in Klingberg, G (ed.) *Children's Books in Translation: The Situation and the Problems.* Stockholm: Almqvist & Wiksell International

Venuti, L (1995) *The Translator's Invisibility: A History of Translation,* London: Routledge

Venuti, L (1998) *The Scandals of Translation: Towards an Ethics of Difference,* London: Routledge

Zając, M (2000) *Promocja Kksiążki Dziecięcej,* Warszawa: SBP

Website

Interview with Bartosz Wierzbięta (n.d.) Retrieved February 20, 2006 http://www.dubbing.pl/index.php?option=com_content&task=view&id=61&Ite mid=74

Bridging the Gap between Cultures: Slovenian Translations of American Children's Literature

Darja Mazi-Leskovar

Introduction

From its nineteenth-century beginning until the present day, Slovene literature has always made abundant use of translated texts, and literature for children is no exception to this characteristic. Recent statistics reveal that in the year 2004, out of 415 new fiction books published for young readers, 255 (61%) were translations (Jamnik, 2005). Even though the trend is for a steady rise in Slovene authorship – for example, in the year 2001, translations represented 63% of the new titles – the awareness of the role that translations play in 'the evolution and interaction of literatures and cultures' (Lefevere, 1994: 3) has not been decreasing. On the contrary, literary translation, including translation of children's literature, appears to be gaining in importance. Since 1991, when Slovenia attained the status of an independent and sovereign state, new literary awards for translators have been founded and among several symposia dealing with translation of literature, there have been two on translating children's literature, organised by the Association of Slovene literary translators.

Slovenes have traditionally believed in the importance of literary translation as a means to transfer information from a specific source culture to the target Slovene culture. While in 2004 new translations for children came from 24 countries (Mlakar, 2005: 105), in the nineteenth century, when the importance of children's books began to be recognised in the Slovenian environment, most texts were translated from German. The German influence, though beneficial at the start because it encouraged Slovene authors to start writing for children, became less welcome with the growing need to emphasise the Slovene national character. Consequently, source texts originating in foreign semiotic spaces which were seen as presenting less potential danger to Slovenian identity acquired new significance. Among these ranked books from the United States of America.

This paper, which is mainly based on my MA research into Slovene translations of American children's fiction, will show how translations of selected earliest prose texts opened new cultural horizons to Slovene readers. By presenting books that have been retranslated in various periods, it will also uncover 'the mechanisms of canonisation, integration, exclusion and manipulation that are at work on many levels – not just of literature, but of society,' as Andre Lefevere claims in his book *The Study of Translations* (1994: 3). I aim also to show how retranslations testify to the increasing similarity between the Slovenian target culture and the source cultures presented in the American books. The term culture will be used here to denote 'the way of life and its manifestations that are peculiar to a community that uses a particular language as its means of expression' (Newmark, 1988: 94).

The early translations of American books are particularly interesting because of their multicultural nature. Each translation bridges the gap between the target Slovene culture and the semiotic space of the source-text readers who, as a rule, share that of the American author. On the one hand they played a major role in bridging the gaps between Slovene culture and the English-speaking world, while on the other they contributed considerably to the raising of general intercultural awareness for generations of young Slovenian readers.

Translation and Slovenian National Identity

Renowned Slovene scholars and translators have stated that 'The history of Slovene literature is also the history of the literature translated into Slovene' (Stanovnik, 1993: 18) and 'Translation is a constituent part of national identity' (Moder, 1993: 14). Throughout history, Slovene literacy developed from the reading of a combination of original Slovene texts, translations and foreign texts. This specific cultural situation is closely linked to Slovene geographic and historic reality. The Slovene territory, which was originally four times larger than today, has been surrounded by four nations: Italy in the West, German-speaking Austria in the North, Hungary in the East and Croatia in the South. The Republic of Slovenia represents not only the crossroads of four linguistic groups but also of several different geographical entities: mountain chains including the Alps, the Mediterranean Adriatic Sea, and the Panonian Plain.

Exposure to foreign languages and cultures has resulted both in the acceptance of translation and interpreting as an important means of communication, and in a distinctive blend of national culture and character. Moreover, it has given rise to a strong feeling about the link between the Slovene language and national identity. The name of the nation itself, *Slovenci*, means *the people of the word*, and in this case *nomen est omen*. Accordingly, despite centuries of foreign rule, Slovene has always been spoken in the national territory and the written language has developed within the European tradition. One of the proofs of this particular language sensibility, as well as being a reason for special pride, is the translation of the Bible in 1584, which made Slovene the twelfth language to receive scripture in the mother tongue. James Gow and Cathie Carmichael compare the role that this translation played for Slovenes to that of the renowned English translation, 'It raised the quality of the written language rather as the King James Bible elevated the English of the early seventeenth century' (2000: 63). Translation established itself also in other spheres of life. It was

156

promoted both by the fruitful development of Slovenian literature, and by the general everyday 'relationships with the more dominant cultures of Vienna and the Adriatic [which] were complex and not simply ones of dominant versus stubbornly independent' (Gow & Carmichael, 2000: 62).

Mutual enrichment was obvious also in the field of children's literature. Translations from the German language, most of them made in the time of the Habsburg Empire, were gradually followed by translations from other languages. Intercultural communication, promoted today by slogans such as 'No global communication without translation' (used by Newmark as a headline for his contribution to *Translation Today,* Anderman and Rogers, 2003: 55), had already started for young Slovene audience in the nineteenth century.

The first literary text translated from the English language into Slovene Benjamin Franklin's *Poor Richard's Almanac* (1812). This might at first sight seem surprising but it fits well into the cultural history of both Slovenia and of central Europe as a whole. Franklin's book was an early portent of the possibilities realised forty years later. American literary texts addressed a larger reading public in the mid-nineteenth century, when the Slovene regions became involved in the immigration wave from Central Europe to the United States of America. At that stage a whole series of translations from American literature appeared in the Slovene book market, resulting both from a common Europe interest in America as 'the promised land,' and from a specific Slovene phenomenon, the effect of the writings of the Slovene missionary Friderik I Baraga. His texts describing encounters with the native Indians addressed readers of all ages and thus prepared the ground for books written by American authors. The American books too were not meant for any specific age group: their authors were 'great writers [who] wrote books for an audience composed of both children and adults' (Griswold, 2004: 248). Slovene translations targeted the entire reading public, even though they gradually started addressing young readers above all, so that these texts eventually became part of the canon of children's literature. This term (the Slovene equivalent of which is *mladinska književnost* - literature for the young) is used here in its widest sense, denoting texts addressing readers who due to their youth are not entitled to adult rights.

Translations of Uncle Tom's Cabin

The first American book to establish itself among Slovenes was Harriet Beecher Stowe's *Uncle Tom's Cabin or Negro Life in the Slave States of America.* This nineteenth-century American bestseller entered the Slovene market in 1853, only a year after its publication in the USA. As well as literature, this book represents a translation of culture, as defined by Evans-Pritchard: 'Making the experiences of other peoples understandable to us ... without making it into something other than it really is for the people who live

157

it' (Morris, 2003: 88). The culturally diverse American experience took various shapes and forms, and functioned as a source of novelty.

Uncle Tom's Cabin has a special position within Slovene children's literature; even though the author's aim was primarily to address American adults in order to influence the public attitude to the abolition of slavery, and therefore a year later the Slovene translators could not have considered the work as children's literature, the book became one of the milestones of Slovene children's literature. It also has a special position among translations of American prose into Slovene: firstly, because it responded to the *Zeitgeist*, to the general European interest in the USA, encouraged by immigration and Baraga's writings; and secondly, because it was translated in the same year by two translators, published by two different Slovene publishers in two Slovenian cultural centres, Celovec/Klagenfurt, a town in today's Austrian Carinthia, and Ljubljana, the current Slovene capital.

Both these translators, Janez Božič and Franc Malavašič, used the German translation as their point of departure, which reflects the cultural dependence of the then Slovene semiotic sphere on the cultural sensitivity of the larger Habsburg area. However, even though the two Slovene translators shared the same semiotic place characterised by a racially homogenous population where slavery was a completely unknown issue, their versions differ in many respects. Neither racial heterogeneity, nor the acknowledgement of the rights related to national identity, were really part of the then Central European culture. The new sensitivity resulting in the 'springtime of nations' (1848) only gradually started to manifest itself. Circles of Slovene intellectuals accordingly formulated a manifesto but did not have much impact on the nineteenth-century view of the world of the majority of the population. Hence, loyalty to the Habsburg crown, and respect for authority and existing laws, continued to be a part of everyday behavioural practice. On the other hand, Christianity with its teaching about God's love for everybody and the necessity for individuals to respect and love each other in the spirit of brotherhood, had a strong impact on the formation of Slovene culture. These features of the target audience are of vital importance when considering the cultural dimensions of *Uncle Tom's Cabin*.

Perhaps because of their expectations or their readership, and of the role that intertextuality inevitably plays in translation, each of the two translators put specific stress on the presentation of the cultural issues to be found in the source text. Divergences resulting from the individual viewpoints are however evident already on the title pages. Božič entitled his translation *Stric Tomaž ali življenje zamorcov v Ameriki (od Henrijete Stowe)* which would read in English as *Uncle Tomaž or Negro Life in America* (by Henrijeta Stowe). Franc Malavašič entitled his translation *Stric Tomova koča, ali življenje zamorcov v robnih državah severne Amerike,* which would read in

English as *Uncle Tom's Cabin or Negro Life in the Slave States of North America*. Božič's domestication of the title consists in deleting any information that may have seemed to be too detailed for an average reader. The cultural clue of the title is thus restricted to the 'Negro life,' and the target-text readers were thus spared from dealing with the multiculturally foreignising effect of the title. Moreover, the adaptation of Harriet Beecher Stowe's name to the rules of Slovene grammar enabled the target readers to learn that the author was a woman. Malavašič, on the other hand, showed his desire to expand the cultural knowledge of the target readers by introducing the word 'North' in front of the name America. This additional precision about the location reveals the translator's wish to provide information about the geographical setting which is absolutely superfluous for source-text readers.

Recognition of the need for acculturation of the text is particularly obvious in the Prefaces that the two translators wrote to facilitate the reading. These also reflect the truth that 'translators mediate between literary traditions ... with some goal in mind' (Lefevere, 1994: 6). Malavašič starts by informing the readers about the importance of *Uncle Tom's Cabin* in the international book market. The second cultural bridge he builds is even more important as he explains the signs related to racial characteristics which were absent in the Slovenian semiotic space. The third bridge is the explanation of the background of the title of the political name of the 'United States of America' and of the geographical concept of 'North American'. The information about the American currency may not seem important unless we know the content of the novel. The second part of the preface is a strong example of the acculturation effort of the translator, since Malavašič links the issue of slavery to that of the treatment of servants, by stressing that even though slavery is not permitted in Slovenia, there are masters who treat their domestic servants worse than some American masters do their slaves. The awareness of the human condition and the fairness of treatment of the underprivileged thus build a bridge between two different social systems.

The other translator, Janez Božič, also initially highlights the importance of *Uncle Tom's Cabin,* but his next step is directed towards enlarging on the idea of unknown, using the places mentioned in the book. The three American states are localised with basic geographic data. The building of historic knowledge is the third bridge facilitating the understanding of the novel. The issue of slavery, which was completely strange to Slovenian culture, is presented through the condemnation of slavery that Beecher Stowe expresses in chapter 45, 'Concluding Remarks.' The aim of the parallels drawn between American and Slovenian culture is to sensitise target readers to the cause and to put them in tune with the experience of source-language readers. The encouragement of empathy with the persons who have to suffer immoral and unfair treatment is based on the familiarity that young Slovene readers might have with the consequences of alcoholism, recognised as an evil that should be eradicated by joint efforts of society. In this context, the necessity to teach people responsibility for the treatment of servants is stressed. The domestication revealed in the encouragement to combat injustice and show compassion for their fellow citizens is much in line with Beecher Stowe's intention in writing the book. The final stroke to bring American and Slovene culture close is a suggestion to engage personally in a Slovene-American cause by supporting financially the Slovene missionaries working among the 'Natives' in the USA.

These two Prefaces thus not only manage to domesticate the fundamental issues of the book but also enable the original to acquire new, Slovene connotations. The application of the issue to the Slovene cultural context contributes to its universalisation, and at the time of publication presented bright promises for the survival of the book among Slovene target readers.

Additionally, the positioning of the novel as an international bestseller gives the translation a special status in the target cultural sphere from its very entering the market. On the other hand, by offering varied basic factual information related to the narrative, these Prefaces have enlarged the Slovene cultural sphere with new concepts and thus prepared the basis for the application of the procedure of foreignisation in the translation of the text. These first two translations were abridged considerably, but still preserve the integrity of the story about Uncle Tom and the young Negro family, as well as the spirit of the novel.[1]

After the First World War, *Uncle Tom's Cabin* was issued for the third time. The translator Silvester Košutnik devised a new title: *Stric Tomova koča: Povest iz suženjskega življenja* or *Uncle Tom's Cabin: A Story about Negro Life*. From the point of view of cultural perception, it is important to observe that this title is followed by a note, 'Translated from the German original'. At this time, Slovenes were no longer a part of the Habsburg monarchy and it can be concluded that awareness of the influence of the translation that here is used as a source text instead of the original has become more obvious.

In 1934 the most important Slovenian translation of the novel was published. Its significance is not due just to the new title, *Koča strica Toma* or *Uncle Tom's Cabin,* which became the standard, but to the translated text as a whole: it reveals a new approach towards translation, and consequently towards domestication and foreignisation. On the front cover of this translation, there are two important cultural clues: for the first time the author's name is written correctly in its complete form, and the readers are told that the book is an adaptation. The translator Olga Grahor is also the author of the Preface and the notes. The former contains the biography of

Harriet Elisabeth Beecher Stowe, and a reference section called 'A Key to Uncle Tom's Cabin' (1853).

Cultural bridges are additionally built in the fields of geography and socio-political history. The target readers are thus informed about the institutions and points of reference, such as the Anti-Slavery Society, John Brown's rebellion and the Fugitive Slave Act. The foreignising elements are thus presented as facts that the reader should be familiar with in order to understand the novel. Besides, Beecher Stowe's own Preface to the European translations is added as another source of insight into the American cultural sphere. The reference section is important for the expansion of the linguistic aspects of the culture as it brings additional details about a few culturally bound terms, presumably unknown to the average Slovenian reader, together with the translator's commentary on the usage of proper names. From the cultural point of view, the variety in the treatment of proper names is indicative: the names of protagonists, spelt in the original form, are presented with a phonemic transcript; this is culturally important since Slovene as a Slavonic language does not share all the sounds of English or American. In this context only the name 'America' is not transcribed as such, because it has already become familiar to Slovenes as 'Amerika'.

Thanks to such complex guidance into the cultural dimensions of the novel, a relatively high degree of foreignisation of the text was possible. On the other hand, it can be speculated that the earlier translations of this work and the rest of the translations from American literature which were available in Slovene (or even in German) at the time of the publication, resulted in a considerable bridging of the gulf between American and Slovene culture, literature and language. This book became the basic text for all subsequent editions of *Uncle Tom's Cabin* in the Slovene language.

After the Second World War, *Uncle Tom's Cabin* was first republished in 1954. If the preceding Slovene translations of *Uncle Tom's Cabin* primarily addressed a dual audience, the illustrations and the introduction of this edition are clearly aimed at children. The foregrounding of the images of children, of the mother and family, of home and shelter, all belonging to the child reader's semiotic space, reveal the orientation towards a precisely targeted public (Nikolajeva, 1996: 27-34). The 1954 book has remained one of the elementary school canonical texts, for children aged 6 to 14.

This edition, published at a time of intensive communist propaganda, carries all the features of the totalitarian period and could therefore be seen as pulling down one of the bridges that had already connected American and Slovene culture. 'Domestication for political ideas' (Oittinen, 2000: 99) is obvious in the editor's foreword and drastically exposed in the text itself.

Such a type of alteration is foregrounded by the editor, Kristina Brenkova, a children's author herself, who claims that despite the adaptation 'the whole story and the way of narration, and above all the basic idea and the intention of the writer are preserved' (*Koča strica Toma*, 6). However, all the sections of the text where Beecher Stowe claims that Christianity and slavery cannot exist together have been omitted. The domestication conditioned by the communist regime has thus completely changed the 'meaning, truth and morality' (Weston, 2003: 140) of the novel. Today, 16 years after the fall of communism in Slovenia, young readers are still waiting for a new translation to rebuild the bridge between the two literatures and cultures, enabling them to receive the real message of H B Stowe; the 1993 edition of the book is only a reprint of the edition edited by Kristina Brenkova and translated by Olga Grahor.

Other Translated American Texts

The start of the twentieth century was marked with the translations of *Leatherstocking Tales* (J F Cooper), which introduced other types of American culture to Slovene readers – the culture of the Native Americans and that of various European newcomers who were starting to form a composite white American culture. The presentation of Native Americans from the point of view of an American author and not from the perspective of a Slovene missionary, dictated a domesticating stroke that would ensure a new reading public. Hence, the books were marketed with the cover notice 'Tales for young people.' Another successful move that helped towards success with the audience was the order in which the translations were published. The best known book about Natanael Bumppo, *The Last of the Mohicans, Natanael Bumppo/Poslednji Mohikanec* (1900) was translated and edited first. Since the book displays all the features of the series, the building of bridges that resulted thanks to the translation of this series can be understood through a focus on this novel.

The Last of the Mohicans, Natanael Bumppo, like all Cooper's books, was in this translation reduced to a story full of action. The commentaries on the historical, geographical and socio-political issues that are integral parts of the stories are reduced to a minimum. The commentary is as a rule deleted and only if it is indispensable is it briefly summarised. For instance, in the first chapter of *The Last of the Mohicans*, Cooper describes the historical circumstances on which the story is based and comments on the stance of Europe with regard to the wars and the fights with Indians. He even criticises 'the cold and selfish policy of the distant monarchs of Europe...' (p1). The Slovene translator leaves out the author's reflection altogether and sets only the time frame for the story: 'In the third year of the war between England and France...' Such domestication clearly indicates that the translator's aim was to reduce the text to a minimum, which he manages by condensing parts of the tales and by leaving out whole episodes and chapters. Citations from literary works which were presumably not expected to be known by Slovene young readers were omitted as well. Even the footnotes that Cooper wrote for the source readers are not translated for the target readers immersed in another cultural context.

Despite such a reduction, the books had a strong foreignising effect, resulting from: 'the so-called *realia*, words and phrases that are so heavily and exclusively grounded in one culture' (Robinson, 1997: 222); the natural environment, to a great extent different from the Slovene landscape; the protagonists belonging to various European nations and several tribes of Native American; and issues completely foreign to Slovene culture. The books thus introduce a new picture of North America, as a continent where wars are not only the consequence of the competitiveness between the English and French but also of the clashes between the civilisation of the Native Americans and the Whites.

The treatment of names, however, reveals that the cultures have already made quite a few steps towards one another. Some proper names retain their original form, particularly the name of the main hero, featuring on the cover page of each book, and this contributes considerably to foreignisation. However, names which have Slovene counterparts are Slovenised, Alice for instance becoming Alica. The third type of treatment is displayed with names which carry a meaning, which are also translated. A fourth group of names is represented by cases where there seems to be no rational cause for changes in names, and this may reflect a convergence of the two cultures, particularly when the spelling is altered, presumably with the intent of facilitating the pronunciation. On the other hand, the translator tends to use Slovenised forms of the geographical names, which were likely to be already familiar among Slovenes. From the point of view of domestication, it is however indicative that French names retain their original form. Among Slovenes, French had by this period established itself as a language of culture, having previously been during the Napoleonic period one of the official languages, so that sentences in French are also not translated. An average reader was expected to understand them.

In the 1926 translation of *The Last of the Mohicans*, entitled *Zadnji Mohikanec,* some of the inconsistencies of the first translation give way to more satisfying solutions. The translator Alojz Benkovič prepared footnotes explaining historical and geographical data, the meaning of signs that are untranslatable in Slovenian because they belong to a completely different semiotic space, either that of the Indians or that of the white Americans. The corresponding pronunciation of the words is included in the explanation. One of the references presents a short prayer composed and written by the Slovenian missionary Friderik I Baraga in the language of the Chippewa Indians. The annotation has a strong domestication effect as Baraga was widely known and his missionary endeavours had been generously supported[2].

In the 1960s the *Leather Stocking Tales* were translated anew. At this date, the entire text is translated, and the books also include the culturally significant literary citations. *The Prairie (Prerija)*, published in 1965, for instance, includes terms that Cooper explained for source readers. Readers were also offered explanations of terms strange to the Slovene community because of their cultural specificity. A real novelty in the domestication effort is an attempt not only to translate wordplay, but also to provide intertextual cultural reference. For example, hints are given at the links between the word 'buffoon' and the French encyclopedist, Buffon.

Compared to these advances, the 1973 translation of *Leatherstocking Tales* presents a step backwards, since it is a translation of a German adaptation, published by Herder K G Heilderberg. It is not the content and the spirit of the text that are to be questioned but the references that evoke the German cultural sphere which is foreign for the targeted Slovene audience. German references thus present a hindrance to the reception of the American literary text. Hence the editions based on the earlier translations from the American original remain the ones that can powerfully address the contemporary audience.

Conclusion

Tracing the translations of selected books by Beecher Stowe and Cooper reveals a few general traits to be seen in the translation of American books for Slovene children. The earliest translations of American books present texts that gained popularity among Slovenes, with each new translation narrowing the gap between the cultures. The image of the USA may be seen as evolving from that of the promised land to a country with its own problems and challenges. Finally, the socio-political framework within which translations were published has dictated the adaptations to the extent that the Slovene texts do not always excel in either fidelity to the original or an honest approach to the target reader.

American culture and Slovene culture have remarkably expanded 'the zone of translatability' (Nikolajeva, 1996: 29), spheres which the source and the target readers share everyday experience. Cultural gaps have been bridged by these translations. Naturally, the expansion of translatability has not taken place only thanks to literary translation but also to other reasons, among which the ubiquitous presence of English and its association with the modern media industry seems to be significant. However, even though the diversity of racial, national, ethnic and religious aspects of American culture is accessible today through various media, translated books, especially those that have undergone several translations, remain of special importance from the cultural standpoint. In particular, a number of American books have entered the elementary school reading canon, and a few have even become part of the Slovene cultural repository. Beecher Stowe's *Uncle Tom's Cabin* ranks in both of these areas. Due to its inculturation, it represents a plank that has enabled several generations not only to obtain access to the bridges which have already been built between American and Slovene culture by previous generations, but also to extend them and to build new ones when new requirements have been set by changed cultural circumstances. This became significant when retranslation did not meet the demands of the original as in the period of communism. Translations then had first of all to ensure that children's books would help 'to create a new personality, the 'new socialist being" (Thomson-Wohlgemuth, 2003: 241). Their main aim was to safeguard the priorities of the totalitarian society. Today, in the democratic environment, translation ethics has anew found its way into professional translating, for the need to make 'a new creation' for the target audience enables genuine 'cross-cultural communication (Oittinen, 2000: 6).

Even though the democratisation of society and the internationally acclaimed importance of translation enable high standards of linguistic achievement, this is only one of the prerequisites needed to foster intercultural encounters. Second equally important is the choice of texts offered to children. As in any other field of human endeavours technique or knowledge do not suffice if not combined with wisdom in the choice of intercultural books which 'promote empathy and our ability to evaluate' (Bredella, 2005: 54). It is not enough to put readers in touch with the American reality by enabling them to read American cultural signs. Even more urgent is the need to encourage readers to see the world through the eyes of the other. I totally agree with Bredella who claims that empathy can be evoked by presenting 'experiences and conflicts which do not only reveal something about the culture and period in which they were written but also about the culture and period in which they are received' (Bredella, 2005: 55). Therefore I hope that the American children's books that were translated in the last two years: 45 in 2003 (Mlakar, 2004: 101) and 27 in 2004 (Mlakar, 2005: 105), will display all the prerequisites necessary for the genuine promotion of further intercultural understanding between Slovenes and the many cultures represented in the American children's literature.

Notes

1. An extensive analysis of the translations of the *Uncle Tom's Cabin* is available in the *Meta Translator's Journal* (2003) under the title 'Domestication and Foreignisation in Translating American Prose for Slovenian Children.'

2. Friderik I. Baraga (1797-1868), the first Bishop of Marquette (Diocese of Michigan), was a missionary in the area of Great lakes and Ottawa river. He was not just an evangeliser but also a great promoter of Indian

cultures. He spoke several European Languages and learnt Indian languages spoken in the area he cared for. One of his great endeavours was to help his tribes to get a written language and he succeeded in establishing the literary language of the central Algonquian tribes: Chippewa and Ottawa Indians. Among the books he wrote are primers and prayer books. The Chippewa book from which the prayer is taken was published in Ljubljana in 1843.

Bibliography
Primary Sources

Cooper, J F (1989) *The Last of the Mohicans*. London: Bantam Books

Cooper, J F (1980) *The Deerslayer*. New York: New American Library

Cooper, J F (1992) *The Prairie*. New York: Oxford University Press

Cooper, J F (1960) *The Pathfinder*. New York: Washington Square Press

Cooper, J F (1964) *The Pioneers of the Sources of the Susquehanna*. New York: A Signet Classic

Cooper, J F (1900) *Natanael Bumppo, Strelec*. Ljubljana: Janez Giontini

Cooper, J F (1900) *Natanael Bumppo, Poslednji Mohikanec*. Ljubljana: Janez Giontini

Cooper, J F (1901) *Natanael Bumppo, Naseljenci*. Ljubljana: Janez Giontini

Cooper, J F (1901) *Natanael Bumppo, Stezosledec*. Ljubljana: Janez Giontini

Cooper, J F (1901) *Natanael Bumppo, Na preriji*. Ljubljana: Janez Giontini

Cooper, J F (1926) *Zadnji Mohikanec*. Maribor: Tiskarna sv. Cirila

Cooper, J F (1973) *Naseljenci*. Ljubljana: Mladinska knjiga

Cooper, J F (1973) *Divjačinar*. Ljubljana: Mladinska knjiga

Cooper, J F (1973) *Stezosledec*. Ljubljana: Mladinska knjiga

Cooper, J F (1973) *Zadnji Mohikanec*. Ljubljana: Mladinska knjiga

Stowe, H Beecher (1981) *Uncle Tom's Cabin*. London: Bantam Books

Stowe, H Beecher (1853) Stric Tomova koča ali življenje zamorcov v robnih državah svobodne severne Amerike. Ljubljana: Janez Giontini

Stowe, H Beecher (1853) *Stric Tomaž ali življenje zamorcov v Ameriki.* Celovec: Janez Leon

Stowe, H Beecher (1932) Stric Tomova koča. Povest iz suženjskega življenja. Ljubljana: Anton Turk

Stowe, H Beecher (1934) *Koča strica Toma.* Ljubljana: Založba tiskarne Merkur

Stowe, H Beecher (1954) Koča strica Toma ali življenje črncev v suženjskih državah Amerike. Ljubljana: Mladinska knjiga

Stowe, H Beecher (1973) *Koča strica Toma.* Ljubljana: Mladinska knjiga

Stowe, H Beecher (1993) *Koča strica Toma.* Ljubljana: Mladinska knjiga

Secondary Sources

Anderman, Gunilla & Rogers, Margaret (2003) *Translation Today.* Clevedon, Buffalo, Toronto, Sydney: Multilingual Matters Ltd.

Bredella, Lothar (2005) 'Intercultural Understanding with Multicultural Literary Texts' in *Intercultural Communicative Competence in Europe and Beyond.* Koper: Univerza na Primorskem

Gow, James & Carmichael, Cathy (2000) *Slovenia and the Slovenes,* Bloomington, Indiana, US: Indiana University Press

Griswold, Jerry (2004) 'Kiddie Lit: 'The Cultural Construction of Children's Literature in America by Beverly Lyon Clark'' *Children's Literature Association Quarterly*, Vol 28, No. 4. (2004): 248

Jamnik, Tilka (2005) 'Kar 499 novih mladinskih knjig, 56 več kot leto poprej: nova mladinska dela 2004 / 499 new children books, 56 more than the previous year: 2004 new children's books' in *Delo, Književni listi*, 11th May 2005 (12)

Lambert, Jose (ed.) (1998) *Routledge Encyclopaedia of Translation Studies,* London: Routledge, p131

Lefevere, Andre (1994) *Translating Literature: Practice and Theory in a Comparative Literature Context.* New York: The Modern Language Association of America

Mazi-Leskovar, Darja (1998) '140 Let Prevodov iz Ameriške Mladinske Proze/140 Years of Translations of American Children's Literature in Prose' in *Prevajanje Otroške in Mladinske Književnosti/Translation of Children's Literature and Adolescent Literature.* Ljubljana: Društvo Routledge *Encyclopaedia of Translation Studies,* Slovenskih Književnih Prevajalcev/Association of the Slovene Literary Translators, pp62-68

Mazi-Leskovar, Darja (2003) 'Domestication and Foreignization in Translating American Prose for Slovenian Children' in *Meta, Traduction Pour les Enfants, Translation for Children.* Montreal: Les Presses de l'Universite de Montreal

Mlakar, Ida (ed.) (2004) *Pravljični Vrtovi, Seznami Zelja in Druge Dobre Zgodbe/Fairytale Ggardens, List of Wishes and Other Good Stories.* Ljubljana, Pionirska knjižnica

Mlakar, Ida (ed.) (2005) *Klicarji Zzvezd/Heralds of the Stars.* Ljubljana: Pionirska knjižnica

Moder, Janko. (1993) 'Prevod kot Sestavni del Narodove Identitete/Translation as a Constituent Part of National Identity' in *Prevod in Narodova Identiteta/Translation and National Identity.* Ljubljana: Društvo Slovenskih Književnih Prevajalcev/Association of the Slovene Literary Translators

Morris, Marshall (2003) 'With Translation in Mind' in *Translation Today.* Clevedon: Multilingual Matters Ltd.

Newmark, Peter (1988) *A Textbook of Translation.* New York and London: Prentice Hall

Nikolajeva Maria (1996) *Children's Literature Comes of Age, Toward a New Aesthetic.* New York and London: Garland Publishing Inc.

Robinson, Douglas (1997) *Becoming a Translator.* London and New York: Routledge

Stanovnik, Majda (1993) 'Original Fear of Translation' in *Translation and National Identity.* Ljubljana: Društvo Slovenskih Književnih Prevajalcev /Association of the Slovene Literary Translators

Thomson-Wohlgemuth, G (2003) 'Children's Literature and Translation under the East German Regime', in *Meta, Traduction pour les Engants, Translation for Children,* Montreal: Les Presses de l'Universite de Montreal

Weston, Martin (2003) 'Meaning, Truth and Morality in Translation' in *Translation Today.* Clevedon: Multilingual Matters Ltd

Translating Children's Literature Multiculturally: Spanish Translations of Deborah Ellis

Belén González Cascallana

It has been more than thirty years since Mildred L Batchelder's statement from 1972: 'Children of one country who come to know the books and stories of many countries have made a beginning toward international understanding' (reprinted in *The Children's Book Bag*, Winter, 1990: 1; in Metcalf, 2003: 324). Since then, conscious efforts have been made to promote cross-cultural understanding amongst children. To this purpose, translations are undoubtedly a clear medium to facilitating the presence of previously neglected or invisible cultures in children's literature worldwide.

The aim of this paper is to explore how translations reveal voices of other cultures and races and, in doing so, promote cultural diversity. The Spanish translations of Deborah Ellis's *The Breadwinner* and *Parvana's Journey* will be used to illustrate how translating multicultural children's books can help children gain a broader vision of the diverse backgrounds, cultures and religions that make up our world. Adopting a descriptive-comparative approach, the process whereby these children's books are transferred from one culture to another will be analysed. My main focus will be the consideration of whether or not the otherness of the foreign culture is retained in the translation, depending on the translators' choice of strategies. The study will be approached from the angle of Translation Studies and, in particular, will concentrate on research that deals with cultural difference and with the interface between the source culture and the foreign, linking ideology and politics to translation strategies. Finally, it will be suggested that exposure to translated multicultural literature certainly helps children appreciate the idiosyncrasies of other ethnic groups, eliminate cultural and racial intolerance, and develop multiple perspectives.

Translating Multicultural Literature

When McGillis set out to introduce his seminal book, *Voices of the Other: Children's Literature and the Postcolonial Context* (1999), he emphasised his commitment to 'hearing the voices of those who have been silenced by various forces in our culture' (McGillis, 1999: xxii). Multicultural literature for children, that is to say, books that 'deal sensitively and accurately with cultures other than the dominant Anglo-European culture that has until recently assumed unquestioned priority over much of the English-speaking world' (McGillis, 1999: xxv), indeed pays attention to previously invisible or unheard cultures.

Ironically, this promotion of 'minority' cultures still involves other political and economic forces, since these multicultural books are often transmitted in the language of power, English. Politically and economically less powerful cultures are frequently either originally depicted in the English language or translated from minority languages into English. Moreover, in a postcolonial context, as Bassnett and Trivedi have pointed out, the asymmetrical power relations are reflected in the unequal struggle of various minority languages against 'the one master-language of our postcolonial world, English' (1999: 13). A close linkage of translation to postcolonialism can then be perceived in the imbalance of power relations between different languages, between coloniser and colonised. Furthermore, 'translation is thus seen as the battleground and exemplification of the postcolonial context' (Munday, 2001: 135). In this sense, translation comes into a direct engagement with other matters since it widens the horizons of multicultural literature with a wealth of new insights.

Bearing in mind that translating multicultural literature can further cross-cultural understanding, it is important to stress that, in our current multicultural society, the presence or absence of multicultural literature has a great influence on children's understanding of themselves and others, on the formation of their own identities and the recognition of others. By introducing children to multicultural literature, we are giving all people an equal voice, since it gives everybody the opportunity to listen to all diverse voices. Hence, the role of translation acquires exceptional importance.

Cathy Hirano, who translated the 1997 Batchelder Award Winner, *The Friends* by Kazumi Yumoto, from Japanese into English, offers a very interesting perspective on translation: 'Translation of literature is far from mechanical, and ... requires fairly strenuous cultural and mental gymnastics' (in Matulka, 2004). During the translation process, the translator faces numerous challenges, but the greatest endeavour of translators consists is to come up with an accurate version of the original text in such a manner that it also captures its voice.

Multicultural books representing other countries contain voices that speak of other ethnicities, other traditions, other religions and other places, and therefore speak for their own culture. In the case of multicultural literature, although the form and the content are equally important to both the reader and the author, cultural references have a greater significance since, to a large extent, they contribute to bring to the fore the diverse voices in the text. In this sense, an accurate rendering of culture-bound elements is essential if translators are to provide readers with an accurate portrayal of a different culture.

Portrayal and Authenticity

When introducing children to multicultural books from other countries, there is a need for books to be authentic. When books lack authenticity, readers can be misinformed, which may lead to misconceptions about the culture and the people. A persistent question for the children's book world is the identity of the author. Some critics and authors themselves believe that only people from a particular race, culture or nation of origin should write about their own group. On the other side of the argument is the view that a well-researched work will reflect values and traditions of a culture, regardless of the race or nationality of the author. The question remains: Is a children's book about a certain culture more authentic if it is written by an individual from that culture? Can authors research or immerse themselves into a culture that is not their own, producing a book that accurately presents another culture? (Matulka, 2004).

The argument can then be extended to translators. How important is it for a translator of a children's book to have the same cultural background or extensive knowledge/ experience with the culture or ethnic group being depicted in the book they are translating? How far can a translator understand and appreciate all the cultural norms that are presented in the book? Although these questions may seem unanswerable, it is important to highlight that translation is not the mere process of transferring one word from one language into another; it is a complex procedure that involves, apart from a great command of both languages, a solid cultural background. Since languages express cultures, translators should be not only bilingual, but also bicultural.

Case Study: Novels by Deborah Ellis

This study of multicultural books in translation will focus on Canadian writer and political activist Deborah Ellis, whose work has been translated into 17 languages, looking particularly at the Spanish translations of her first two books within *The Breadwinner Trilogy*: *The Breadwinner* (2001)/ *El Pan de La Guerra* (2002) and *Parvana's Journey* (2002)/ *El Viaje de Parvana* (2004). In her books Ellis brings alive the voices of Afghan people and gives readers a realistic portrait of life for women in modern day Afghanistan under the Taliban Regime.

After having spent some time helping at an Afghan refugee camp in Pakistan and interviewing women for her book of oral stories *Women of the Afghan War* (2000), Ellis decided to write *The Breadwinner*.[1] In fact, the stories she heard and the people she met in those camps were the inspiration for her trilogy. *The Breadwinner* is the story of the starvation and survival of an eleven-year-old girl, Parvana, under the Taliban rule. In this book, Parvana disguises herself as a boy to earn money to feed her family after her father is arrested. In its sequel *Parvana's Journey*, our strong heroine, Parvana, has lost her father and travels across Afghanistan to find her mother and sisters. *Mud City* (2003), which has not been translated into Spanish yet, completes the trilogy and tells the story of Parvana's friend, Shauzia, and her determination to follow her dream of getting away from the refugee camp in Pakistan and travelling to France.

Children's fiction awards make books gain in popularity, which also increases the possibility of their being translated into other languages. In fact, the success of Ellis's books amongst children and in the critical world has been a determining factor in their selection for translation and publication in Spain. Deborah Ellis has indeed been the recipient of numerous awards, including the 2000 Governor General's Award for Children's Text, one of Canada's premier literary awards, for *Looking for X*, the 2003 Jane Addams Book Award for *Parvana's Journey*, and, most recently, a Jane Addams Book Award Special Commendation for *The Breadwinner Trilogy*.

Even though Ellis deals with topics such as life under the Taliban, issues of women's rights, foreign intervention and war, her books are very popular with young readers.[2] The popularity of her books suggests that there has been a change in the assumptions about what childhood can bear and understand, as she explains herself in an interview:

> I don't generally write books with the audience in mind. I write because of what interests me. Initially, I was pretty surprised that kids would want to read this. I've become less surprised, because of my respect for children has grown over the years. Kids are really hungry to learn about what's going on in the world. The fact that they would read a book like this on their own, not necessarily prompted by teachers, and they write to me on their own, without being prompted by teachers and parents, has raised my respect level for them tremendously. They are capable of understanding very complex things that are happening in the world and they are hungry for it as well. I don't think we give them enough credit. (Maxworthy O'Brien, 2005).

For a description of the relations between the originals and the translations, it is indispensable to look at the shifts that have been established during the translation act and the main factors that determine and shape the translator's strategy in solving problems. The analysis thus will focus on the way the translator Herminia Bevia handles culturally-bound items on a macro- and micro-structural level. By examining the translator's treatment of culturally specific elements, my study will aim to show whether the multicultural voice of the original has been maintained or not in the translations or target texts (TT), whether the foreign identity of the original or source text (ST) has been enhanced or minimised.

An examination of preliminary data indicates that both TTs are presented and accepted as translations with the original title and the translator's name on the title pages and the copyright pages. The translator's choice of strategy with regards to titles is very significant, as exemplified by the first book, *The Breadwinner*. In this case, Bevia's use of compensation, *El pan de la guerra* ('The bread of the war'), suggests the main theme of the book: survival from starvation and war.

The design of front and back covers is different. In both cases, the photographs incorporate elements which belong to a different culture: women dressed in burqas and the girl covered with a chador are clear indicatives of the Muslim culture. However, the Spanish publisher Edelvives manages to create a stronger visual dialogue between author/translator, text and reader.

The fact that the books are for children is only indicated in the Spanish translations by the presence, on the back covers, of the name of the series they belong to, 'Colección Alandar,' one that is for older children (from twelve onwards). Although both translations are full renderings of the originals, there are several differences and omissions on the macro level. The inclusion of a world map in both STs with a clear educational intention of introducing readers to Afghanistan and Asia, only appears in *El viaje de Parvana*. The same applies to the Author's note at the end of *The Breadwinner*. This additional information on Afghanistan is omitted in the translation. Marketing strategies, such as the addition of details about the other two books that belong to the trilogy, and the first chapter of *The Breadwinner*, included at the end of *Parvana's Journey*, differ from its Spanish counterpart, which only includes a summary of the first book in its final page. All these examples are indicative of the power exerted by the publishing industry and its influence on the final product.

One of the most striking features of the books concerns the inclusion of a glossary at the back of the books to explain the meaning of unfamiliar cultural elements, mostly culturally bound items that reflect the Afghan culture. Herminia Bevia deals with these cultural references in a similar way, including the glossary at the back. The terms therefore are retained in the translation, although italicised to emphasise their foreignness.

The close adherence to the ST structure is distinctive of the translation strategy foreignisation. Following Lawrence Venuti's work (1995), the foreignising method of translation, a strategy that Venuti also terms 'resistancy' (1995: 305-6), makes visible the presence of the translator by

174

stressing the foreign identity of the ST. Conversely, domestication negates the foreign in translation and therefore minimises the foreignness of the TT. This translation strategy entails the absence of any linguistic or stylistic peculiarities, making the translation read fluently. Although Venuti concentrates on translation into English, the general trend towards a translation policy of fluency, of domestication, also affects other languages, such as Spanish. Pym even suggests that translation is, at the current time, typically domesticating, irrespective of the relative power of source and target cultures (Pym, 1996: 170). Although Spanish translations do tend to follow the translation method of domestication, there is an increase in translators and scholars of translation who advocate a translation policy of 'visibility' (or 'foreignisation'). Thus, foreignisation emphasises the 'otherness', captures the voice of the original and introduces the reader to cultural difference, revealing the foreign as foreign.

The translator's use of foreignisation is manifested in her rendering of culturally specific elements. In some cases, the translator's choice of other domestication strategies such as generalisation, omission and addition also suggest that strategies are not exclusive of each other. In fact, the translator needs to opt for those strategies that fulfil a similar function to that of the original. Through the Spanish translations, Spanish readers find out about the Afghan culture: names, clothes, religious traditions, objects, languages that belong to a different culture, a foreign culture. The translator's choice of translation strategies and its implications with regards to the presence or absence of the foreign in the translations will be illustrated through a selection of representative examples.

Names

Proper names are always retained in the translation (Parvana, Nooria, Ali, Maryam, Kaseem, Hossain, Shauzia). Names of places are either rendered by their phonetic adaptation (Afghanistan / Afganistán, Mazar-e-Sharif / Mazar i Sharif) or retained as they appeared in the ST (Kabul, Kandahar, Jalalabad, Kunduz). This choice of strategy reflects the translator's aim to preserve the ST's idiosyncratic characteristics.

Clothing

'burqa/*burka* - A long, tent-like garment, which the Taliban have decreed women must wear whenever they go outside. It covers them completely and even has a narrow mesh' (*The Breadwinner*, Glossary: 169). In the Spanish translation the term has been adapted phonetically, yet maintains its foreignness:

How do women in burqas manage to walk along these streets? (*The Breadwinner*, p17)

175

¿Cómo se las arreglan las mujeres con *burkas* para andar por estas calles? (*El pan de la guerra*, p15)

'chador/*chador* - A piece of cloth worn by women and girls to cover their hair and shoulders. Girls wear this outside' (*The Breadwinner*, Glossary, p. 169). The term is retained in the translation, insisting on the foreign nature of the text:

'I can read that letter as well as Father can,' Parvana whispered into the folds of her chador. (*The Breadwinner*, p7)
'Yo puedo leer esa carta tan bien como mi padre- susurró Parvana entre los pliegues de su *chador*' (*El pan de la guerra*, p7)

'shalmar kameez/*shalmar kameez* - Long, loose shirt and trousers, worn by both men and women. Men's are all one color, with pockets in the side and on the chest. Women's are different colors and patterns, sometimes elaborately embroidered or beaded' (*The Breadwinner*, Glossary: 170). This is another example of the translator's use of retention of a culture-specific term of the source language:

'My good shalwar kameez! We can't sell that!' (*The Breadwinner*, p24)
'¡Mi shalwar kameez bueno! ¡No podemos venderlo!' (*El pan de la guerra*, p21)

Religion

'Eid/Eid - A Moslem festival coming at the end of Ramadan, month of fasting' (*The Breadwinner*, Glossary: 169). This is the only instance where the translator's lack of cultural knowledge has lead to a misinterpretation of a cultural reference, having mistaken a religious festival with a proper name:

It had been an Eid present from her aunt in Mazar-e-Sharif, a city in the north of Afghanistan. (*The Breadwinner*, p24)
Había sido un regalo de su tía Eid, que vivía en Mazar i Sharif, una ciudad del norte de Afganistán. (*El pan de la guerra*, p21)

'mullah/*mulá* - A religious expert and teacher of Islam' (*Parvana's Journey*, Glossary: 198). On this occasion the term is also phonetically adapted to Spanish and the translator includes a footnote to remind readers that those words in italics appear in a glossary at the end of the book. This type of intervention makes the translator visible and suggests readers that they are reading the translation of a foreign work.

'jenazah/*jenazah* - A Muslim prayer for the dead' (*Parvana's Journey*, Glossary: 198). On this occasion, the source text includes an explanation of

176

the term, literally reproduced in the translation, which improves the reader's comprehension:

> The village mullah had already recited the jenazah, the prayer for the dead. (*Parvana's Journey*, p9)
> El *mulá** de la aldea había entonado ya el *jenazah*, la plegaria por los muertos. (*El viaje de Parvana*, p7)

Food

'**nan/nan** - Afghan bread- flan, sometimes long and sometimes round' (*The Breadwinner*, Glossary: 169). The treatment of this term has involved the use of two different translation strategies: generalisation and retention respectively. By recurring to a generalisation strategy an immediate comprehension is produced, whereas in the second instance the reader needs to resort to the glossary at the back of the book in order to decode the cultural reference.

> Ali was dozing on Mother's lap, a piece of nan in his little fist. (*The Breadwinner*, p26)
> Alí estaba adormilado en el regazo de su madre, con un trozo de pan en la mano. (*El pan de la guerra*, p23)

> … most days they ate just nan and tea. (The Breadwinner, p91)
> la familia comía, aunque algunos días solo fuese *nan* y té (*El pan de la guerra*, p77)

'**pilaf/pilaf** – A rice dish that usually contains vegetables, meat and spices' (*Parvana's Journey*, Glossary: 198). In line with previous examples, the translator selects a retention strategy to maintain the foreignness of the text:

> 'How about some golden rice pilaf, with extra raisins, and huge chunks of roasted lamb buried in it?' (*Parvana's Journey*, p36)
> ¿Qué te parece un arroz *pilaf*, con muchas pasas y grandes trozos de cordero asado? (*El viaje de Parvana*, p30)

'**bolani/bolani** – a kind of dumpling' (*Parvana's Journey*, Glossary: 198). In the glossary of the Spanish translation, the translator opts for adding an explanation to the term '*bolani* - una especie de bola hecha con una masa que se cuece o hornea.

> Puede ser dulce y rellena de fruta, o salada de carne y verduras' (*El viaje de Parvana*, Glossary, p171)

As previously discussed, there are occasions where the translator opts for generalisation ('sweet noodle pudding' becomes 'un montón de pastel'= 'a

177

lot of cake') or even omission strategies ('dumplings'), which illustrates the translator's desire to make the text more fluent.

> Then we'll have some bolani dumplings, and some tomatoes and onions, and lots of sweet noodle pudding. (*Parvana's Journey*, pp36-7)
> Luego tomaremos *bolani*, y tomates y cebollas, y un montón de pastel. (*El viaje de Parvana*, p30)

Languages

'**Dari and Pashtu/dari y** *pastún* – Two main languages in Pakistan' (*The Breadwinner*, Glossary: 169-70; *Parvana's Journey*, Glossary: 198): the latter has been phonetically adapted in the target language. In the Spanish glossary of *El Viaje de Parvana*, the translator's intervention is clear, as further information on the origins of these languages is added (*El Viaje de Parvana*, Glossary: 171-72).

> Most spoke Dari, the same language Parvana spoke best. When a customer spoke Pashtu, she could recognize most of it, but not all. (*The Breadwinner*, p10)
> La mayoría hablaba dari, el idioma que mejor conocía Parvana. Ella entendía bastante si utilizaban el *pastún*, pero no todo. (*El pan de la guerra*, p9)

Objects

'**karachi /** *karachi* – A cart on wheels, pushed by hand, used to sell things in the market' (*The Breadwinner*, Glossary|: 169). The use of retention and generalisation strategies respectively is also exemplified in the following instances:

> 'We have the loan of a karachi for the afternoon,' Mrs. Weera said. (*The Breadwinner*, p85)
> 'Nos prestan un *karachi* esta tarde –explicó la señora Weera' (*El pan de la guerra*, p73)

> Parvana loaded a few quilts and cooking things onto the karachi. (*The Breadwinner*, p85)
> Parvana cargo unos cuantos edredones y cacharros de cocina en el carro. (*El pan de la guerra*, p73)

'**toshak/***toshak* – A narrow mattress used in many Afghan homes instead of chairs or beds' (*The Breadwinner*, Glossary: 170). Once again, retention is the strategy the translator recurs to:

Father (...) stretched out on a toshak for a rest. (*The Breadwinner*, p19)

Luego se tendió a descansar en el *toshak*. (*El pan de la guerra*, p17)

An examination of these culturally bound elements suggests a pattern of translational choices, the forces that have influenced these choices during the translation process and the overall orientation of the translations, which is indicative of the translator's behaviour towards translation in general. Thus, Herminia Bevia's choices of strategies discloses the interaction between her educational aim of introducing a text of foreign nature to the target young audience (hence the constant use of a foreignisation strategy such as retention), with the aim of presenting a text that reads as well as possible (hence the presence of domesticating strategies, such as generalisation, omission and addition).

In the translation of children's literature, explicit cultural references, which make a text recognisably foreign, are often eliminated or adapted. Although this practice has been very common in Spanish translations, the translations analysed are indicative of how the presence of culture-specific terms do not necessarily hinder the young readers' enjoyment of a book, but can actually further the international and multicultural look and understanding of young readers.

Conclusion

Translation essentially bridges the gap between two different cultures and two different languages. Translating multicultural children's literature offers an avenue to help children develop an understanding of differences of ethnicity, colour, religion or culture. Furthermore, children should be exposed to multicultural literature since it helps them deal with personal and social issues, develop positive and accurate attitudes towards people of different backgrounds, and express their feelings regarding problems they may encounter in their lives. In fact, Dowd argues: 'From reading, hearing, and using culturally diverse materials, young people learn that beneath surface differences of color, culture or ethnicity, all people experience universal feelings of love, sadness, self-worth, justice and kindness' (1992: 220). It is therefore important that multicultural books continue to be translated so that children have access to the diverse voices revealed through authentic and accurate portrayals of other cultures.

Notes

1. All the royalties from *The Breadwinner* are being donated to the education of Afghan girls in the refugee camps in Pakistan either by funding teacher training programmes and health care centres, or building schools and hiring teachers.

179

2. Deborah Ellis's latest book *The Heaven Shop* (2004), a remarkable account of an AIDS orphan in Africa, also shows Ellis's commitment to presenting children with the realities of our world.

Bibliography

Primary texts

Ellis, Deborah (2001) *The Breadwinner*. Oxford: Oxford University Press

Ellis, Deborah (2002) *El Pan de la Guerra*; Bevia, Herminia (trans.) Zaragoza: Edelvives

Ellis, Deborah (2002) *Parvana's Journey*. Oxford: Oxford University Press

Ellis, Deborah (2004) *El Viaje de Parvana*. Bevia, Herminia (trans.) Zaragoza: Edelvives

Secondary texts

Basnett, S & Trivedi, H (eds.) (1999) *Post-Colonial Translation: Theory and Practice*. London and New York: Pinter

Dowd, F S (1992) 'Evaluating children's books portraying Native American and Asian cultures'. *Childhood Education*, 68: 4, 219-224

Gonzalez- Cascallana, B (2005) 'Translation of Stories and Tales: Hearing the Voices of the Other'. *Érase una vez... en Andersen. II Congreso Internacional de Traducción, Literatura Infantil-Juvenil y Didáctica*, Universidad de las Palmas de Gran Canaria, 16-18 marzo 2005 (in print)

Hade, D (1997) 'Reading Children's Literature Multiculturally,' in Becket, S. L. (ed.) *Reflections of Change: Children's Literature Since 1945*. Westport, Connecticut, US: Greenwood Press, pp115-122

Hunt, P (2001) *Children's Literature*, London: Blackwell

Klein, G (1985) *Reading into Racism: Bias in Children's Literature and Learning Material*. London: Routledge and Kegan Paul

McGillis, R (1999) *Voices of the Other. Children's Literature and the Postcolonial Context*. New York, London: Garland

Metcalf, E M (2003) 'Exploring Cultural Difference Through Translating Children's Literature', in *Meta* vol. 48, no 1-2, pp322-327

Munday, J (2001) *Introducing Translation Studies.* London: Routledge

O'Sullivan, E (2003) 'Narratology meets Translation Studies, or, The Voice of the Translator in Children's Literature,' in *Meta* vol. 48, no 1-2, pp197- 207

Oittinen, R (2000) *Translating for Children.* New York, London: Garland

Pascua Febles, I (2003) 'Translation and Intercultural Education,' in *Meta* vol. 48, no 1-2, p. 276-284

Pym, A (1996) 'Venuti's Visibility' (Review of *The Translator's Invisibility*), *Target,* 8:1, pp165-177

Venuti, L (1995) *The Translator's Invisibility: A History of Translation.* London: Routledge

Websites

Lu, M (2001) *Children's Literature in a Time of National Tragedy.* ERIC Digest
http://www.ericdigests.org/2002-2/time.htm

Matulka, D I (2004) *Passport: Defining International Children's Literature*
http://passport.imaginarylands.org/introduction.html

Maxworthy O'Brien, Andrea (2005) *The Power of Voice. An Interview with Deborah Ellis*
http://education.wisc.edu/ccbc/authors/experts/dellis.asp

Translating Sound in Children's Literature

Gillian Lathey

Sound and rhythm play a fundamental role as children discover the powers of language and narrative. Young children *hear* stories rather than read them; as Maria João Goucha pointed out in *Translating Today* no.3, much writing for the young child is read aloud. Indeed, Danish translation scholar Cay Dollerup has argued that translating for reading aloud 'is an art requiring great competence of translators' (2003: 82). Moreover, young children are eager imitators of whatever sound-systems surround them; they learn language naturally through practice and play, with the encouragement of their fluent elders. Ruth Weir's classic account of her son Anthony's pre-sleep monologues, *Language in the Crib* (1962), demonstrates the sheer joy of a two-and-a-half-year-old's experimentation with sound patterns as he rehearses the phonology of his native language. Repetition, rhyme, onomatopoeia, wordplay and nonsense are, therefore, all common features of children's texts and require a linguistic creativity that is a challenge to any translator.

Take, for instance, the representation of animal noises that is a common feature of children's rhymes and stories. When translating literary effects that depend on aural qualities, as in the case of animal sounds, translators have to switch from one phonological system to another, transposing the barks, squeals, roars and neighs of a complete menagerie into the commonly accepted equivalents in their own tongues. As long ago as 1659, London schoolmaster Charles Hoole grappled with this conundrum in the first English translation of one of the earliest picture books for children, the *Orbis Sensualium Pictus* by Czech philosopher and educationalist Johannes Amos Comenius. This dual-language text (originally published in German and Latin) includes a section designed to teach the sounds of letters of the alphabet. Captions in Latin and in English (in Hoole's translation) accompany pictures of animals and birds, together with an indication of the sounds they utter. Hoole renders the alliteration and onomatopoeia of the source text as best he can, with some curiosities:

Anſer gingrit, *ga ga*	*The Gooſe gagleth.*	G g
Os halat, *bà'h, bà'h*	*The Mouth breatheth out.*	H h
Mus mintrit, *ì ì ì*	*The Mouſe chirpeth.*	I i
Anas tetrinnit, *kba, kba*	*The Duck quacketh.*	K k
Lupus ululat, *lu ulu*	*The Wolf howleth.*	L l
Urſus murmurat, *mummum*	*The Bear grumbleth.*	M m

Figure 1

How human representation of animal cries in different languages began, or how conventions are established, can only be the subject of speculation, but an articulated cry such as that of a cockerel does at least maintain its characteristic rhythmic pattern across a number of languages: 'Cock-a-doodle-doo' in English; 'coquerico' in French, 'qui-qui-ri-qui' in Spanish and 'kikeriki' in German. And in some instances there is an aural equivalent between two or more languages: a Spanish pig in the Venezuelan picture book *Cui-cui-cuidado! Animales al volante* by Marilyn Pérez Falcón and María Elena Repiso, happily utters an 'oinc oinc' that matches the English 'oink oink'.

But there are differences, too: the Spanish-barking dog in the same the book utters in 'guau' a sound very different from an English 'woof woof', 'ruff ruff', or the quaint 'bow-wow'. Differences in some cases are even more marked. According to the comprehensive Georgetown University website on animal noises, 'gonggong' is the sound customarily attributed to Indonesian dogs; 'mung-mung' to Korean and 'hav, hav' to Turkish canines. There is not space to list further examples here (see website reference below), but it is common translation practice to use the conventional equivalent in the target language. I can't help wondering, however, whether a more playful approach might catch children's imaginations. A transliteration of a Spanish or German cockerel's cry into 'kikeriki' in an English translation would certainly intrigue a young child already familiar with 'cock-a-doodle-do'. A touch of foreignisation in such instances is likely to spark interest in sound and language and enhance the metalinguistic awareness that many monolingual British

183

children so sadly lack. I write this with some conviction, after hearing of the enthusiastic response of a colleague's daughter to the transliteration of Japanese animal noises in *Where Are You Going? To See My Friend! A story of friendship in two languages* by Eric Carle and Kazuo Iwamura. These two great illustrators came together to create a book that reads in English from the front and Japanese from the back. It depicts the progress of two bands of animals, all uttering typical cries and marching towards a grand finale in the central, fold-out section of the book. Four-year-old Milly wanted to hear the story again and again, listening, enthralled, to animal noises in two languages!

Figure 2: Carle/Iwamura

Nonsense and sound poetry for the young present an even greater challenge. Can pure sound poetry be translated? Umberto Eco gives a negative answer in the case of 'invented language like the poetic languages of Morgenstern and Hugo Ball, where no translation is possible, because the phonosymbolic effect depends precisely on the absence of any semantic level – and therefore it is pointless to translate' (2001: 108). Yet Anthea Bell's translation for children of Christian Morgenstern's (1871-1914) sound poem 'Das Grosse Lallula' ('The Big Laloola'), illustrated in an appropriately quirky manner by Lisbeth Zwerger, ensures that at least some of the sounds uttered in English will replicate the aural quality of the German original. In the third line of the poem Bell renders the German 'Bifzi, bafzi' as 'Biftsi, baftsi', thereby reproducing in English the 'ts' sound of the German 'z'. Bell does not adopt this strategy throughout the poem, however, as can be seen from the rest of the verse:

German	English
Kroklokwafzi? Semememi!	Kroklokwoffzie? Seemimeemi!
Seikronto – prafriplo:	Siyokronto – prufliplo:
Bifzi, bafzi; hulalemi:	Biftsi baftsi; hulaleemi:
Quasti basti bo...	quasti basti bo...
Lalu lalu lalu lalu la!	Laloo laloo laloo laloola!
	(Morgenstern 1992, 1995: 21)

She chooses, for example, not to represent the voiced fricative represented 'v', represented by 'u' in the German digraph 'qu'. This may well be because translation of this kind of poetry has to take account of the visual element that reaches its extreme form in concrete poetry: the arrangement of letters on the page is part of the appeal of nonsense verse. To return to Eco's comment, I would argue that this process can be called translation, since Bell *is* operating between two languages, making choices that are appropriate both to the aural and visual qualities of Morgenstern's original poem, and to the needs of its target-language audience.

Bell's idiosyncratic translation indicates that there can be no hard and fast rules that will ensure a child-friendly translation of sound; the only sure test is the response of children to a trial reading or performance. It is imperative in this aspect of translation to enter into a dialogue with a child audience as translator and academic Riitta Oittinen (2000) recommends. Sound may be play for the child, but it is not child's play for the translator.

Bibliography

Carle, Eric & Iwamura, Kazuo (2001) *Where Are You Going? To See My Friend! A Story of Friendship in Two Languages*, New York: Orchard Books

Comenius, Johann (1677, first published 1659) *Orbis Sensualium Pictus*, trans. Charles Hoole, London: S Leacroft

Dollerup, Cay (2003) 'Translation for Reading Aloud', *Meta*, Vol. 48, nos. 1-2, pp81-104

Eco, Umberto (2001) *Experiences in Translation*, Mc Ewen, Alastair (trans.) Toronto: University of Toronto Press

Falcón, Marilyn Pérez & Repiso, María (2002) *Cui-cui-cuidado! Animales al Volante*, Caracas, Venezuela: Ediciones Ekaré

Goucha, Maria João (2005) 'Translating Illustrated Poems for Children', *Translating Today* no.3, pp22-24

Morgenstern, Christian (1992) *Kindergedichte und Galgenlieder,* illus. Lisbeth Zwerger, Frankfurt: Neugebauer

Morgenstern, Christian (1995) *Lullabies, Lyrics and Gallows Songs,* illus. Lisbeth Zwerger, Bell, Anthea (trans.), New York: North-South Books

Oittinen, Riitta (2000) *Translating for Children,* London and New York: Routledge

Weir, Ruth Hirsch (1962) *Language in the Crib,* The Hague: Mouton

Website

www.georgetown.edu/faculty/ballc/animals/animals.html

Text and Picture:
Translation and Illustration

Translation and Illustration

The link between the articles in this section is that all of them deal in some way with visual as well as verbal text. The translation of picture books between different languages and cultures is by no means a straightforward exercise, and there have been many instances where elements in the pictures in the source text have had to be manipulated or omitted for the target culture. Mieke Desmet has examined the problems encountered when translating into Chinese the work of two of the most prestigious contemporary British author-illustrators, Babette Cole and Anthony Browne. There are obvious difficulties about the placing of text on the page and about the unfamiliarity of some of the scenes illustrated. More significant however is the virtual impossibility of rendering the humour created by the interplay of word and picture, especially when sometimes there are significant gaps that are to be filled by the reader. Desmet's particular caution is against regarding the translated text as 'transparent', though she recognises that certain changes may result from the publishers' realistic assessment of their market.

A similar emphasis on 'domestication', in this instance of both picture and text, is to be found in André Moura and Renata Junqueira de Souza's study of a tale by Hans Christian Andersen. They show how the demands of a young audience quite unfamiliar with Denmark have been borne in mind throughout.

The other articles in this section are less directly related to the question of 'translating' a pictorial text than with the effect of the illustrations within it. Maria-Venetia Kyritsi's main focus is on narrative aspects of those Grimm tales that Wanda Gág chose for her ground-breaking translation, and how she treats issues such as violence and sexuality. A very important aspect of Gág's work, however, is the fact that she was an illustrator, with the result that the illustrations to her collections are among the most faithful to the stories.

Sue Neale makes an interesting comparison between the French and English editions of Daniel Pennac's *Eye of the Wolf*. Because the French publishers seem to see the book as primarily for use in schools, the rather literal illustrations occupy a subordinate position, whereas in the English text they are larger and give much more scope to the reader's imagination.

In the recent Neapolitan versions of the children's classics *Alice in Wonderland* and *Pinocchio*, the pictures too have been in effect translated. Stefania Tondo shows how the covers bear the image of Vesuvius, while the local figure of Punchinella serves as a mediator of the story.

These articles touch on just a few of the many issues involved in the translation of picture books and illustrated text, a subject which really deserves a conference in its own right!

Road-Blocks and Broken Bridges: Translations of Picture Books into Chinese

Mieke K T Desmet

Translations are often seen as a way of bridging the language and culture gaps between different peoples, and translation of children's literature is especially considered to be one of the means to make global connections. On the surface it may seem that in countries where there is much material translated from abroad there must be an open attitude towards other cultures. Translation is seen as transparent, as bringing the original text (source culture text) to the target culture without any loss of meaning. However, that view of translation may actually be misleading. A closer analysis of what exactly happens in translation shows the fissures between the cultures and sometimes the impossibility of covering the gap. Although it is possible that translation of children's literature creates bridges between literatures from different countries, the traffic on the bridges is in many cases only going in one direction, from majority cultures to minority cultures.

From a quantitative perspective, it is obvious that there is an imbalance in the number of books that are exchanged and translated between countries. It is well-known that the main English speaking countries (US, UK, Australia and Canada) are not importing that many children's books from other cultures (Flugge, 1994), whereas minority cultures generally import more material from other cultures, often for a variety of reasons (Desmet 2002). One such reason is that translation is often an important strategy to establish children's literature in a culture lacking a strong children's literature tradition. What is missing in the target culture can be imported and translated and be the impetus for the development of the local children's literature. Yet the members of the target culture also holds the power over how they want to shape their own children's literature, which that means that translated children's literature is likely to be adapted to fit target culture views. In this paper I will firstly introduce some general facts about publishing children's literature in Taiwan before going on to look at one particular publisher in the context of the case studies: translations of picture books by Babette Cole and Anthony Browne.

Publishing Children's Literature in Taiwan: Abundant Wonderland

The publishing of children's literature in Taiwan has changed dramatically in the last decade, and the publishing industry is currently blooming, with many publishers actively engaged in bringing children's books to their home audience. Both the number of publishers and the number of books published each year rival the situation in major cultures with more readers. Taiwanese publishers not only bring out translations of English language children's books, but also publish translations from French, German and other languages. Children's literature written in Chinese is also slowly developing (Gao, 2002; Teng, 2003; Bradbury & Liu, 2003; Desmet & Duh, 2004).

At the moment, Grimm Press is one of the major publishers of children's literature in Taiwan, with a special focus on picture books. This company is relatively young, having been established in 1993. Its aim, as reflected in its name, is to bring Western children's literature to Taiwan. They publish roughly twice as much translated material as that of Chinese or Taiwanese origin. This publisher has made connections with more than 200 illustrators over the years and built bridges with 30 countries. However, despite their wide range of connections, and a range of works originally in German, French and a few other languages, it is obvious (and acknowledged by the publisher in a questionnaire) that the dominant language from which works are translated is English. Their focus is on America and Western Europe, rather than countries in Asia or Africa. In general terms the priority in their selection process for translation is the aesthetic aspect and the creativity of the author/illustrator. The publisher wants to be known as the top Taiwanese publisher of children's and adult's picture books; they therefore aim to find quality books, especially those which have won awards, for translation. Their list of authors and illustrators selected for translation is a veritable 'Who's Who' of illustrators in Britain, America and Australia, including, among others, Babette Cole and Anthony Browne[1]. In this paper I shall focus on the translations into Chinese of one book by each of these author/illustrators, and through a careful page by page comparison of the English source text and the Chinese target text, to reveal relevant features about the translation strategies.

Babette Cole and Anthony Browne: Creativity Constrained

Translating a good many children's picture books from other countries may indicate an open attitude to other cultures and a desire to build bridges between countries, but the target culture may also put constraints on the translations. Previous research has indicated that in the case of award winning novels there may be less radical change in the translation process than for other types of books (Desmet, 2002). However, such an attitude does not hold in the case studies presented below. Scrutiny of the translations into Chinese of *Princess Smartypants* by Babette Cole and *Voices in the Park* by Anthony Browne shows that even though these are award winning books, many changes have been made during the translation process.

It is helpful to start with a note on the Chinese writing system which is obviously very different from a Western alphabetical system. In Taiwan, people use traditional complex Chinese characters rather than the simplified ones in use in Mainland China. Moreover, the Taiwanese also use their own

Mandarin Phonetic System (known as Bopomofo). Printed material for adults normally only shows the Chinese characters, while material for children can either provide these characters alone, or show them with the phonetic pronunciation guide next to them. Children's books without the phonetic pronunciation guide are mainly aimed at older readers who can read independently, or at parents planning to read to their children; children's books with the phonetic system printed next to the characters can be read by anyone who has mastered the Mandarin Phonetic System, which is taught in kindergarten and is definitely mastered by the first grade of elementary school. Both the texts under discussion here use the phonetic system and can thus be read by young children independently.

Babette Cole: Princess Smartypants Smothered

The avowed aim of Grimm Press is to choose the best and most creative picture books from abroad and to translate them so that Taiwanese children can explore and enjoy them (Desmet, 2005). *Princess Smartypants* was selected for translation because it had won the Kate Greenaway award, a fact that is duly advertised on the cover and the title page of the book in order to promote sales. The book is also clearly marketed as a translation, since the translator's name is also on both the cover and the title page. This heavy promotion by the publisher makes evident that the foreign is seen here as exotic and desirable.

Babette Cole's work exhibits a range of different forms of humour, and in *Princess Smartypants* this is created in several ways. Part of the fun lies in recognising the double entendres in the names of the princess's different suitors, whereas another aspect is the contrast between the text and the pictures. Unfortunately not all these features are recreated in the translation.

The changes start with the title. The source text title gives little indication of the subject matter of the book, although the princess's name indicates that she is likely to be more exciting than the traditional fairy tale princesses. The target text title, on the other hand, reveals the main point of the book by entitling it, 'Naughty princess doesn't want to marry'[2]. Any suspense that readers might have had on reading the title has disappeared. The target text readers can no longer discover what will happen in the book, but know the ending before they have opened it.

Wordplay in the text and in the names of characters is also almost completely absent in the Chinese translation. The motto of the princess with its mock Latin ('Smartypantus Rulus O.K.us'), located at the beginning of the book, has been replaced by a repetition of the title. For the translation of the English text 'She enjoyed being a Ms,' (in contrast to Mrs. with its various connotations), the Chinese translator, in the absence of any differentiation

193

between Ms and Miss, opts for a Chinese phrase which loosely translates as 'single noble,' meaning someone who enjoys being single.

Most of the wordplay in the source text lies in the names of Smartypants and her suitors. There are only a limited number of strategies to translate names, although these may in turn give rise to many changes in the names. Names may not be translated at all (verbatim copying), they may be adapted to target spelling, deleted, substituted by a target culture name, replaced by a noun or pronoun, or the meaning of a name may be translated literally. Keeping a name in English alphabetic form in a Chinese text would immediately draw attention to it as a translation, so that this strategy is not often used in Chinese books. A more common strategy with names is to transliterate the foreign name into Chinese on the basis of its sound. If such a transliteration has more than three characters, then it equally stands out as being a foreign element since Chinese names are usually three or two characters long (four in the case of married women in former times). Even when transliterated names are only three characters long, they are also generally recognized as foreign elements in the Chinese target text because they do not sound like 'real' Chinese names. If English names are being transliterated into Chinese characters, it seems preferable that those which carry meaning should be translated into a similarly creative name into Chinese, rather than simply imitating its sound. In some instances the translator might be able to replicate both the sound and the meaning of the English name in the Chinese characters used for transliteration. In this way the wordplay and the humour resulting from it would be preserved to the enjoyment of target text readers. Here the name 'Smartypants' is obviously a pun, alluding both to the fact that the princess always wears trousers, and that she is someone who always knows best. The translator has however paid attention only to the sounds of her name and those of her suitors, completely disregarding their meanings. As a result, the humour of the names is completely absent, which results in a flatter and duller text that loses the effect of the names of Prince Compost, Prince Pelvis and the rest.

Cole also creates humour by an ironic interplay between the words of the text and the pictures on the page. The source text uses basic terms - pets, animals, slugs, tower, firewood, etc. – the apparent simplicity of which is undermined by the visuals which clearly show pictures of exaggerated monsters. The Chinese target text constantly adds words such as 'monster' and 'big monster fish' which explicate what the visual layer of the book aims to tell. The reader of the target text is not allowed to enjoy this contrast between words and images, as the ideas that the images are intended to convey are spelled out in the text.

Another aspect of the source text is that, in many cases, readers of the source text have to draw their own conclusions about what the image actually tells, as the ideas are implied rather than being directly stated. Instead, the translator here has added explanations, so that readers have no room to make their own interpretations of the text. For example, in the source text, Princess Smartypants challenges Prince Pelvis to a 'roller-disco marathon,' and readers see him flattened with exhaustion, but in the target text the phrase 'to see who will be defeated (and give up) first' is added. Prince Vertigo is called to rescue Princess Smartypants from her tower, but in the Chinese edition the tower is described as 'a slippery glass tower' (which is already evident in the picture) and, just to ensure that readers get the point, an additional phrase is supplied: 'but Prince Vertigo cannot climb the tower.' In the source text, the image shows Prince Swashbuckle safely feeding the dangerous pets from a helicopter, but in the target text the phrase 'flying his helicopter' is added. Consistently, text is added to explain what is already shown in the image.

Overall, the translation is characterised by strategies such as the transliteration of names, explication of features in the visual part of the text and additions to explain aspects of the story. All of these translation strategies show that the translator has little confidence in the ability of the child readers to explore the visual and written text on their own. This viewpoint of the ability of the child reader is of course in contrast to that embedded in Babette Cole's work. *Princess Smartypants* is a instance where the translation process has smothered the creativity of the source text and produced a weak imitation of it. Children in Taiwan only have access to a Chinese version of the book in which the humour and creativity are markedly toned down and diluted.

Anthony Browne: Voices Silenced

Like Babette Cole's work, Anthony Browne's leaves much scope for readers to explore and discover meanings for themselves. However, *Voices in the Park* has been translated using a number of strategies which again tone down the creativity of the source text and limit the interpretation possibilities.

Most immediately obvious is the change in title. *Voices in the Park* becomes (in back translation) *When Nai-Ping Met Nai-Ping*. According to one of the editors at the company, this change was adopted partially because this new title would sound similar to the movie title *When Harry Met Sally*, though questions might well be asked about the relationship of this film to a children's book. The main (and perhaps the only connection) between them is that they have both been imported into Taiwanese culture. The argument of the editor was that parents buying the book would recognise this wordplay and would therefore buy the book. The result of this change in title is that the focus on 'voices' from the source text changes into a focus on two child characters meeting. This shift represents a reduction as there are four voices in the book, but only two are highlighted in this title. The children become the main protagonists in the Taiwanese book rather than there being four people whose lives intersect in this visit to the park. This change addresses the child readers more specifically as children by focusing on the part the children play in the story and by disregarding the roles of the parent figures. The intertextual connection to the movie *When Harry Met Sally* also adds the idea of romantic love which is absent from the source text.

It is also clear from the title that the names have been altered. As mentioned before, there are various possible strategies for this; here it is immediately clear that the names of the characters have been changed into proper Chinese names rather than merely transliterations of the English names. The translator has opted to use almost similar (homophonic) names for the boy and the girl. The cultural connotations in the source text, of the boy, Charles, being from a well-off family, whereas the girl's, 'Smudge', is a nickname which refers both to her lower social status and her enjoyment of being dirty, have vanished. The class distinction reflected in the names in the source text has been removed and has shifted into a boy and a girl having similar personal names in the target text. Although the two Chinese names sound the same, they are partly written in different characters, so that readers can distinguish them. Charles has become Nai-Ping, with connotations of milk bottle and flat, whereas Smudge has been changed into Nai-Ping, with connotations of floating on water and duckweed. An alternative strategy would have been to have translated Smudge literally and to have rendered Charles as a transliteration. The change has made meaningless Charles's comment on spread 11 in the source text that the girl's name is funny, so in the translation he says instead that it is funny that their names sound similar. The idea of having a similar name can of course imply that the characters share something and that there is somehow a connection between them which implied in the source text and explicated in the target text.

Staying with names, there is Charles's pedigree dog, Victoria, and Smudge's mongrel, Albert. Cole's choice of names can be seen as a tongue in cheek link to Queen Victoria and Prince Albert. 'Victoria' has been translated as a straightforward transliteration whereas Albert becomes 'A Buo', a name with lower class connotations. By translating these dog names in two different ways, the association between their names is completely lost, but the idea of different social class is added to the names of the dogs. What was implied in the names of the children in the source text has been transferred to the names of the dogs in the target text instead. Translation can be seen as a compromise in which lost meaning on one level is replaced or recreated on another level. This compensation strategy may not be the best way to translate, but by using it, the translator is able to keep some level of complexity in the target text.

At one point in the story, Charles picks flowers for Smudge and in that passage Smudge calls Charles 'Charlie'. This can be seen as a term of endearment, showing how they have become close, as well as representing the class background of Smudge. The translator could have made a similar choice: Charles versus Charlie could be rendered as Nai-Ping versus A-Ping. Instead the translator uses a pronoun and the connotations of Smudge calling Charles 'Charlie' have disappeared from the target text.

The word 'voice' is replaced by a musical term 'piece, song, tune', rather than being translated literally, but the musical term retains some of the meaning of 'voice'. It is not a complete match. In the English text the typography for the different voices in the source text tells us something about the particular voice who is speaking. It reflects both the character and the social status of the different protagonists. The voice of the upper-middle-class mother is in standard type; the voice of the lower-class father is in bold, as a reflection of the robust type of man he is; Charles's voice is in a very thin font reflecting his powerlessness; and Smudge's happiness is reflected in the dancing letters used for her. This typographical difference is absent in the Chinese text and the Chinese characters for all the speakers follow the same format and font without differentiation, although it would have been perfectly feasible to have recreated this aspect in the target text. There could be several reasons for this omission: it might be more expensive to use different Chinese fonts, or it may have been felt that beginning readers would not yet be able to distinguish between different kinds of characters (although the use of the Mandarin Phonetic Script negates this reason). Whatever the reasons, the loss of this element removes a level of interpretation and playfulness in the text.

Another small change which carries a less identifiable effect is that in general the register of the Chinese text is more polished and literary. For example, the child calling his mother 'mummy' is changed into the more distant 'mother'. This could be linked with the educational aspect of children's text and the hierarchical structure of traditional Chinese families. Furthermore, there is hardly any attempt at representing the social differences linguistically between the characters, apart from the dog's name as mentioned above.

There are also a number of other smaller additions to the target text, which, just as in the case of *Princess Smartypants*, are designed to help the reader with the interpretation of the text. For example, in spread 3 the annoyance of the mother is implied in the source text, but is explicated in the target text with the addition 'really angering me.' In the same spread, the translator adds the words 'turning my head to Nai-Ping' which is clearly contradicted by the picture. Mother and son look away from each other indicating their emotional distance and loneliness. The translator/editor must feel that a mother should love her son and look at him when speaking to him and these additions undermine the message of the picture. Further words are added to make the mother seem more motherly, and show her talking more lovingly to her son. The loneliness and distance between the mother and her son is negated in the target text, and mother and son are shown in a more loving relationship. This of course undermines the messages of the source text and changes the interpretation of the parent-child relationship in the target text. This kind of change shows the different views on parent and children relationships in British and Taiwanese culture.

When Charles expresses the hope that he will meet Smudge again and says, 'Maybe Smudge will be there next time?' the Chinese text keeps the 'maybe', expressing doubt and hope, but deletes the question mark. The feeling of uncertainty regarding meeting with Smudge in the future is thus less strong in the Chinese text. Another cultural item that is changed is the cup of tea that Smudge makes for her father, which has turned into a cup of chocolate milk. It is possible that tea is considered too Chinese and chocolate milk is considered more foreign and exotic. Another possible reason for the change is that since the tea ritual in Chinese society is only performed by adults and not by children, a child making tea would be considered strange in the target culture.

Although there are only a few minor changes in the target text for *Voices in the Park*, their effects can be as far-reaching as the more drastic ones in *Princess Smartypants*. The translation shifts show that there are differences between the Taiwanese children's literature system and the British one. The Taiwanese publisher has less faith in the ability of Taiwanese children (and parents) to make sense of the text and has in some cases narrowed down the interpretation possibilities. In *Voices in the Park,* the visual images undermine and contradict the text, whereas in *Princess Smartypants* the images are explained to the reader. The loss of cultural specificity in the text may seem less important in the case of picture books, because the pictures can still provide the cultural difference for the target text reader, since they have not been changed.

Conclusion

Translations may work to create bridges between cultures, yet the actual practice of translation may undermine some of those ideals. Although the shifts discerned in the translated case studies do not really neutralise cultural differences in an extreme way, and the pictures still allow the books to celebrate cultural differences, it would be easy to argue that these changes are extremely regrettable and that the translations are betraying its source. Yet we should not forget that translations are part of the target culture system and function within that system. What seems as a betrayal of the source text may well be an astute commercial move by the local publisher, who needs to sell the product in the Taiwanese market; the view of Taiwanese parents and the way they select books may well be a realistic one. The attraction of a foreign book which has received many accolades may be enough to encourage Taiwanese parents to select these translated books for their children. Only parents making a detailed analysis of the English source texts and the Chinese target texts would discover the discrepancies between the two. Such a comparison would easily be possible as both the English version and the Chinese version are available in book stores in Taiwan, but most people believe in the transparency of translation and accept the translated book as the 'real' thing. These two case studies show that even in a culture that translates many texts, translation loss may occur when the target culture tries to retain some sense of local cultural identity or is not able to tolerate the creativity and openness of the source text.

Note on Language

Both works discussed in this paper are published in Taiwan and are thus written in complex characters of Mandarin Chinese. The translations of the Chinese book titles into English are my own as all are other translations from Mandarin Chinese. I would like to express my gratitude to Ivy Tsai, my research student assistant, who provided valuable help during the translation process.

Notes

1. See Desmet 2005 for a full analysis of this publisher's list.

2. All translations are my own.

Bibliography

Primary texts

English Source Texts:

Browne, A (1998; 1999) *Voices in the Park*, London: Transworld Publishers

Cole, B (1986; 1988) *Princess Smartypants*, London: Picture Lions

Chinese Target Texts (Translations in Chinese and Back translation into English):

布朗安東尼 (2001) 當乃平遇上乃萍, 譯彭倩文, 台北 格林
(Browne Anthony (2001) *When Nai-Ping Met Nai-Ping*, Chien-Wen, Peng (trans.) Taipei: Grimm Press)

柯爾巴貝 (1994; 2004), 頑皮公主不出嫁 譯吳燕凰 台北格林
(Cole, Babette (1994; 2004) *Naughty Princess Doesn't Want To Marry*, Yen-Huang, Wu (trans.), Taipei: Grimm Press.)

Secondary texts

Bradbury, S & Feng-Hsin Liu, F (2003) 'Everywhere a Children's Book: The View from Taiwan', *The Horn Book Magazine*, Vol. 79.2, pp239-248

Desmet, M K T (2002) *Babysitting the Reader: Translating Narrative Fiction for Girls from English into Dutch (1946-1995)*, London: University College London [unpublished PhD thesis]

Desmet, M K T & Ming Cherng Duh (2004) 'Taiwan' in: Hunt, P (ed.) (2004) *International Companion Encyclopedia of Children's Literature Second Edition*, London and New York: Routledge, pp1241-1245

Desmet, M K T (2005) 'Connecting Local and Global Literatures or Driving on a One-Way Street? The Case of the Taiwanese Grimm Press' in Reynolds, K, O'Sullivan, E & Romøren, R (eds.) Children's Literature Global and Local: Social and Aesthetic Perspectives, Oslo: Novus Press, pp218-226

Flugge, Klaus (1994) 'Crossing the Divide: Publishing Children's Books in the European Context' *Signal* 75,pp209-214

Gao, Pat (2002) 'Not Just Kid Stuff' *Taipei Review* 52.4, pp.50-57

O'Sullivan, Emer (2000) *Kinderliterarische Komparatistik*, Heidelberg: Universitätsverlag C Winter

Teng, Shu-fen (2003) 'A Reader's Paradise, A Publisher's Inferno' Sinorama 28.5 (2003), pp6-15

Brazilian Ugly Duckling: Diversity and Tradition in the Hans Christian Andersen Classic

André Muniz de Moura & Renata Junqueira de Souza

Introduction

In 2006, readers, writers, teachers and specialist critics all over the world remembered Hans Christian Andersen and his work. The situation in Brazil was the same - we had seminars and exhibitions, together publications of some Andersen anthologies. In my country, the best known Andersen story is definitely 'The Ugly Duckling,' even if we allow for the recent rise in popularity of Disney's version of 'The Little Mermaid,' the theme of many girls' birthday parties.

There are many Brazilian versions of 'The Ugly Duckling' but a special one was released in May as homage to Andersen's Bicentenary. Its text, by José Francisco Borges (usually known as J Borges), is illustrated by Jô Oliveira; both are astonishingly creative. But this book is quite different from others. It is not simply a translation that takes the classic, original story from Hans Christian Andersen to the different environment of Brazil. Its uniqueness lies in the fact that it is an adaptation written in verse, in a very typical Brazilian form, the 'cordel'. J Borges, a wood-carver and poet, is one of the most important artists of the 'Literatura de cordel'.

'Cordel' are pamphlets or booklets that hang from a piece of string ('cordel') in the places where they are sold. They are long, narrative poems with woodcut illustrations on the cover, often done by the poet himself. Their subjects include traditional themes (romances, fantastic stories, animal fables, traditional religious tales) and themes based on current events, famous people, life in the cities, etc. The largest concentration of this type of popular literature is in northeastern Brazil, where the artists J Borges and Jô Oliveira were born. Recent studies have investigated the European background of the 'Literatura de Cordel'. Its probable origin, from the Middle Ages until the sixteenth century, was probably the 'Littérature de colportage,' which is found mainly in France but also in other countries. For instance, experts have reported that in seventeenth-century Spain, there was material called 'pliegos sueltos,'[literally 'loose folds'] or 'pliegos de cordel,' while in the Netherlands, the name was 'pamflet'. In England they were called 'cocks' or 'catchpennies', when they were romances, and 'broadsides' when they dealt with historical facts.

To avoid confusion, I should emphasise that J Borges is a Brazilian poet and wood-carver who was born in 1935, not the Argentinian writer, Jorge Luis Borges. J. Borges is well known in Brazil, having sold one hundred thousand copies of a cordel book, *The Arrival of the Prostitute in Heaven*. He also illustrated the cover of *Walking Words* by the Uruguayan writer and essayist, Eduardo Galeano. A really versatile artist, indeed.

Rhyme and Reason: Diversity and Tradition

J Borges is widely known for his woodcarvings but in the book I am analysing, he is responsible for the text. The illustrations, made by Jô Oliveira, are based upon the style of typical woodcarvings from Northeast Brazil. I have used the term 'Diversity' in my subtitle because this book is really innovative. This diversity has three main aspects. Firstly, the use of poetry is certainly unusual and is a radical change from the original form. While maintaining the main plot, it contributes to a new reading of the classic Hans Christian Andersen tale. The whole story is organised in six line stanzas. Secondly, there is also diversity in the language - the style is very Brazilian. In fact, it is so specifically from the Northeast of Brazil that there are some words that even a reader with a very wide vocabulary needs to search for in a dictionary. This feature is a device that can help children who live so far from the place where this story was originally written to make connections with it. Finally, there is diversity in the setting. The environment in this Brazilian adaptation is that of a drought region, with two seasons: the summer when the air is dry and the temperatures are high, and the so-called winter, a season when there is rain, but the temperatures are quite different from those in the Northern Hemisphere. This environment is totally different from that of Denmark or indeed any European country.

The other word I have used in my sub-title is 'Tradition'. Although it has many differences from the original and presents a brand new point of view, this Brazilian version of 'The Ugly Duckling' has also some characteristics that make it a traditional retelling or adaptation. José Francisco Borges has not provided a 'rupture', a 'carnivalisation', or a 'deconstruction' of the original version. In this he differs, for instance, from the version in *The Stinky Cheese Man* by Jon Scieska and Lane Smith: 'The really ugly duckling.' In Scieska's text, the ugly duckling does not become a swan at the end, but stays ugly. This is a good-humoured deconstruction of the happy ending typical of fairy tales. But this does not happen in the text by José Francisco Borges; it would have been inappropriate in a book celebrating Andersen's two hundredth birthday.

While I cannot discuss all the illustrations by Jô Oliveira, I shall select for comment some of the most interesting aspects. Right at the beginning, on the title page, the reader is shown the shadows of Hans Christian Andersen and José Francisco Borges chatting; it is important to notice that is Borges who is holding a book, signifying that an intertextual dialogue has only been made possible through the book. A later picture shows how the Ugly Duckling escapes from the cat and the hen. This illustrates the incident when

202

the Ugly Duckling talks about the pleasure of diving to the bottom of a lake, and the hen considers him crazy. The hen and the cat say that he is not allowed to give his opinion; they despise him and he escapes from the house. All that happens in the original story is exactly portrayed in the Brazilian version.

On the Ugly Duckling's journey, the seasons are portrayed: the summer with its drought, low humidity, and high temperatures, and then the 'winter' flood, when the ugly duckling can swim happily and dive. Though the climate differs from that in the Andersen tale, the story and illustrations are faithful to its spirit. The setting plays a very important role, being responsible for much of its diversity. It also enables the literatura de cordel to win a wider public.

The following table displays the differences between the two stories.

Hans Christian Andersen (Original version)	José Francisco Borges (Brazilian version)
Autumn	Summer
Winter	So-called Winter
Ugly Duckling gets stuck on ice	Ugly Duckling gets stuck on swamp roots
A peasant saves Ugly Duckling	A peasant saves Ugly Duckling
The peasant takes Ugly Duckling home	The peasant takes Ugly Duckling home
Ugly Duckling flies into the milk, the butter, and the flour and children tease him	Ugly Duckling flies into the milk, the butter, and the flour and children tease him
Ugly Duckling flies off	Ugly Duckling flies off
The author shortens Ugly Duckling's sufferings	The author suppresses Ugly Duckling's sufferings
Spring comes	Spring time already
Ugly Duckling waits for Death	Ugly Duckling waits for Death
Ugly Duckling asks to be killed	Ugly Duckling doesn´t ask to be killed
Ugly Duckling realises that he is a Swan	Ugly Duckling realises that he is a Swan
Children cheer him	Children cheer him
Happy Ending	Happy Ending

Conclusion

In producing this version of Andersen's tale, I believe that the main goal of the writer and the illustrator was to make it known to a wider group of children, and also to make them aware of a traditional aspect of the Brazilian culture that has become almost unknown today. The originality of the text in verse form, the use of language that speaks directly to children, and the illustration of elements familiar to a Brazilian audience mean that they have surely succeeded in their aims.

Bibliography

Primary sources

Andersen, H C, trans. Borges, J (2005) *O Patinho Feio Adaptado em Cordel*. Rio de Janeiro: Zit Editora

Andersen, H C. (1974) 'The Ugly Duckling', in *The Complete Fairy Tales and Stories*, Haugaard. E C (trans.), London: Gollancz

Wanda Gág: the first 'innovative' translator of the Grimms' *Kinder- und Hausmärchen*

Maria-Venetia Kyritsi

Gág's Selection and Translation Background

The first non-comprehensive collection of translated tales from the Grimms' *Kinder- und Hausmärchen (KHM)* which stands out from the multitude of 19th- and 20th-century translations, versions and adaptations both because of its style and its translation approach, was made by Wanda Gág. It was the first translation up to that time to have been made and published in the USA by an American translator. Gág's work was reprinted by a British publishing house, Faber and Faber, and reached British audiences in a relatively short time after its publication in the USA. In fact her first volume of translations entitled *Tales from Grimm* (1936) was published in the UK in 1937, only a year after its American release, although its follow-up, *More Tales from Grimm* (1947) – published in the USA after Gág's death in 1946 – appeared in the UK for the first time in 1962, a full 15 years after its American publication. The contents of the first volume of translations were derived from only sixteen of the original *KHM*, but the success of the book seems to have encouraged Gág to produce more translations for her second volume which contained thirty-two tales in total, thirty-one taken from the Grimms' *KHM* and one, 'The Sorcerer's Apprentice' taken from unknown sources. Although this tale has the same title as Goethe's poem 'Der Zauberlehrling' and Disney's animated film sketch from *Fantasia* (1940), it has a different plot; it is now known (Zipes, 2000: 96) that it was written by Gág herself who was inspired by the similar story in 'De Gaudeif un sien Meester' or a variant of the latter (Tale Type 325, 'The Magician and His Pupil', in the Aarne-Thompson Index).

In this paper, I shall comment on Gág's two volumes jointly, with appropriate references to the time of publication of each separate story under analysis. I hope that this may facilitate a better understanding of the translator's strategies and approach than would totally separate treatment.

The importance of Gág's books lies not only in the novelty of the dual publication but also in the irregularity and originality of the translation itself, as will be seen further on in the paper. Critics who have commented on Gág's work include, among others, Brian Alderson (1978: 6), who designates it a 'free' translation. Gág herself conceded this, both in her introduction and in the title pages of the two volumes where it is noted that the stories were 'freely translated and illustrated by Wanda Gág.' Alderson considers it one of the best 'modern versions of the tales [which] take heed of the character of the original telling and try to reflect it.' Jack Zipes (2003: xxxvii) puts Gág's rendition in the same category as most 20th-century translations, which 'seek to streamline the language according to present-day usage and often negate the historical features of the tales'.

Gág's translation holds another first in the publication of the KHM in the English language. Although her books are clearly intended for an audience of children, she does not refrain from prefacing her first volume with an 'Introduction.' In this, more or less in the self-deprecating manner of Edgar Taylor (1823: xi-xii), she states fairly lengthily that she has made changes to the original stories and explains the reasons for those interventions. In order to solve the presumed language difficulties of young readers, she has also added an explanatory afterword in Tales from Grimm (Gág, 1936: 245) with the title 'In case you want to know: The meanings or pronunciations of the unusual words in this book.' This lists the pronunciations and, where necessary, the meanings of German words present in the text. However, since no reference is made to this 'glossary' throughout the texts of the tales, it must be assumed that the readers would only discover it either by looking at the contents or by accident after reaching the end of the book.

Another irregularity in Gág's work arises from the fact that her initial intention (as described in her Introduction to the first volume) had only been to produce illustrations for the Grimms' work rather than a translation. However, while in the process of reading the original German text in order to find inspiration, she discovered that she also wanted to produce a new translation, at least of the tales she intended to illustrate. Her illustrations are inspired and memorable, and certainly contributed to the success and popularity of the two volumes both in the USA and in the UK. That both the translation and the illustrations were created by the same person is also significant, since in no other translated KHM collection do the illustrations appear to be so faithful to the text of the story. Alderson (1978: 6) notes that 'part of the warmth that one feels for the editions by Wanda Gág is occasioned by the unusual integrity of her chunky, folksy pictures'; according to Carl Zigrosser's Foreword to More Tales from Grimm (1962: 7-8), Gág has achieved 'a compelling unity of effect in a work such as the Grimm's, which somehow seems to call for pictorial embellishment ... [her work] belongs in that rare but ideal category of the illustrated book where the writer and artist are one.'

From the Introduction to the first volume, the reader can also deduce that although Gág was an author and illustrator rather than a translator by profession, she seems to have studied the history of the Grimms and their work very carefully. She also presents a very clear idea of what she considers to be the 'fairy-tale age limit' (1937: 9) which, as she correctly states, has 'shifted considerably' (1937: 10) over the years. With her intention being to translate for a four-to-twelve age group, as she states in her Introduction, she naturally cannot not help finding it 'advisable to simplify some sections in order [for a child of that age to get] the full value of the stories' (1937: 10). She reassures her readers that she does not 'believe in 'writing down' to children' or, even more extremely, using words of one or two syllables in order to facilitate a child's understanding of the story (1937: 10). In a letter to her friend Alma Scott (Scott, 1949: 177), Gág writes that

> I am translating the original and authentic Grimm's Fairy Tales ... I find this very interesting and, in many cases, difficult, because what can one do with such words as *Kindlein*, *Weibchen*, *Käppchen*, etc? Little child, small wife, wee cap - are just not the same. Some words lend themselves to the *kin*, *ken* or *let* ending, but all too few have that form. Well, I do the best I can. Mine is to be a *free* translation, true to the spirit rather than the letter, because I want to show just what *Märchen* meant to *me* as a child.

She also stresses in her preface that although she has made free translations of some stories she has not 'carelessly made free with the material at hand', because 'after reading the Grimms' painstaking annotations, no one could, with a clear conscience, shuffle their material indiscriminately' (1937: 11).

Translation Alterations

Religious Allusions

Although Gág's translation was published at a time when the strength of religious superstition of American audiences had already started to wane, there is still a definite avoidance of religious allusions permeating her work. Thus, although in the tale 'Von dem Fischer un syner Fru' ('Of the Fisherman and his Wife') – transcribed by the Grimms in the original Low German dialect – the wife is allowed to say openly for the first time in a 20th-century translation that 'she wants to be like God,' the statement is almost imperceptibly softened by the added phrase 'she wants to make the sun and moon rise' (1937: 178) which immediately precedes it. This gives her wish a more neutral tone, since she is primarily driven by the urge to control astral movements. The title of 'Der Teufel und seine Grossmutter' ('The Devil and his Grandmother') has however been changed into 'The Dragon and his Grandmother' in a similar way to that of some 19th-century translators such as J E Taylor (1846) and Mrs H H B Paull [c.1872]; this change can almost certainly be attributed more to Gág's (1937: 14) intention to produce a magical-sounding book for children, than to her reluctance to pronounce the Devil's name in front of children. Similarly, the omission of the wind's description as 'das himmlische Kind' ('the heavenly child') in 'Hänsel und Gretel' ('Hansel and Gretel') can be also attributed to Gág's endeavour to produce a successful rhyme, 'It's only a breeze/Blowing down from the trees'

207

(1937: 32), which would not have been as easy with the use of the phrase 'the heavenly child'[1].

'Goriness'

Although in her Introduction Gág does not seem to have any views on matters of sexuality or violence in children's literature, she appears to be quite concerned with matters of 'goriness', as she terms them, which have provoked 'conflicting opinions' (1937: 11) with their use in 'juvenile literature.' Very modestly she concedes to having consulted 'several authorities' on the matter, since she did not 'want to rely solely on [her] own judgement', and reaches the conclusion that:

> too much bowdlerising creates a spineless quality which is not characteristic of the [Grimms'] tales, and more depends on the method of narration than on the actual details of such episodes. A certain amount of 'goriness', if presented with a playful and not too realistic touch, is accepted calmly by the average child. In this way sanguinary passages can be rendered harmless, without depriving them of their salt and vigour. (1937: 11)

In view of this comment it would be plausible to assume that Gág's translations would encompass a modest amount of violent and terrifying elements, especially those related to 'sanguinary passages.' However, it comes as a surprise that Gág not only has omitted the gory ending of 'Aschenputtel' ('Cinderella'), in which the eyes of the two stepsisters are pecked out by pigeons ('da pickten die Tauben einer jeden das eine Auge aus'), leaving the 'fairy-tale ending' as happy and carefree as possible, but she has also cut down substantially on the blood and goriness of the shoe trials in the same story (1937: 126,127). Thus she describes how the first sister 'had to nip off a bit of her big toe to get it in' although in the original 'Das Mädchen hieb die Zehe ab' ['the girl cut the toe off']. Similarly, the prince 'saw a little blood trickling out of the golden slipper' instead of the original 'Da blickte er auf ihren Fuss und sah, wie das Blut herausquoll' ['he looked at her foot and saw how the blood was gushing out']. Again, the second sister's heel 'was too fat, so she had to nip off a little bit of it' replaces the original 'Das Mädchen hieb ein Stück von der Ferse ab' ['the girl cut off a piece of the heel']; the prince sees that 'A few drops of blood were trickling out at the heel', which is much less bloody than the original '...sah wie das Blut aus dem Schuh quoll und an den weissen Strümpfen ganz rot heraufgestiegen war' ['saw how the blood gushed from the shoe and rose up the white stockings turning them completely red']. Also, the pigeons' revealing song 'rucke di guck, rucke di guck,/Blut ist in Schuck (Schuh):/Der Schuck ist zu klein,/die rechte Braut sitzt noch daheim' ['Looky look, looky look, /there's blood in the shoe: /the shoe is too small /the right bride still sits at home'), which triggers the prince's reaction has been reduced to a cryptic 'Dee rookety goo/Just look at that shoe!'

Violence and Sexuality

It is quite noteworthy that Gág did not seem to hold any particularly strong views on the subjects of sexuality and violence in children's literature. The only sexual reference present in one of the stories she has included in her collections comes from 'Rapunzel' ('Rapunzel'), where the incident of the heroine bearing twin children ('wo Rapunzel mit den Zwillingen, die sie geboren hatte') as a result of her illicit coupling with the young prince is kept intact (1937: 154).

Gág's treatment of violence and terror does not provide much of note, since it seems that the stories in both of her volumes lack these elements, whether by her conscious decision or because the stories she chose to translate and to provide illustrations for happened to be the more neutral 'innocent' ones with which she had already acquainted with from the time of her own childhood. The only violent incident that has been suppressed in her translation is the notable treatment of the frog in the story 'Der Froschkönig oder der eiserne Heinrich' ('The Frog King'), in which the princess picks up the frog with her two fingers and carries him to her room where, at his request to sleep on her bed, she throws him against the wall with all her might, the prince emerging in place of the frog as soon as he hits the floor ('Da ward sie erst bitterböse, holte ihn herauf und warf ihn aus allen Kräften wider die Wand ... Als er aber herabfiel, war er kein Frosch, sondern ein Königssohn mit schönen und freundlichen Augen'). This can easily be explained if it is taken into consideration that Gág based her translation of the story on different versions of the original, as she readily admitted in her introduction (1937: 12): 'There are many versions of the Frog Prince. One of these sanctioned by the Brothers Grimm, has the ending which I have used.' Why Gág chose not to translate the tale from the 1857 edition remains unknown, but her prefatory admission to having used different source texts does not necessarily imply the absence of further unacknowledged alterations to the story. Apart from small textual changes, the main narrative of the story is much longer than that of the 1812 or 1815 editions, mainly because the three-night-long odyssey of suffering (on the part of the princess) is quite repetitively extended with the frog sleeping on the foot-end of her bed for the first two nights and under her pillow on the third. After this he miraculously wakes up as a 'young prince with handsome friendly eyes' (1937: 197), thus justifying the princess's long patience. What is quite noteworthy is that Gág's translation is dense with didactic elements emanating from the princess's noble attitude, since although she is 'bitterly angry' (1937: 195) she manages to control herself and fulfil her honourable promises without hesitation, something which could be interpreted as a lesson in self-control for children.

Puns, Rhymes and Repetitions

The formula of tripling in fairy tales, which Gág evidently chooses to emphasise in 'The Frog King,' was also widely employed by the Grimms themselves. Gág could thus be partially justified in departing from the strict textual content of the 1815 edition. Tripling (Dreizahl), according to Lüthi (1984: 44) is a fairy tale 'stylistic and structural formula' which 'occurs not only in conjunction with figures and props ... but also with episodes' and 'In the western world the number three is woven in many ways into the general cultural structure. It is a mythic number, it has a central place in higher religion (the Trinity), it is a magical number ('Thrice must the words be spoken!'), and it occurs in children's games ('One, two, three, who's got the ball?') just as in serious art (the triptych).' Thus it is usually three brothers who set out on an adventure ('Die drei Brüder'), three languages that have to be learnt ('Die drei Sprachen'), three spinners who spin flax ('Die drei Spinnerinnen'), three sons who set out to find their fortune ('Die drei Glückskinder'), three nights during which Cinderella goes to the dance ('Aschenputtel') and hundreds of other occasions when the number three is of substantial significance to the plot of the *KHM*. As all of the aforementioned stories are part of Gág's collection, we can only assume that she was particularly eager to conform to the rule of tripling, which she presumably felt would mystify children and engage their attention for the story. As Lüthi (1984: 44) further observes, 'The listener to fairytales can rely on the fact that these numbers [i.e. the number three] will keep turning up; they are one of the many constants in the fairytale. They give security not only to the narrator, who relies on them and takes pleasure in making use of them, but to the listener, as well.' It seems that in tripling Gág discovered a very effective formula for storytelling, since her books were extremely popular and continued to be read in both continents until at least the 1980s (The last reprints of the two volumes circulated in both the UK and USA seem to have appeared as recently as 1981).

Another characteristic of Gág's collection of stories is that the majority contain some sort of rhyme or poem, which Gág herself is not afraid to translate, unlike her predecessors who frequently turned rhyme into prose, or unsuccessfully rendered it into a non-rhyming version. As an example of successful rhyming we can take the little verses from 'Hansel and Gretel', where 'knuper, knuper, kneischen/wer knupert an meinem Häuschen?' is translated as 'Nibble, nibble, nottage,/Who's nibbling at my cottage?' Its answer, 'der Wind, der Wind,/das himmlische Kind' as we have seen, becomes, 'It's only a breeze,/Blowing down from the trees'. In the same tale, Gág has lengthily intervened by adding two more rhymes of her own devising to the original three of the story; this is common practice[2] for a translator who by her own admission has endeavoured to preserve the magic that the Grimms' fairy tales held for her personally (1937: 14). It is quite noteworthy that in her Introduction she makes a point of accentuating how the fisherman's rhymed supplication to the fish from 'Of the Fisherman and his Wife' (transcribed by the Grimms in the original Low German dialect) had enchanted her even before she could read; although she understood very little of it literally it was 'potentially fraught with magic meaning' for her (1937: 14). Thus she strove to preserve 'as many of its magic sounds as possible' in her translation, which is juxtaposed here with the German original,

German Original	Gág's Translation
Manntje, Manntje, Timpe Te,	Manye, Manye, Timpie Tee,
Buttje, Buttje in der See,	Fishye, Fishye in the sea,
myne Fru de Ilsebill	Ilsebill my wilful wife
will nich so, as ik wol will.	Does not want my way of life.

The translation of the rhyme is not only faithful in meaning but also true to the style and sound of the original.

One final instance in which Gág has provided the reader with an explanation in her Introduction comes from 'Doktor Allwissend' ('Doctor Know-it-all'), in which she has changed the peasant's name from 'Krebs' ('Crab') into 'Fish'. The name Krebs 'was apparently chosen so that it could be punned upon at a critical point in the story' and according to Gág (1937: 15) the 'idiomatic equivalent of Du Armer Krebs! is You poor fish!' in English; therefore she could not but substitute one name for the other.

Conclusion

Although Gág translated a total of only forty-seven of the Grimms' original stories, her translation stands as a landmark in the translation history of the *KHM*, since it was the first one to have been published and achieved success in two different English-speaking countries. Up to 1936, the only translations of the Grimms' *KHM* available in the USA were translations by British translators which were merely reprinted in the American continent (Hoyle, 1994: 58). According to Zipes (2000: 83), the creation of the first American translation of the *KHM* was due 'in large part to the rise of an interest in American folklore, a growing interest in American subjects on the part of American writers for children, librarians, and editors ... and the rise of patriotism during World War II'. Before the time of Gág's translation many people in the US considered fairy tales 'frivolous, subversive, pagan, escapist, and potentially dangerous for the health and sanity of children - attitudes that mirrored puritanical sentiments in England' (Zipes, 2000: 84) but her translation helped in 'making fairy tales popular for an American public during the 1930s and 1940s just at a point when anti-German sentiment was once again on the rise' (2000: 82). Overall, Gág was true to her word of creating brand new translations – even if they were of a highly

211

adaptive character and could in some instances be classified as alternative versions of the original *KHM* – since, unlike her predecessors, she was the only translator who did not extensively copy elements from other 19th- and 20th-century translations.

Notes

1. In truth, up to this day only Magoun and Krappe (1960:61), Manheim (1977:59) and Alderson (1978:128) have managed to produce a translation of the rhyme which encompasses the phrase 'the heavenly child', and only Manheim's translation could be regarded as a successful one, especially if it is considered that Alderson's is an exact copy of it.

2. She has also added rhymes to 'Aschenputtel' ('Cinderella), 'Jorinde und Joringel' ('Jorinda and Joringel') and 'Der Eisenhans' ('Iron Hans').

Bibliography

Primary Texts

Gág, W (1936) *Tales from Grimm*. New York: Coward-McCann

Gág, W (1937) *Tales from Grimm*. London: Faber & Faber Ltd.

Gág, W (1947) *More Tales from Grimm*. New York: Coward-McCann

Gág, W (1962) *More Tales from Grimm*. London: Faber & Faber Ltd.

Grimm, B (1812) *Kinder- und Hausmärchen gesammelt durch die Brüder Grimm*. Vol. 1. Berlin: Realschulbuchhandlung

Grimm, B (1815) *Kinder- und Hausmärchen gesammelt durch die Brüder Grimm*. Vol. 2. Berlin: Realschulbuchhandlung

Grimm, B (1857) *Kinder- und Hausmärchen gesammelt durch die Brüder Grimm. Grosse Ausgabe. Siebte Auflage*. Göttingen: Dieterich.

Secondary Texts

Alderson, B (1978). 'Boy-stew and Red-hot Slippers'. *The Times*. May 6. p6

Alderson, B (1978) *The Brothers Grimm. Popular Folk Tales*. London: Gollancz

Aarne, A & Thompson, S (1961) *The Types of the Folktale: A Classification and Bibliography*. Helsinki: Suomalainen Tiedeakatemia

Fantasia (1940) Animated Film. Directed by: Armstrong, S. USA: Walt Disney Pictures

Hoyle, K N (1994) *Wanda Gág.* New York: Twayne

Lüthi, M (1984) *The Fairytale as Art Form and Portrait of Man.* Bloomington: Indiana University Press

Magoun, F & A Krappe (1960) *The Grimms' German Folk Tales.* Carbondale: Southern Illinois University Press

Manheim, R (1977) *Grimms' Tales for Young and Old. The Complete Stories.* New York: Doubleday

Paull, M H H B [1872] *Grimm's Fairy Tales.* London: Frederic Warne

Scott, A (1949) *Wanda Gág: The Story of an Artist.* Minneapolis: University of Minnesota Press

Taylor, E (1823) *German Popular Stories.* Vol. 1. London: C. Baldwyn

Taylor, J E (1846) *The Fairy Ring: A New Collection of Popular Tales, Translated from the German of Jacob and Wilhelm Grimm.* London: John Murray

Zipes, J (2000) *Sticks and Stones: The Troublesome Success of Children's Literature from Slovenly Peter to Harry Potter.* London: Routledge

Zipes, J (2003) *The Complete Fairy Tales of the Brothers Grimm.* New York: Bantam Books

Daniel Pennac's *Eye Of The Wolf*: An Insight into Other Cultures

Sue Neale

My enthusiasm for the work of Daniel Pennac started when I chose to study his pastiche crime fiction saga of the Malaussène family in French for my undergraduate dissertation. These books have now all been published in English so that a larger readership can enjoy them. As an art director who has worked with children's books since the seventies, I also view books with a professional eye. I was impressed and delighted to receive copies of the English translations of Pennac's earliest children's books – *Dog* and *Eye of the Wolf* - when Walker published them in 2002. Though they had originally been published in France in 1982 and 1984 respectively, the universality of the stories they relate gives them a timeless quality. As the organiser of the Red House Children's Book Award in Oxfordshire I discussed these books with young readers in schools and was impressed by their enthusiasm. What I found particularly interesting is the fact that in English these books have an appeal that transcends age boundaries. The illustrations for *Eye of the Wolf* are both atmospheric and ethereal, so when I obtained a copy of the French version (re-illustrated in 1994) I was rather disappointed to see how firmly this book was defined - by its typography, illustrations and format - as a school reader. My objective in this paper, therefore, is to show how sometimes a book can be so transformed in translation that it is much better than the original.

Daniel Pennac

Daniel Pennac was born in 1944 in Morocco. His father was in the army and he spent much time in Africa in his youth. A lifelong interest in reading and storytelling developed from his period at boarding school. In 1997 in an interview for the *Magazine Littéraire* he indicated that writing was essential for him as well as the extension of the excitement he found in reading. Pennac trained as a teacher and continued to teach older teenagers in Paris until the late 1990s.

Pennac is very popular in France for his children's and adult books and has been translated into many languages. He says that his aim has always been to pass on to the reader his happiness at writing – finding the 'mot juste' and the right rhythm for the story he has to tell. He wants his readers to get away from the mechanics of deconstructing a text towards enjoying reading for the amazing places it can take them. He defines himself as a storyteller first; when discussing how he writes, he has indicated that he invents the story orally and polishes it before he commits it to paper. A writer may create stories but it is up to readers to interpret as they want.

Eye of the Wolf

Transport yourself from northern Europe to Africa and Alaska and share in the magic of this book. In a cold northern zoo a wolf and a boy face each other through the bars of a cage. Having recently lost his companion, the wolf is disgruntled and the boy's staring irritates him. We hear him mentally communicating with the boy although he has sworn not to have anything to do with humans since a bad experience in the past. Even on a day when the zoo is shut to the public, the boy appears and the staring contest reaches a crisis. The problem is that the wolf only has one eye. When the boy decides to shut one of his eyes, and they are equal, they stare into each other's single eye. Like a moth to the flame, the boy is drawn into the sparkling black pupil in the centre of the wolf's yellow eye. Here he meets Black Flame, the mother of the wolf in the zoo, whose life story is played out to him. In a litter of seven cubs, five have pelts that are rust-red; a sixth with a pelt resembling a ray of gold is called Shiny Straw; the blue-red one, now the one in the zoo, is called Blue Wolf. The mother, Black Flame, tells them scary stories about humans, about the hunters who track them to kill them for their pelts. The wolves are always on the run as the humans colonise more land and reduce the space available for the animals. Shiny Straw has such a wonderful coat that she is just what the humans wish to possess. Sadly, she is also reckless: one day, when she tries to discover about humans close up, she is caught in a net. Blue Wolf frees her but is shot whilst doing so then captured and knocked out with a flaming branch, injuring his eye.

Over the next ten years he is moved from zoo to zoo. He is put with a she wolf, Perdrix, who brings him news of Shiny Straw. The boy learns that Shiny Straw's coat changed colour when she lost her brother and now she is only Yellow Straw. Blue Wolf lives happily with Perdrix for some years until she dies, the week before he encounters the boy. Now the only person with whom he can share his memories with is the boy. He tells him all about the zoos, the seasons, the sad animals and his most recent memory, the boy standing by the cage.

Now the wolf wants to know about the boy, his story and his name. The boy, who initially had no name, has been laughed at by the children at his school in the cold dark land where he now lives, because he is seen as being different. Looking into his eye, the wolf can see the boy's first memory – 'panicked cries, flashes of light splitting the darkness in every direction, followed by a series of explosions' (*Eye,* 58). His parents have been killed and Toa, a trader who sells all sorts of objects from the back of his camel, is paid to take him on and effectively rescue him from possible death. Toa appears to dislike the burden he has taken on and would happily lose the boy. However, the dromedary, whom the boy nicknames Saucepans, warms to the boy and will not allow Toa to abandon him even though he often tries to do so. Saucepans nicknames the boy Sand Flea, and the two of them endure their hard life together with growing love and friendship: 'They learned how to laugh on the inside a long time ago. Seen form the outside, they are both as smooth and serious as sand dunes' (2002b: 65).

From the start, we are shown that the boy has the special ability of telling magnificent stories. Adult readers understand that Pennac is suggesting that this boy possesses a fairy-tale quality which will help him survive. His storytelling attracts customers to Toa's camel shop when they are in the nomad camps. It even means that he is fed because the nomads want to hear his stories about 'an Africa filled with sands and sunshine and solitude and scorpions and silence' (p67). The people who listen to his stories see 'a different Africa from high up on their camels' and these stories are so powerful that they stay with them.

An old Tuareg chief gives the boy the name Africa. When they reach Grey Africa – with burning stones and thorny bushes – Toa sells Saucepans, and then, without anyone to protect him, Africa is also sold. He has to work for a goat keeper as a shepherd. He does this for two years, teaching the old man that in order not to lose animals you have to offer the predators alternative food. In this way he befriends the lion and the cheetah and even persuades the cheetah to work with him protecting the goats from hyenas. Africa is so popular that men and beasts gather around to hear his stories about Yellow Africa and Grey Africa, but one day, the young goats are killed and eaten, and Africa loses his job.

An old gorilla tells the boy about another Africa - Green Africa – and he manages to find the driver of a rough bus willing to transport him there free, in exchange for cleaning the lorry and cooking meals. His storytelling is also useful to entertain the passengers. But one day when they spot the tropical rainforest in the distance, the driver becomes so excited that he accelerates and takes a bend too fast. Africa is knocked out and almost killed; he wakes up in the house of Ma and Pa Bia who care for him and make him well again. As he recovers, he decides he would like to look at the forest and goes outside. As he is in a house on stilts he falls off, but happily Pa Bia is there to catch him. Africa settles down to life with them and takes his storytelling to the local market. When the Bias understand that he is an orphan, they choose to adopt him as their fifteenth child.

Sadly the forest is being cut down and sent to the Other World and so the land is drying out. The gorilla he has befriended and the crocodile he meets both realise that they must move before their habitat is lost. In order to survive, the Bia family also have to move, but they travel a long way to the Other World where Pa Bia finds work in the zoo's tropical hothouse. Africa feels sad and alone in this unfriendly town that seems like a prison. However, when he arrives in the zoo he finds all his old animal friends:

Saucepans, the dromedary, the hyena, the cheetah, the special goat, the grey gorilla, the old lion and the crocodile. As the wolf is the only one he does not recognise, he has chosen to watch him and to find out more about him.

Having revived the boy's memories as well as his own, the wolf now feels able to think about his own family and friends again and becomes happy. He opens his second eye and thus allows Africa to open his own eye, which was closed in sympathy with the wolf, something which has caused concern to the Bia family. Now, although the animals are in the zoo, through the boy and his storytelling skills they can share their stories and be revitalised.

Reading *Eye of the Wolf*

Searching on the internet, it is clear that, rather than being experienced and enjoyed, this book is being used as a text to be dissected in order for children to understand about the process of writing. Many French websites are dedicated to showing how teachers can direct the attention of their young readers to analyse the characters, the story and so on. Exploring the mythical nature of the story seems to be the last thing to be considered. This tendency to deconstruct children's literature in schools is something that irritates Pennac and was one reason that he wrote his book *Comme un roman,* currently being translated by Sarah Adams and available soon. Whatever Pennac's aims, *Eye of the Wolf* is a book that makes readers think about how different people deal with loss and about the experience of being transplanted into a strange place. That they can still find happiness and inner strength is a message that shines through.

In the English version, the black and white illustrations by Max Grafe are each given a whole page. In terms of style they are softly grainy and dreamlike, leaving much for the imagination of the reader to fill in. The page is laid out with plenty of space between the lines and the margins are generous. Chapters begin on new pages and there are four sections, dealing with how they meet in the present, the wolf's story, the boy's story and the arrival of the Bia family in the Other World. The paper is thick and off-white, so that there is little 'show through.' The format is wide for a paperback and all this makes the book a pleasure to hold and to read from. All these elements combine to make the English version less specific to a target age group. In addition, the way in which the thoughts of the boy and the wolf have been removed from the speech marks they bear in the French version, and integrated into the text make it more thought-provoking, encouraging the reader to empathise with each of the main characters. This also makes the text appear appropriate to an older age range.

The French version on the other hand was originally published in the early 1980s, and was reissued with new illustrations in 1994. It is in a tall, narrow format as a school reader and looks like a book to use for work rather than to be read for pleasure by 8 – 12 year olds. The illustrations are in strong black and white ink and appear relatively realistic. They are small and seem squeezed into the text which itself has chapters running on from each other rather than starting a new page. The typeface is a standard serif face, with little additional interlinear spacing to encourage ease of reading. The cover, mainly white, implies a school target readership, and does not invite young readers to pick it up for pleasure.

In the English version, the cover shows a blending of images of both the wolf and the boy, leaving viewers a choice to interpret it as they wish. The back cover continues with this theme, showing the shadow of the boy with the wolf overlaid at his heart. I see the English version as a triumph, as it leaves readers to interpret the novel in their own way, while highlighting the importance of storytelling as a way to achieve an understanding of others. Children and adults can enjoy the book on many levels and it could lead to discussions about belonging, displacement and otherness:

Life is strange … Someone tells you about something you didn't even know existed, something unimaginable, something you can't bring yourself to believe in, and the words are hardly out of their mouth before you find out all about it for yourself (2002b: 80)

Bibliography

Pennac, D (1999), *The Scapegoat*, Monk, Ian (trans.), London: Harvill

Pennac, D (1999), *The Fairy Gunmother*, Monk, Ian (trans.), London: Harvill

Pennac, D (2000), *Write to Kill*, Monk, Ian (trans.), London: Harvill

Pennac, D (2001), *Passion Fruit*, Monk, Ian (trans.), London: Harvill

Pennac, D (2002a) *Dog*, Adams, Sraah (trans.), London: Walker

Pennac, D (2002b) *Eye of the Wolf*, Adams, Sraah (trans.), London: Walker

Pennac, D (2003), *Monsieur Malaussène*, Monk, Ian (trans.), London: Harvill

Pennac, D (2004) *Kamo's escape*, t Adams, Sraah (trans.), London: Walker

Recent Translations of Children's Classics into Neapolitan

Stefania Tondo

'All mankind is of one author and is one volume; when one man dies, one chapter is not torn out of the book, but translated into a better language; and every chapter must be translated. God employs several translators; some pieces are translated by age, some by sickness, some by war, some by justice; but God's hand is in every translation, and his hand shall bind up all our scattered leaves again for that library where every book shall lie open to one another ... No man is an island, entire of itself; every man is a piece of the continent, a part of the main. If a clod be washed away by the sea, Europe is the less, as well as if a promontory were, as well as if a manor of thy friend's or thine own were' (Donne, 1623-4)

The more I read this short extract from Donne's 'Meditation XVII', the more surprised I am to discover how well it links with the topic of Children's Literature and Translation. The title of the Conference and consequently of this book, 'No **Child** is an Island,' makes an intertextual reference to Donne's famous words, 'No **Man** is an Island', and this thought seems to have so much in common with children's literature, in which translation is an essential element. It is well known that as a religious poet and a preacher Donne drew his themes from the secular world and analysed the relationship between the individual and society. In a world dominated by change and death, he explored humanity and love at depth, and his words share with translated children's literature a hope for a united world which is at one. Both in Donne's metaphysics and in the field of children's literature, this idea of being in touch involves the idea of universality, with each person being connected to everyone else, as in a book made up of chapters. His famous image rejecting human insularity suggests a borderless space, and relates effectively to the ever reversible interplay between adult and child, while the whole passage emphasises the importance of the work of translation. Donne's words chime in well with what Kimberley Reynolds says in her Introduction to *Modern Children's Literature* (2005): that children's literature includes books translated from a range of languages; that the subject is characterised by an absence of boundaries between it and other areas of knowledge; that a concern about aesthetics is vital; and that within it there is a good deal of child-adult negotiation and interchange

Children's literature in translation acts against human isolation because it is made of books travelling across frontiers, of new books and new authors becoming familiar to new readers, and of cultures encountering each other. It reveals humanity in a world dimension, the world as a 'library where every book shall lie open to one another.' It is in this context of world community that I see **love** as the key word for the recent translations of classics for children into Neapolitan. Italian translation studies scholar Laura Bocci describes translation as an act of literary generosity, one of true love for a dead author and for a future reader, and, above all, of true love for one's own mother tongue into which the literary work is translated.

These two motives, the love for literature of the past and the desire to make it available to one's own people, are to be detected in Roberto D'Ajello's recent translations of children's classics into Neapolitan. D'Ajello is a judge by profession and has chosen these classics for their universal comprehensiveness and for their being part of his own childhood and his very being, but above all for their artistic quality. Through translation and illustration, these classics for children have become sources for a real artistic 'metamorphosis'. This is supported by the way in which, in his books, the illustrations are integral to the text, so that the pictures and the words become interdependent: the written text cannot live without the illustrations and it is no longer possible to distinguish between the illustrated book and the picturebook[1].

The choice of the well-known Neapolitan artist Lello Esposito as the illustrator of these books is a significant part of the project. Esposito's sculptures and paintings metamorphise Neapolitan cultural icons and the images of bygone traditions and memories - Vesuvius, the egg, the 'corno'[2], the skull, San Gennaro[3], Pulcinella - into contemporary, more avant garde, innovative terms[4].

Roberto D'Ajello's first experiment in this form was *Pinocchio in Lingua Napoletana* [*Pinocchio in the Neapolitan Language*] (1997). This was followed by a translation of Antoine de Saint-Exupéry's *Le Petit Prince*, *'O Princepe Piccerillo* (2000). In this case, artistic cooperative support could not totally be achieved because copyright obligations make it impossible to re-illustrate this text. Nevertheless, the idea of a new cultural and artistic form was achieved by incorporating a personalised numbering of the pages, with Pulcinella being portrayed as an intermediary.

In *Alice's Adventures in Wonderland*, translated as *Alice 'int' 'o Paese d' 'e Meraveglie* (2002), a complete artistic metamorphosis of the text was achieved, as I have indicated in my own Introduction to this book: 'The translation entirely involved illustration. It was both linguistic and visual. The illustrator intended to translate the original illustrations by Lewis Carroll for the manuscript version *Alice's Adventures Underground*' (see Figures 1 & 2).

Figure 1

Figure 2

Figure 3

Figure 4

The cover of the Neapolitan version of Carroll's masterpiece, showing Alice moving into the deep blue Neapolitan sea, with Vesuvius on the background (Figure 1), has an affinity with that of *Pinocchio* (Figure 3). As always, Pulcinella, who appears in the first illustration in *Alice*, where Alice is seen with her sister, is present as the symbol of Neapolitan translation and culture: he is a figure of the translator, the illustrator, and the reader. Thus within this new text there are graphic and visual signs that it is a cross-cultural version of one of the most famous classics for children in the world (Figure 4).

This book is an example of translating arising out of both aesthetic and literary devotion: for what Barthes describes as 'the pleasure of the text.' There is no ideological manipulation of the source texts or of the source cultures; cultural interfusion, pleasure and love, alone, are the motivating factors of the translation. This translation is made from the original English; there are only a few cases of manipulations when cultural elements from Neapolitan culture linguistically meet and interplay with English culture, as for example in the names of the characters, the Cheshire Cat becoming 'A Gatta 'E Zi' Maria'.

Cultural interfusion occasions the next translation by R D'Ajello, Dickens' *Christmas Carol, Na cantata 'e Natale* (2006), which is ready to be officially launched for the reading public next December[5]. A relevant point, for instance, is the idea of death as a leveller, seen both in Dickens and in Neapolitan thought, as encountered in Totò's *'A Livella.*

A question remains about the value of these translations into Neapolitan and the audience for whom they are produced, raising issues about the target text and the target culture[6]. The experience of publishing them has led to the identification of several potential audiences. These include members of an older generation who encounter in these books the classics of their childhood in a language which is also from their past, and are thus able to

222

mediate the experience to their grandchildren. There is also the audience of young people who are meeting the classics of their recent childhood in a language which they don't speak but which is a part of their culture. A further potential audience, significant to those who are committed to cultural transmission, is that of migrant communities of Neapolitans living abroad. There are also many new possibilities for the identification of connections between literatures across cultural and national boundaries and across time. Additionally, there are people from all over the world who are interested in art and literature, and want to achieve a sense of community with others in their love for the children's classics.

Figure 5

Because of the commitment of all those involved with these recent translations into Neapolitan – the original author, the translator, the illustrator, the reader, and those who study children's literature within the flowing sea (Figure 5) of world literature and art – these children's classics are continuing to travel and to add new volumes in the great library that is the world, passing the torch on again across time and space. As suggested by Bassnett (1993) and O'Sullivan (2005), children's literature really can cross linguistic and cultural borders, because it is composed of translated books which can therefore move throughout the world and give new life to world literature.

Notes

1. See the articles about picture books by Lisa Sainsbury and Judith Graham in Reynolds, K (ed.) (2005).

2. Literally 'horn' but here more often with the meaning of the pointed hat appearing in many of Esposito's figures.

3. A Bishop-martyr the relic of whose blood, according to traditional belief, liquefies on his feastday.

4. See http://www.lelloesposito.com for more information.

5. R D'Ajello (2006), C. Dickens, *Na cantata 'e Natale*, Naples, Franco Di Mauro Publisher, edited by and introduced by Tondo S, 'Transformations', pp7-13, and illustrated by L Esposito.

6. This is interestingly explored in Gillian Lathey's essay 'Comparative and Psychoanalytic Approaches', in Reynolds K. (ed.) (2005), *Modern Children's Literature*.

Bibliography

Bassnett, S (1993) *Comparative Literature: A Critical Introduction*, London: Blackwell

Bocci, L. (2004) *Di Seconda Mano*, Milano: Rizzoli

D'Ajello, R (1997) *Pinocchio in Lingua Napoletana*, Naples: Grimaldi Editori

D'Ajello, R (2000) *'O Princepe Piccerillo*, Naples: Franco Di Mauro Editore

D'Ajello, R (2002) *Alice 'int' 'o Paese d' 'e Meraveglie,* Naples: Franco Di Mauro Editore

D'Ajello, R (2006) *Na cantata 'e Natale*, Naples: Franco Di Mauro Editore

Graham, J (2005) 'Reading Contemporary Picturebooks,' in Reynolds, K (ed.) *Modern Children's Literature*, Basingstoke: Palgrave Macmillan, pp209-226

Hunt, P (ed.) (2005) *Understanding Children's Literature*, London: Routledge

Lathey, G (2005) 'Comparative and Psychoanalytic Approaches' in Reynolds K (ed.) *Modern Children's Literature*, Basingstoke: Palgrave Macmillan, pp74-88

O'Sullivan, E (2005) *Comparative Children's Literature*, London: Routledge

Reynolds, K (ed.) (2005), *Modern Children's Literature*, Basingstoke: Palgrave Macmillan, 'Introduction', pp1-7

Sainsbury, L (2005) 'Picturebook Case Study,' in Reynolds K (ed.) *Modern Children's Literature*, Basingstoke: Palgrave Macmillan, pp227-249

Translation and Culture:

Other Cultural Areas Involved in Translation

Translating Cultures

The three articles in this final section may serve as a reminder of the variety of aspects of translation and culture which remain to be considered. Gaby Thomson-Wohlgemuth looks at Afterwords, a feature relatively rare in children's books generally but abounding in East German translations from 'Western' sources. She shows how this communist society was very careful to ensure that the young readership was not contaminated by a bourgeois ideology – and the effects that this policy had on authors and publishers.

Perhaps inevitably, the majority of contributors to the conference represented languages and cultures of European origin, though we were fortunate enough to have the chance to look at the relationships between English texts and readers in Taiwan (in Mieke Desmet's paper) and Alaska (in the paper by Tricia Brown and Teri Sloat). It was a disappointment, however, to learn at the last moment that neither of the two expected participants from Africa could come. We were lucky that one of these, Abasi Kiyimba, was able to let us have a copy of his paper, which was read and consequently is included here. It enables us to learn about a well-known Ugandan writer, Barbara Kimenye, who, although she writes in English, is clearly someone whose works can provide Western readers with a really illuminating perspective on that culture.

Finally, Robert Ornstein's discussion of the teaching story from Afghanistan opens a window on another way in which the West can learn from other culture. His examples reveal how the wealth of stories from around the world, with the different attitudes towards pedagogy that they embody, can support the use of story in education. This tallies with the conviction that many educators already possess, that narrative is an irreplaceable means of instruction, without which children will be impoverished. Psychologist Jerome Bruner contends[1] that narrative is one of the two primary modes of human thought, in no way inferior to the scientific mode which is too often given supremacy in modern society. Increased translation from sources all over the world could be an invaluable way of adding fresh perspectives from unfamiliar cultures for the immense enrichment of young readers, not only in terms of imagination but also of cognitive development.

Notes
1. In *Actual Minds, Possible Worlds* (Harvard University Press, 1986)

The Role of Afterwords in East German Translated Literature for Children and Adolescents

Gaby Thomson-Wohlgemuth

On the whole, literature for children and young adults does not abound in paratexts. However, when analysing books that were translated and published in the German Democratic Republic, the wide-spread use of a particular paratextual text type, the Afterword, becomes evident. This phenomenon may result from the fact that many of the translated books from Western countries originated from a period long gone or from parts of the world far away and thus needed these Afterwords to render them accessible to readers, as well as to reveal the cultural significance of certain points in the source text. A second reason for the use of Afterwords in translated texts relates to the fact that every book had to pass a censor before it could be published. In East Germany the written word was considered a potential danger to society and, ultimately, to the existence of the socialist system. It was for this reason that Afterwords were of invaluable help to publishers, as they provided the readers with the 'correct' interpretation of the texts and thus guided the books past the censor.

Translated texts bring with them a number of unknown cultural concepts and alien ideas with which the audience in the target culture may not be familiar. Paratexts, including Afterwords, aid in placing a translated work in its cultural context. They point out reasons for a text's cultural importance, and they explain textual elements which would otherwise cause problems of interpretation for target text readers; in short, they aim to smooth out things which may disturb the reading experience.

Given a child's limited knowledge of life, annotation can help child readers to comprehend the text in front of them. In the case of the German Democratic Republic (GDR), paratexts (and in particular Afterwords) without doubt fulfil a major function in making texts more accessible to children. A vast number of books published in the GDR originated from periods long gone. Equally, it should not be forgotten that, because of the Iron Curtain, the country was cut off from a large part of the globe, and the cultural distance between East Germany and other areas of the world was relatively wide. Books originating from these inaccessible regions or from other times brought with them unfamiliar terms and ideas. Afterwords made the foreignness less of an obstacle for East German child readers. Hence, glossaries were frequently added to classic texts, explaining archaic measures, currency, customs, titles and objects of everyday life.

It appears, however, that offering supplementary information on the texts was neither the sole nor the main aim of afterwords, since the majority of

227

them provide interpretation with a clear ideological bias. The GDR was a satellite state of the Soviet Union and, as such, was dedicated to Marxist-Leninist ideology. One key aspect of Marxist doctrine was the aim to transform society and bring it closer to its final destination: Communism. As a consequence, East Germany was a country with a societal mission. In order to achieve this goal, every section of society, including the Arts, was conscripted. Every work of art had to support the creation of the New Socialist Being. As a corollary, art was intended to educate. Children's books therefore were used not only as tools of entertainment, but also of education and socialisation, assisting in shaping the worthy citizens of the future into the new socialist personality.

Books from Western societies had attached to them the stigma of otherness, conveying an outlook on life that was ideologically opposed to that of the GDR. This entailed not only difficulties in explaining to children alien concepts and attitudes, but also the danger of disruption to the building of the new society. The solution for the GDR was therefore a careful selection of the titles to be translated and, equally important, an appropriation of the books to East German culture. In this scenario, Afterwords functioned as a valuable aid. Home-grown East German books were hardly ever given any explanatory sections, yet a great many of the foreign translated ones were, and this demonstrates how seriously the authorities took the task of cultural and political ideological mediation. Rarely were the translators of the stories given a platform to voice their opinions in Afterwords; rather it was the specialists in English language and culture, and the social historians, who provided information and critical comments on the socio-historical background of the story, on the biography of the authors and on the protagonists' motivations for their actions. The Afterwords explained the foreign books from a socialist angle and with socialist notions and, in so doing, placed a non-socialist text firmly in the context of the socialist environment.

Producing such Afterwords from a Marxist perspective inevitably led to a division of the world into two camps: the capitalist and the socialist, the **us** and the **them**. The message to the child reader was clear: the communist ethos was superior to capitalism. Regardless of the historical period in which a book was set, Afterwords communicated the concept that capitalist, imperialist and bourgeois societies epitomised evil wrong-doers, while socialists and communists represented all that was noble, combined with concern for the general good of the world. It is perhaps not surprising that the finger is pointed predominantly at Great Britain and the United States – the former for its leading role in the Industrial Revolution and its desire to rule the globe politically and economically, the latter for its status as a world power with imperialistic claims.

Hence, discursive techniques in Afterwords consistently employ criteria from the Marxist-Leninist belief system and from the cultural paradigm of Socialist Realism: for instance, praise of an honest work ethic; a collective spirit and a defiant stance; and condemnation of violence, money and materialism, passivity, religion and superstition. The two principal criteria used for interpretation, however, are two socialist realist concepts, namely Realism and Humanity. Indeed, every single Afterword makes use of them, in order to describe the ideological position of a book and the viewpoint of the author. To illustrate this, I will give brief attention to three categories in the discussion of Afterwords: authors; historical and socio-cultural context; and protagonists.

Authors

The Afterwords devoted to authors make the notion of Humanity immediately evident. Daniel Defoe is called 'the courageous champion of the rights of the poor' who was therefore 'celebrated by the poor' and, because of his actions, ended up in the pillory three times (Biester, 1963: 328, my translation here and throughout). Similarly, the 'amateur detective and advocate of victims of justice' Arthur Conan Doyle is described as performing noble deeds, such as 'acquitting a life convict from his imprisonment by proving a verdict of not-guilty for the prisoner' (Hillich, 1982: 371). In relation to his Christmas Stories *(Weihnachtsgeschichten)*, Charles Dickens is explicitly described as 'Anwalt der Menschlichkeit' (Advocate of Humanity; Wirzberger, 1970: 213). Walter Scott, although a landowner with a title, is characterised as having been 'fond of the people who lived on his land,' as 'never displaying the condescension of a lord of the manor' and as being 'hospitable not only to friends but also to farmers, shepherds and manual workers' (Krenn, 1964: 468).

Humanity, essentially, is interpreted as having a love for people from the lower social classes and for the exploited and disadvantaged, and it would seem from studying the Afterwords, that all the authors published in the GDR had done their share in this respect. For example, Erskine Caldwell is said to 'have already rebelled as a child against social injustice and outrages' (Petersen, 1968: np); later, he is described as working in many jobs in the Southern States of America and there experiencing:

> the misery of negroes and white people with part-leases on meagre land who had to earn their sparse livelihood ... negroes being persecuted and even killed by white people, poor white farmers and workers being cheated out of their earnings and white gentlemen and landowners preaching racial hatred in order to maintain their rule in the South

As a result of this, so the reader of *Molly Baumwollschwänzchen* (Molly Cottontail) learns, 'in this book, as in his other works, he [Caldwell] settles the score with the inhuman attitudes of those Southerners' (Petersen, 1968: np).

The Afterword to Frederick Marryat's *Peter Simple* describes the author as 'becoming aware of the dubious morality of British hegemony on the oceans, when he made contact with the simple people on the ships on which he was serving' (Wirzberger, 1969: 262). The Afterword proceeds:

> His attitude toward coloured people, who at that time represented only objects of exploitation for the colonial masters, is without any prejudice. He recognised, already in his times, the power which sleeps in the coloured peoples.

It finishes, 'In his private life, Marryat showed this sympathy by bringing home with him a negro boy and providing him with a good education' (Wirzberger, 1969: 262).

These Afterwords also demonstrate utilisation of the other key aspect, Reality; Conan Doyle is portrayed as assisting people in need, while Scott is shown as 'despite all romanticism in his oeuvre', creating 'pioneering acts with his works by writing about historical events' (Ilberg, 1965: 541). His heroic figures appear 'genuine and true to life, as can only be created by someone who watches people accurately and who understands them deeply' (Krenn ,1964: 466, 467).

Other characteristics which make authors worthy of an East German publication are their industry and tireless work (Scott, Robert Louis Stevenson, Edgar Wallace) or their realisation of the uselessness of money and possessions (e.g. Conan Doyle, Stevenson, Rabindranath Tagore).

Historical and Socio-cultural Context

When analysing Afterwords, many that can be categorised as including historical and socio-cultural context give the immediate impression of being marked by a strong emphasis on Humanity and Reality, together with an even stronger one on the division between East and West. A few extracts from the Afterword to *Unser weißer Hirsch* ('Our white stag'; Petersen 1978:256-259) may serve as an example. This book is an anthology of contemporary American short stories, published in 1978. The Afterword begins by stating,

> The largest part of American children's and adolescent literature reveals a picture of reality that is all too friendly. In order to show to our young readers experiences of their peers in the United

States, a collection of short stories by authors who look at their country objectively and critically has been compiled.

With these words, Petersen, editor of the book and author of the Afterword, tells children that, on the whole, American literature is partisan and that the GDR has now selected what it considers objective and representative from its point of view. Petersen continues by attributing status to the authors of the short stories and portraying them as knowledgeable and trustworthy:

These authors love their country, however, their love has not made them blind. They know how the American people live and work, because they have looked around at all spheres of life and many professions. The existing conditions are in need of improvement – the authors become aware of this fact wherever they go and look. With their works they want to contribute to a more beautiful America, a motherland for all Americans, irrespective of their origin, skin colour and religion.

After this introduction of the authors as reliable figures, Petersen speaks about the stories themselves, their content and the various problems prevailing in the US. By these descriptions, a seed has been planted in children's minds about the conditions and qualities of America which, it was hoped, would lead them to believe that this country was not a desirable place to live. These contributions are

realistic, accusatory, poetic, funny [and] show how young Americans grow up – in cities, in the countryside, at home and at school. The thematic scale is broad. It ranges from racial segregation, child exploitation, hatred of foreigners and people of other races to the dangers of big cities, the relationship between children and adults or animals ... We meet young Americans and older ones, Whites and Blacks, Indians and Chinese, cowboys, one rich 'dirty swine' (or more) and poor devils, sportspeople, teachers and waiters, a huge space cow on Mars, animals caught up in a criminal case and – not to be forgotten – a *white stag*. [emphasis in the original]

Next, the afterword turns to one particular author who reports about her personal experiences in the US:

The Afro-American author Kristin Hunter who had made efforts in earlier times to write 'objectively', i.e. to treat Blacks and Whites with the same regard, now states, 'since about 1968 I have been feeling a subjective anger and simultaneously I began to understand the situation in our society.' ... Her story breaks down the old legend of a peaceful coexistence of Blacks and Whites and, in so doing, takes up the battle for equal rights of the Afro-Americans. As her first-person-narrator knows, in the ghettoes, murders and robberies in fact belong to the 'normalities of everyday life.' Some capable young people manage to break away from this environment, others stay and seek solace in drugs. The sportsman Papa Go in Mari Evans's *Friends* is already completely at the mercy of his dealer, he experiences his world only from a *dazed state*. [emphasis in the original]

This paragraph continues to build up the negative propaganda. What is more, sportspeople in the GDR had a special status and were hailed as heroes and fighters for their country; hence, it may be assumed that the depiction of a sportsman completely dependent on drugs was to serve as a further means of alienation. In this Afterword, there is no ambiguity; the readers are not permitted to fill in any gaps or create their own meaning for the text. In fact, what follows instructs the children explicitly in what is missing from American society and gives them the reason for why this is the case, 'Mostly negative examples show what American society lacks and what this young generation is missing: love, understanding and a warmth that comes from the heart.' Following this, the reader hears that it is 'the absolute and dreadful power of money' that stands in the way of deep and honest feeling and leads to 'young people from secure bourgeois circumstances [being] exposed to psychological pressure with which they cannot cope.'

In a concluding paragraph, the child readers are instructed how to react to the stories,

> Certainly, an anthology like this one cannot provide a seamless overview of the social and political situation in the United States. The selected stories are supposed to provoke questions, questions about North America and the people who live in the largest and most powerful capitalist state of the world, and about the social circumstances there. We will take sides first emotionally, then in thought – for the Indians, who have been robbed of their land, and against xenophobia, which Phillip Bonosky describes effectively in *The Chinese Boy*; for full equality of Afro-Americans and against the venality of the police; for sport activities which serve to develop the personality, and against cruelty.

The above example is indicative of the fact that the overall target of Afterwords was not only to give information to readers but to make it absolutely clear to them how they were to read and interpret the content of books, and how socially responsible citizens should think.

Protagonists

With this category again, the attempt to instil into the readership a 'correct' way of behaving becomes evident. What most protagonists have in common is the active stance of a fighter, a healthy portion of wit, courage and sympathy for the weak, suffering and oppressed. Thus, the Afterword to *Das Flaschenteufelchen* ('The Bottle Imp') explains that the guilty characters perish, having been overthrown as a result of their intrigues, whereas the only ones who are victorious are those who are courageous enough to act in a just, reasonable and humane manner (Malberg, 1967: 60). In a similar fashion, Sherlock Holmes is depicted as a hero who possesses courage and intellect, who acts without fear and blemish and not in pursuit of his own, personal advantage, but with the aim of restoring justice and bringing criminals to their deserved punishment. The female protagonist Anne in Mary Benson's *Im Augenblick der Stille* ('At the Still Point') is described as feeling resigned and powerless at the outset of the story in viewing the oppressed natives in South Africa, a country that, according to the Afterword, in part bears resemblance to the German fascist and racist state (this is indicated by denoting the 'Ossewa Brandwag' as a Boer parallel to the national-socialist stormtroopers, Villain, 1974: 239). Anne comes to realise that passive sympathy leads nowhere, and therefore becomes involved, being particularly encouraged by a group of communists whom she has befriended and who believe in and fight for their political goals.

It is however not only the human protagonists who are attributed with positive characteristics. The same applies to animal heroes, like for instance Brer Rabbit in *Geschichten von Onkel Remus* ('Stories by Uncle Remus'). Rabbit, as the Afterword points out, is simple and physically weak, yet smart and full of a will for freedom, but he is surrounded by powerful enemies who are after him and it is only through his wit and the desire to live that he can escape them. As such, the Afterword states, he resembles Black people who also have to fight for their freedom (Petersen, 1984: 148).

So far, I have attempted to show that Afterwords are used as a device to acculturate the readers and to promote socialist culture. Ideologically unambiguous messages ensure that the 'correct' socialist point of view is made visible and children are guided in the 'right' direction. It is worth note too that for every text published there was not only an obvious target reader, the child, but also another, covert, reader inserted between the stages of production and dissemination of the book: the censor. Since books, and the culture of reading in general, were attributed with such an important function, the authorities made absolutely certain that only approved fare would reach the public. Consequently, publishers had an eye not only on the child reader, but also on the censor. They aimed to give pleasure to their young audience and also to satisfy the censor.

Just like the actual book itself, the text of the Afterword was also vetted for its suitability for home readers. A clear, partisan Afterword in the right spirit increased the chances of publication. With the exception of classics and a few newer, ideologically suitable, books, the majority of titles had yet to be acknowledged as a true cultural asset and to be included in the East German canon of children's literature. On the other hand, making accessible to their audience international books lay close to the hearts of the publishers; one way of achieving this goal was the production of an effective Afterword. Commensurate with this objective, publishers were at pains to find the most suitable writers for their Afterwords - ones who would provide a thorough, critical and also socially 'correct' interpretation. In particular, books that carried alien concepts - as was the case with translated books - needed to be presented in a way in which officials in the censorship authority could recognise and accept the concepts presented as 'socialist traits.' The aim was to find a convincing argument to show that the viewpoint of the source text author was identical to that of the East German state, or at least acceptable enough for the censors to grant a print permit.

Additionally, publishers were expected to regard themselves as 'servants' to the state (Institut für Bibliothekswissenschaft und wissenschaftliche Information, 1974: 41, 42) and as 'political functionaries' (DR1/1234). This meant that they were made personally responsible for the suitability of every single book. This led to several unusual devices and procedures within the publishing process, one of which was the use of Afterwords as a mechanism of self-protection for the parties involved. By pointing to socialist characteristics in the texts and hence, appropriating them to the GDR political system, they could make the books acceptable, so that their choice of which books to produce was legitimated. What is more, while Afterwords were used by the publishers to appease the censors, the censors themselves used them to appease the Party bureaucrats and to protect themselves, since they were accountable for their decisions to the Central Committee of the Unity Party. 'Protecting one's own skin' (Darnton, 1991: 213) was a vital strategy in a non-pluralistic state, in which all decisions were based on the judgment of a handful of functionaries. Two features in Afterwords reveal the dual necessity of having to address the next-highest level in the hierarchy and to defend one's own position: anticipation and toning down of ideological political objections; and intertextual references.

Anticipation of Ideological Political Objections

The first category, anticipation of ideological political objections, implies identifying all areas that might cause objections from censors and toning them down or invalidating them. For instance, the Afterword to R. L. Stevenson's *Der schwarze Pfeil* (*The Black Arrow*) states:

> Stevenson himself never thought highly of his story *The Black Arrow*. [And] the bourgeois literary history mentions this masterly piece only in passing. But for us, who view the works of authors of the classical cultural heritage with other eyes and who approach them no longer on the basis of form but because of the benefit they have for us, this piece is of eminent value. Structural shortcomings are more than compensated for by the contents and the realistic portrayal of the characters and the period of the Wars of the Roses. We recognise that *The Black Arrow* is one of the few pieces of world literature in which the life of the Middle Ages is portrayed almost authentically. (Berger, 1969: 254)

As this passage signals, the writer of the Afterword was aware that this story might be considered one of Stevenson's weaker works. However, he distances himself from this attitude by stressing the value of this story for the GDR, while at the same time drawing a line between Eastern and Western ideologies. He further adds value by noting the authenticity (Realism) of life in those days which make the book valuable. He then proceeds:

> With this story, Stevenson does not want to show us an 'objective' historical picture in terms of bourgeois historical research. He is partisan! As he was, during all his life, on the side of the oppressed, he now lays all his sympathy with those gagged and deprived of their rights ... He does not show us a happy and cheerful knighthood life with tournaments, with delicate maidens and merry monks but he reveals times both hard and torn by class struggles (Berger, 1969: 254-255)

Another example originates from a Sherlock Holmes book, *Fünf Fälle des Sherlock Holmes: Detektivgeschichten* ('Five cases for Sherlock Holmes: Detective stories') using the key concepts of Realism and Humanity. Because of their closeness to violence and brutality, crime and detective stories had a difficult standing, especially in the earlier years of the GDR. Thus, the Afterword tells the reader that these stories appeared so true to real life that many people believed in Holmes' real existence (Chowanetz, 1988: 153) - so much so that a post-office box had to be installed for all the letters arriving for the detective with pleas for help (Hillich, 1982: 367). As to Humanity, the Afterword claims that it is not the description of the criminal act per se which is of significance but the finding of the solution to the crime. And of course the fact that good is victorious over evil (Chowanetz, 1988: 154).

Equally, some authors' biographies needed to be toned down. This was true mostly for classic authors, as all contemporary literature selected for publication revolved around socio-critical aspects and was written by authors whose leaning to the left did not require further defence. In the aforementioned *Der schwarze Pfeil*, Stevenson is reported to be the descendant of a well-to-do family (Berger, 1969: 246), having had the particular misfortune to be raised by an over-religious nanny who turned him into a sanctimonious child (Berger, 1969: 247); because of this, he had to find a great deal of painful energy later in his life, in order to liberate himself from this mysticism and superstition (Berger, 1969: 247). And the Afterword hastens to say that he did not know any class differences but loved the simple, hard-working people. However, 'despite his political attitude and despite his fearless battle against reactionary thinking, we do not find in his work such representatives of the working classes who are an embodiment of power and future' (Berger, 1969: 249). The Afterword proceeds in Stevenson's defence: 'But there was not as yet a revolutionary Marxist workers' party, which would have been, through class struggle, the only force capable of developing heroes of a kind worth creating and who would have incited and gripped poets and authors alike' (Berger, 1969: 249). Hence, the Afterword comes to the conclusion, 'He did not see the Tomorrow, which is heralded by and developed by the Today; and since he was disgusted by the Today, he buried his view in the Yesterday' (Berger, 1969: 250).

Intertextual References

The second category constitutes intertextual references, which stress the significance of the text, with respect to either its place within the world heritage or its importance as a tool of education. The function of such references is to demonstrate that distinguished people had also recognised the work as momentous, and that it will therefore enhance East German national literature and is worth being published. Although citations from renowned personalities are used, those from left-wing writers and ideologists are preferred. So Karl Marx and Friedrich Engels are frequently quoted. For instance, the Afterword to Charles Dickens' *Weihnachtsgeschichten* (*Christmas Stories*) states that Karl Marx admired Dickens as 'one of England's authors 'whose clearness, vividness and eloquence gave the world more political and moral truths than all politicians, journalists and moralists together" (Wirzberger, 1970: 213). Another example is the Afterword to the German version of Marryat's *Peter Simple,* which quotes from the memoirs of Marx's daughter, in which she mentions that she was given the 'immortal Peter Simple' for her sixth birthday, and in following years other novels by both Marryat and Cooper, and reports that her father had been quite serious about discussing these books with 'the little girl ... And it was not until several years later, due to Walter Scott's novels, that her enthusiasm for Marryat's heroes diminished' (Wirzberger, 1969: 265). Incidentally, the Afterword does not forget to mention Marryat's long-lasting friendship with Dickens, an author well-established in the canon because of his books about social injustice and the poverty of the working classes in the England of his day.

To sum up: like all Afterwords or Prefaces, East German Afterwords first and foremost perform an informative function - informative however to a point where the provision of information is closely associated with the socialisation and acculturation process of the child readers. Owing to the connection of East German book production to the construction of a new social system and to the notion of usefulness of all literary output, the imaginations and thoughts of the young readers are consciously guided in a certain direction. Therefore, Afterwords do not leave readers with any ambiguity. Just like gadgets or other electronic devices which come with instructions on how to operate the machine, Afterwords constitute the manuals to the books, delivering the explanations necessary to read and understand the texts correctly.

Yet the informative task of East German Afterwords went even further. Since the state reserved for itself the control of all printed matter and operated a tight system of censorship, publishers had to **sell** their books to the censors by highlighting socially and ideologically relevant and accepted elements in the various texts. Amongst other devices, Afterwords were one way of doing this. Promoting the books to the censors by directing their attention to the texts' compliance with state ideology points to the third function of Afterwords in the GDR: they served as tools for defence and protection of the publishers, who were responsible to the censors, and also as protection for the censors themselves, since they were accountable for their decisions to the Central Committee. From the standpoint of researching the cultural aspects of translation, paratexts (here Afterwords) provide additional information about a society or a culture and help situate the text in its proper position within the literary system of that culture. East German Afterwords demonstrate the values of their (socialist) society and the restrictions that this society placed on publishers, editors and even censors.

Bibliography

Berger, K H (1969) 'Nachwort', in R L Stevenson, *Der schwarze Pfeil*, 6th edition, Berlin: Neues Leben, pp244-256

Biester, H-L (1963) 'Nachwort', in Daniel Defoe, *Robinson Crusoe,* Berlin: Kinderbuchverlag, pp324-338

Chowanetz, R (1988) `Über Doyle, Sherlock Holmes und Detektive,` in A C Doyle: Chowanetz, Rudolf (ed.) *Fünf Fälle des Sherlock Holmes: Detektivgeschichten*, Berlin:Kinderbuchverlag, pp153-155

Darnton, R (1991) *Berlin Journal 1989-1990* New York, London: W W Norton & Company

DR1/1234, Bundesarchiv Berlin, Files of GDR Ministry of Culture

Hillich, R (1982) 'Der seltsame Besuch: Ein Nachspiel', in A C Doyle: Hillich, Reinhard (ed.) *17 Detektivgeschichten* Berlin: Neues Leben, pp365-371

Ilberg, W (1965) 'Nachwort', in Walter Scott *Ivanhoe,* Berlin: Neues Leben, pp541-545

Institut für Bibliothekswissenschaft und wissenschaftliche Information (1974) *Verlagswesen und Buchhandel der Deutschen Demokratischen Republik,* Berlin: Humboldt Universität

Krenn, R (1964) 'Nachwort', in Walter Scott, *Quentin Durward,* Berlin: Neues Leben, pp465-474

Malberg, H-J (1967) 'Nachwort', in R L Stevenson, *Das Flaschenteufelchen,* Weimar: Knabe, pp59-62

Petersen, H (1968) 'Nachbemerkung' in Erskine Caldwell, *Molly Baumwollschwänzchen,* Berlin: Kinderbuchverlag (np)

Petersen, H (1978) 'Nachwort', in Petersen, H (ed.) *Unser weißer Hirsch,* Berlin: Kinderbuchverlag, pp256-259

Petersen, H (1984) 'Nachwort', in Joel Chandler Harris, *Geschichten von Onkel Remus,* Berlin: Kinderbuchverlag, pp147-149

Villain, J (1974) 'Nachwort', in Mary Benson, *Im Augenblick der Stille,* Berlin:Neues Leben, pp236-244

Wirzberger, S (1969) 'Nachwort', in Frederick Marryat, *Peter Simpel,* Berlin: Kinderbuchverlag, pp261-267

Wirzberger, S (1970) 'Anwalt der Menschlichkeit', in Charles Dickens, *Weihnachtsgeschichten,* Berlin:Kinderbuchverlag, pp213-218

Cultural Dialogue and the Language of the Neighbour's Child: Lessons from Barbara Kimenye's Writing

Abasi Kiyimba

Introduction

This paper focuses on the work of Barbara Kimenye, the leading writer of Children's literature in Uganda, who has published more than 25 children's stories. The majority of Kimenye's stories are part of a series featuring the escapades of a schoolboy named Moses, and are intended for children of lower primary age. They are well written and offer social entertainment and linguistic instruction to children, and also teach them something about the specific cultural roots of the stories. *The Gemstone Affair* (1978) and *The Scoop* (1978) are addressed to older children, while two collections of short stories, *Kalasanda* (1965) and *Kalasanda Revisited* (1966), which contain humorous glimpses of life in a Buganda village, can be read and enjoyed by both older children and adults. These collections provide a particular focus in this paper. One of these stories, 'The Battle of the Sacred Tree,' has been made into a feature film. Kimenye's writings have been widely read both in Uganda and outside.

Like many other African authors, Kimenye writes in English, but the influence of her linguistic and cultural background is in evidence throughout the work in the form of direct reference to Ganda culture, non-native-English-speaker thought-patterns, untranslatable words, names of characters, etc. In this paper I examine how the culture of the Baganda informs Kimenye's writing, and the extent to which the glimpses of Ganda culture enrich her language. I also consider the capacity of this language to communicate with the 'neighbour's child' - the child with a different cultural background - in an attempt to establish whether her work is accessible across cultures, and thus if it can serve as a medium for a dialogue between cultures.

Children's Literature and Contemporary Experience

African children literature today exists in many different forms, and in a variety of languages. The bulk of it is in African languages, but as a result of Africa's colonial experience, there is also a sizeable amount written in foreign languages. This literature can today be categorised as pre-colonial, colonial or post-colonial.

Pre-colonial literature was basically oral. It was valued as 'one of the major means by which societies educated, instructed, and socialised their younger members' (Odaga, 1985:1). With the introduction of formal education, most of that which previously would have been considered oral literature - proverbs, riddles, tales, taboos, legends - is now available in print. Despite this, oral literature is not a thing of the past. In many African societies it is still alive and active. Much of it is still created daily, so that it is constantly being adjusted to new developments and continues to take on new dimensions.

During the colonial period, African children in government and missionary schools were introduced to children's literature that was alien to their experience. Books such as *Black Beauty, Sleeping Beauty, Beauty and the Beast, Alice in Wonderland* and *Snow White and the Seven Dwarfs* have a western background and are based on western values. While some of them present moral teachings, these teachings had to be painfully fished out of the literature, and it is certainly the case that African children would have benefited more if they had read these books alongside others with a familiar background and cultural values. What was even more unfortunate was that those who introduced the alien literature described it as mature and civilised, and referred to oral literature as primitive and lacking in technique.

A large amount of written literature has been produced by African authors during the post-colonial period. These books are widely used in African schools and elsewhere in the world. Despite its specific background, this literature can read and enjoyed by children from many different backgrounds.

George Orwell once observed that when Charles Dickens describes something, you see it for the rest of your life; in another context, Orwell said that when he first read the scene in *Great Expectations* involving Pip's encounter with the convict on the marshes, he thought a child had written it. The reason why Orwell was able to see Dickens' pictures for the rest of his life or to imagine that a child had written the marshes scene was that Dickens was an imaginative writer who, in the words of Walter Ong, could fictionalise himself into his audience. This quality is needed in order to be a successful writer of children's literature in the current inter-cultural situation.

The Context of Kimenye's Writing

All societies have had and implemented a policy on children's literature, consciously or unconsciously. In Africa, as in other oral cultures, stories have been handed down orally from one generation to another. Societies have done this because they recognise value in these stories. Wario (1989: 51) and Bukenya et al (1997: 14) give several reasons why these stories have been told to children and handed down from one generation to another. They particularly stress their entertainment function, and also point out that stories are told for their instructional value, their capacity to mould character. In these stories, good is rewarded and evil is punished. The stories are also instruments of socialisation. They pass on societal beliefs and values, encourage good and decent behaviour and discourage bad and improper behaviour. By so doing, they prepare children for their roles as adults and pillars of society. For this reason, stories are necessarily instruments and vehicles of the cultures of their societies. They strengthen the knowledge, understanding and appreciation of the children's own cultures and in so doing prepare them for the challenges of adulthood in their communities. They also prepare them to co-exist with people of other cultures. Nandwa and Bukenya (1983: 2) also stress that stories are told for the purpose of improving oral expression. They point out that storytelling

> provides a form of speech training for children so that as they grow up, they become good story tellers and good public speakers, people capable of using language effectively. It also trains children to have a good memory. (Akivaga & Odaga, 1982: 9).

This is particularly important when looked at in the context of oral cultures where oral skills were greatly revered.

According to Wario (1989: 52), Okinda (1994: 5), and Akivaga and Odaga (1982: 8), stories are not only told by adults to children, but also by children among themselves, and by children to a mixed group of adults and children. However, the telling of stories to children by adults is particularly challenging, requiring adults to fictionalise themselves into a child audience.

Written children's stories in Africa occur against the background of the oral stories that have been told in the traditional communities for a long time. But they have changed form, and acquired an additional purpose, the purpose of linking children to one another across cultures. Changes in the socio-cultural environment have brought about new means of communication that must be matched by new formats such as books, newspapers and magazines. Children's stories also come to the child through the electronic media: radio and television programmes, and on the internet. This poses a unique challenge. However, the thematic concerns and moral messages in contemporary children's stories have remained much the same as in the past. This has also brought another realisation: that many of the concerns of the child are universal. So if the initial problem of intercultural communication is overcome, the children's world can turn into a global village through sharing stories.

It is necessary however to keep note of the fact that written children's stories are a development, not a beginning. African children have always had stories for entertainment and socialisation. Children's literature is part of Uganda's oral tradition that has been handed down from generation to another, and has existed in all available forms, such as songs and poems, narratives, proverbs, riddles and tongue twisters. Akivaga and Odaga (1982), Nandwa and Bukenya (1983) and Kipury (1983) identify myths, legends, fables, ogre

241

tales and human tales as being popular with African children. These stories may include aetiological tales, trickster tales, monster and dilemma tales and folktales of various kinds. The terminology tends to differ from one scholar to another, but they all agree that communities used these stories for similar purposes, including explaining the origins of a group of people or the early development of specific aspects of life of a group of people. (Akivaga and Odaga, 1982: 20)

Myths go back to the furthest memory of the tribe (Lo Liyong, 1991: 19). Most of them consist of events which happened in the distant, sacred past, frequently related to the time of creation. A common creation myth from Western Uganda among the Banyoro, Batooro and Banyankole tribes explains their origins, referring to gods and creation under the reign of the Abatembuzi. The Baganda also have a creation myth linked to Kintu and Nambi.

Legends or hero stories are similar to myths in that they tell about events out of the past, but they are about heroic persons who actually lived. They are however exaggerated and are linked to important events in the life of a people, such as migrations, wars, victories, deaths of important Chiefs and Kings, and secession in ruling dynasties. An example of a legend, from Northern Uganda among the Langi, is Acholi's story of Labongo and Gipir, describing the beginning of the two tribes.

Another important group of stories are those described as aetiological. Sunkuli and Miruka (1999: 1) and Akivaga and Odaga (1982: 7) define aetiology as the study of the origin or cause of things: how things came to be the way they are today. The tales in this category explain the origin and characteristics of various animals, plants and landscapes. The explanation may not be true but is enough to satisfy the curiosity of children.

These stories are told in different versions by Uganda societies, and they include: 'Why frog has no tail,' 'Why ostrich and giraffe have long necks,' 'Why the dog is a friend of man,' 'How the dog became a domestic animal,' 'Why chickens do not fly,' 'Why hawk and eagle take hen's chicks,' 'Why the moon and sun shine,' 'Why it rains,' 'Why a dog barks and a cat miaows,' 'Why there is thunder and lightening,' 'Why zebra has stripes,' 'Why sun lives in the sky,' and many others. Some of these tales offer fairly realistic explanations of phenomena, while others heavily rely on fantasy. All of them are however generally invented for the entertainment of children.

The other types of stories include trickster stories, monster stories and, significantly, tales about ordinary human beings. Trickster stories are about a character (animal or human) who practises cunning on others to get the better of them. Trickster stories are very common and popular among children in Uganda. Popular animal tricksters in African oral literature are tortoise, hare, squirrel and monkey. The cunning character is usually diminutive while the victim is almost always a bigger and stronger animal such as elephant, hyena, lion and crocodile. The characters in monster stories on the other hand are imaginary evil and ferocious creatures. They interact with humans at various levels, including marriage and war. The stories often have moral messages for children.

The stories with human beings as the main characters directly deal with relationships between human beings in society. These relationships include those between parents and children, husbands and wives, brothers and sisters, brothers and brothers, sisters and sisters, step-mothers and step-children, and friends and enemies. These stories teach specific morals to children. They may show the conflicts that exist between different people, and also propose possible solutions. In the process, they cover a wide range of subjects including hard work and bravery, good behaviour, neighbourly co-existence, and greed.

Stories in present-day Uganda draw heavily on oral tradition or folklore, especially in their content. The sub-genres of myths, legends, aetiological, trickster and monster narratives are still part and parcel of today's children's stories. The only difference is that they have now been captured in written form in addition to the non-written. The thematic content and moral messages of the past persist in the present. Both the oral and written children's stories are valuable components of the children's literature menu because of their beauty, entertainment, moral messages and level of oral expression.

With the coming of formal education, close to seven million children, or a third of Uganda's population are at school. The formal school setting has therefore taken over the functions of the traditional fireplace, and this is what explains the emergence of writers like Kimenye. Traditional stories are still told, but they are told under the changed circumstances of the modern sitting room and classroom. They are also told through the modern media of books, newspapers, magazines, radio, television and the internet. The interaction between children's stories and other oral literature genres such as songs and proverbs has also continued, but even these have been modernised. This interaction enriches the children's stories and makes them more interesting.

Kimenye the Writer

Barbara Kimenye is the most prolific of all Ugandan writers, male and female. Her writing spans a period of more than thirty years, during which she has produced over thirty works of fiction, and at least one work on a non-literary subject.[1] The majority of her books are written for children, even though they make interesting reading for adults, and are not less serious as works as works of art.[2] Indeed, in her latest publications, *Beauty Queen* (1997) and *Prettyboy Beware* (1997), she deals with the contemporary issues of beauty contests and homosexuality, respectively. In *Beauty Queen*, Adela and Keti jokingly enter a beauty contest, but they soon find that they have to confront greater dangers than they had bargained for. In *Prettyboy Beware*, a combination of social misfortunes and financial deprivation leaves Mathew at the mercy of a European homosexual, who takes advantage of him. Eventually, the boy degenerates into a male prostitute, and is infected with the HIV virus by the tourists from whom he has learnt to earn his living. The lessons in these works are quite heavy; and like Kimenye's other writings, these books cannot be dismissed off-hand simply because their primary audience is children.

Kimenye's two earliest literary works, *Kalasanda* and *Kalasanda Revisited* are both set in the Ugandan kingdom of Buganda before the political turbulence of the mid-1960s.[3] They comprise a series of interconnected stories and have the consistency of a novel, tackling issues of political power, family structure, social organisation, religion, culture and day-to-day social interaction. The background to the social analysis is an ordinary village life, but the social comment that Kimenye makes is far-reaching, and is valid for many other villages in Buganda and elsewhere. Her work gives the impression that she is a pro-establishment writer who is amusing herself with the follies of members of society; there are no overtly anti-establishment social protests, such as those occurring in the work of Mary Okurut, Goretti Kyomuhendo and others of a later generation. Nevertheless, Kimenye's work speaks a language of its own which independently communicates on the above issues. For example, the male nature of the political establishment in the society she writes about is quite evident in her work. The king is male, so is the Gombolola chief and the village chief. The Gombolola chief has a string of wives; while the ladies of the Christian Union find this objectionable because it goes against the Christian principle of one man one wife, they do not question his legitimacy as **chief**. Neither Kimenye nor her characters concern themselves with the ideal of **equality** between the sexes.

The family structure that comes through in Kimenye's tale protects the position of the man at its helm. As soon as the women get married, their lives and wishes are interpreted in terms of how they relate to their husbands. The change of surnames to those of the husbands is a status symbol, and they proudly style themselves by their husbands' names, as 'the Lutaayas', 'the Mukasas', etc. Although the women of the Mothers' Union are quite radical when it comes to defending their perception of inviolable Christian values, they are subordinate to their husbands (who are less enthusiastic about these values), as prescribed by the social system. An incident that clearly illustrates this is the stand-off between Mrs Mukasa and her husband. She drives his car to town in his absence, and then leaves it outside the house because the fuel has run out. The tyres are stolen, which invites his cold anger, and he refuses to speak to her. Peace is only restored between them after she has torn up her driving licence, on the advice of the village chief. Similarly, Mrs Kigozi promptly relinquishes her membership of the Kalasanda Mothers' Union when her husband expresses his disapproval of it.

Kimenye also seems to adopt certain age-old sexist stereotypes without questioning them. It goes without saying that the village gossip should be a woman, as in the character of Nantondo. Maria, the bar woman who is feared by all married women 'for taking their men,' is also a common stereotype. Even the scuffle that takes place in her bar when Antoni beats her up after realising that she has been selling his gifts to other people, is quite predictable. But probably the most remarkable aspect of the man-woman power relationship in Kimenye's work is highlighted by Maria's refusal to press charges against Antoni for beating her and causing destruction of her property, despite Daudi's persistent advice to do so. She knows she is carrying Antoni's baby, and Baganda women do not raise their hands (or even their voices) against the fathers of their children. And finally, there is the picture of the westernised woman whom Lamek Waswa brings from the city. She is clearly a social misfit in the community: she wears a wig, and she does not socialise with other people. For this, she earns the wrath of the village. Their attitude towards her is not helped by her action of stealing the clothes of Waswa's customers.

On the other hand, the young men such as Antoni and Waswa who also come from the city are given a favourable depiction. They are quite amiable, and they get along with villagers very well. When they later leave after encountering problems, which incidentally have been caused by women, they are objects of sympathy rather than ridicule. These women however do not seem to develop beyond the stereotypical roles that Kimenye assigns them.

Thus far, Kimenye would seem to have created a society that is almost entirely male dominated. But she also creates a remarkable female character, whose demeanour would jolt even the most bigoted male chauvinist. Victoria, the girl engaged by Antoni as a shop assistant, is a no nonsense woman for whom money comes first. She has no time for gossip, and she alone among the people in Kalasanda stands up to Nantondo's gossipy character by bluntly refusing to answer any of her questions, or even entertaining her very presence on the verandah of her shop. She also sternly points out to Antoni that he has been wasting his money on the bar woman, and he should not wonder that the stock in the shop is getting depleted. Antoni gets angry, but she proves herself his equal in the ensuing quarrel.

When they eventually patch up their quarrel and get married, it is a small practical wedding; she does not believe in big wasteful weddings.

Kimenye does not spare her male characters either. She raises several laughs at their expense, for having power (both social and political), but often for acting in a naïve and stupid manner. Pius Ndawula is driven into marriage by a very forceful woman (cousin Sarah) who takes over the management of his home, while actually cajoling him to believe that he is the one in charge. Then there is Daudi who has become the village laughing stock because of his endless hunt for scholarships. The young dobbi (Lamek Waswa) and the shopkeeper (Antoni), while their predicament is pitiable, also come up for ridicule. One of them is naïve enough to take on a seasoned city crook for a wife, while the other spends his hard-earned money on a bar-woman who has several other men-friends. Then there is the grotesque picture of Mr. Lubowa, the Honourable Member of Parliament who gets snuff into his eyes. And finally, there is the unpleasant character of Mr Kibuuka, the unequivocal male chauvinist who ridicules Daudi's scholarship because the tailoring-related subject that he is going to study is for women. Kimenye may be pro-establishment in many areas that traditionally place men in positions of authority vis-à-vis women, but careful analysis of her work would show that she does not flatter the men, and she certainly does not condone male incongruity.

One of the benefits of children's literature is to bridge the gap between different generations. Children's literature, even in its oral form, has always played this role, but it is particularly necessary today because of the changing socio-political circumstances that make it difficult for children to receive the kind of exposure to traditional story-telling that they received in the past. Today, families no longer live in the same compound, as used to be the case in the past when grandparents passed on the wisdom of the society as a daily activity through oral tradition. In families that live in urban social settings, the children may not even learn the language of their grandparents. The role of writers like Kimenye is therefore vital because it provides a culture to a new generation. This culture will certainly have changed significantly, which is why it is dismissed by some commentators as European. Nevertheless it is in reasonable communion with its ancestral roots. *Kalasanda* and *Kalasanda Revisited* would seem to have been beamed at older children or even adults, but child-friendly episodes are very much in evidence even in these works. Children will, for example, find the antics of adults described in these works quite entertaining and revealing of the adult world that they are destined to enter sooner or later. They will be familiar with, and may even be among the consumers of, the gossip of adults like Nantondo. The episode that involves the bewitching of Damieno will also be found quite exciting, as will be Daudi's ever-twitching nose.

Kimenye's 'Moses' stories

The majority of Kimenye's stories are clearly for younger children. In the Moses stories such as Moses (1967), Moses and Mildred (1967), Moses and the Kidnappers (1968), Moses in Trouble (1968), Moses in a Muddle (1970), Moses and the Ghost (1971), Moses on the Move(1972), Moses and the Pen pal (1973), Moses the Camper (1973), Moses and the Man from Mars (1991) Moses in a Mess(1991), and Moses and the Movie(1996), children will greatly enjoy the escapades of someone of their own age. They will most probably identify with Moses all the way, as they will see a bit of themselves reflected in him.

The stories will also expose them to new worlds. Stories like Moses and the Movie, Moses and the Pen pal and Moses the Camper have the effect of alerting children to the existence of other worlds in addition to the one in which they are growing up. This prepares them to live in the same world with people from other cultures when they are older.

Dialoguing with the Neighbour's Child

Nancy Schmidt has observed that early European children's literature about Africa was steeped in standard stereotypes that make 'Africans appear foolish and simpleminded...' (1975: 175-78). The emergence of works such as those of Kimenye is therefore an important development in the dialogue between cultures. It means that African children have the opportunity to read literature presented by their own. It also gives children from elsewhere in the world the opportunity to learn about Africa as it is presented from the point of view of Africans themselves. By so doing, it facilitates closer communication between members of different cultural backgrounds.

Commenting on one of Kimenye's stories, an American High School student had this to say:

> 'The Winner' by Barbara Kimenye fails to attract and hold the interest of the reader and should not be used in the English 11 curriculum. Through its use of foreign terms, the story puts a barrier in front of the reader and closes the door to our understanding.[4]

It is possible that the use of local terms such as 'Gombolola', 'Sabalangira', 'Ssaza', 'Shamba', and 'Piki-piki' in both Kalasanda and Kalasanda Revisited may temporarily interrupt the reception of the stories, but then, this is a common feature all literature that is either in translation or is conceived in one language and transmitted in another. What is also true is that once the meanings of these words have been worked out (either from the context or from a glossary) they constitute a cross-cultural experience that will make the child from another culture much richer for it.

247

Interestingly, the comment of the High school student cited above negates the view expressed by some critics to the effect that Kimenye's work is grounded in European rather than in African tradition and therefore does not teach youthful readers about more than a 'very limited segment of African life.'[5] These critics seem to be saying that there is no Africa in Kimenye's work, but this student is saying that there is too much of it! The evidence in the text shows that in addition to the Luganda words used in the texts of several stories, there are many other aspects of the culture and belief of the Baganda in Kimenye's work. They include the culture of women kneeling to greet their menfolk, the carrying of the waterpot on their heads, and the reverence for the sacred tree in 'The Battle of the Sacred Tree' in *Kalasanda Revisited*. The near-worship interaction with the Kabaka (King) in the story entitled 'Royal Visit' in *Kalasanda* will tell the child from another culture something about the Baganda as a people, in addition to entertaining them.

The story entitled 'The Visitor' in *Kalasanda* is particularly child-friendly. Mrs Kajumba receives the message that her father is in a critical condition in Mulago hospital and has to go there, leaving Nansubuga and Erisa to look after the home. Nansubuga is only seven, but attempts to boss her brother Erisa who is two years younger. But the child in her is very much in evidence. She has moments when she struggles to decide whether to play the adult or be a child with her younger brother. In the end she decides to be an adult, and Erisa uses the earliest opportunity to escape to go and play with his friend Njuki, leaving her alone at home. In response to this abandonment, the child in her surfaces even more clearly. She bangs things, abandons the digging, and comforts herself with the thought that she will report Erisa when the adults return. But as fate would have it, this is the moment when 'Uncle Kato', the thief, strikes. He has picked up the story about the adults' absence, so he arrives and deceives Nansubuga that he has come to collect Mother to go to Mulago, sends the child to buy a drink for him, and then robs the house of all its property. This incident shows how vulnerable Nansubuga still is as a child, despite her attempt to play adult. A further revelation comes when she stops to write her name and that of Erisa (and also to draw an unflattering picture of Erisa) on Uncle Kato's vehicle to let off her anger, even though she knows she must hurry and bring uncle Kato's drink. Children will find the encounter between Nansubuga and her brother Erisa in the company of his friend Njuki entertaining:

> There she goes! Old Spider legs! The hostile cry came from the upper braches of the old mamgo tree, where Erisa and Njuki were scrambling about like a pair of monkeys. Safe from retaliation, they yelled jeers and threats at Nansubuga, following them with a fusilage of tiny, wizened mangoes. Nansubuga fairly stamped with impotent rage. She flung back a few insults, and even threw a few stones into the tree, but she was clearly at a disadvantage, and

was forced to run away ignominiously, leaving the boys to celebrate their victory by bouncing up and down and screaming war cries. (p56)

Nansubuga is saddened that there is no time to respond to respond to these insults, since she has to take uncle Kato his drink. Children will easily be able to picture this entertaining scene.

Conclusion

The introduction of writing on the African Continent has brought a new literary regime for both adults and children. While oral literature is still enjoyed by a great number of people, the emergence of a body of written children's literature constitutes a major development in the way a particular people interacts with other peoples. Barbara Kimenye, as the pioneer and leading writer of children's literature in Uganda, has played a significant role in fostering intercultural understanding between on the one hand the Baganda in particular and Africans in general, and between the Baganda and other peoples of the world, on the other hand. Her work does not draw extensively on African oral literature, but it is clearly set against an African background and this enables her to communicate from a position of cultural strength and to tell readers from elsewhere something about the Baganda. This is a very good starting point for inter-cultural dialogue.

Notes

1. Kimenye is author of The Modern African Vegetable Cookbook, 1997.

2. In an article about Ugandan Writers, Bernard Tabaire writes at length about the work of several others, dismissing Kimenye in the phrase 'and Barbara Kimenye's children's books.' This is not an isolated incident, and it relates to the notable absence of attention to Kimenye in the criticism of Ugandan literature.

3. The Baganda of central Uganda have had a kingdom for probably about twelve centuries. In 1894, the British government imposed colonial rule over a vast area in this region, and included this kingdom within one political structure that was eventually called Uganda. The kingdom of Buganda was maintained, and the British ruled the Baganda through their king in a system of indirect rule. In the 1962 constitution under which Uganda was given independence, the kingdom of Buganda retained a federal status, while other kingdoms in Western Uganda had a semi-federal status. The remaining parts of Uganda were administered directly by the central government. In 1965/66, a crisis erupted between the central government, led by Prime Minister Milton Obote and the Kingdom of Buganda, led by Edward Mutesa, who was both the Kabaka of Buganda and the ceremonial president of Uganda. He was exiled to

Britain, where he eventually died in 1969. Since that time, Uganda has had a turbulent political climate, sporadically interrupted by short phases of peace.

4. http://www.directessays.com/viewpaper/58121.html (Visited on 20th October, 2005 at 10.00 GMT)

5. Nancy J. Schmidt, 'The Writer as Teacher: A Comparison of the African Adventure Stories of G.A. Henty, Rene Guillot and Barbara Kimenye,' *African Studies Review*, 19 (September 1976) pp.69-80.

Bibliography

Primary Texts *by Barbara Kimenye*

Beauty Queen, Nairobi, Kenya: East African Educational Publishers, 1997

Kayo's House, London: Macmillan, 1996

The Mating Game, London: Macmillan, 1992

Martha the Millipede, Nairobi: Oxford University Press, 1973

The Money Game, London: Oxford University Press, 1992

Moses, Nairobi: Oxford University Press, 196

Moses and Mildred, Nairobi: Oxford University Press, 1967

Moses and the Kidnappers, Nairobi: Oxford University Press, 1968

Moses in Trouble, Nairobi: Oxford University Press, 1968

Moses in a Muddle, Nairobi: Oxford University Press, 1970

Moses and the Ghost, Nairobi: Oxford University Press, 1971

Moses on the Move, Nairobi: Oxford University Press, 1972

Moses and the Penpal, Nairobi: Oxford University Press, 1973

Moses the Camper, Nairobi: Oxford University Press, 1973

Moses and the Man from Mars, Nairobi: Heinemann, 1991

Moses in a Mess, Nairobi: Heinemann, 1991

Moses and the Movie, London: Macmillan, 1996

Paulo's Strange Adventure, Nairobi: Oxford University Press, 1971

Prettyboy Beware, Nairobi: East African Educational Publishers, 1997

The Runaways, Nairobi: Oxford University Press, 1973

Sarah and the Boy, Nairobi: Oxford University Press, 1973

The Smugglers, London: Nelson, 1997

The Winged Adventure, Nairobi: Oxford University Press, 1969

Secondary Texts

Akivaga S K & Odaga, A B 1982 *Oral Literature: A School Certificate Course* Nairobi: East African Educational Publishers

Barongo E I (1996) 'Popular Themes in Children's Literature in Uganda: Some Case Studies' in *Other Worlds Other Lives: Children's Literature Experiences*: Machet, M et al. (eds.), Pretoria: University of South Africa

Bukenya A S & Gachanja M (1996) *Oral Literature: A Junior Course*, Nairobi: Longhorn Kenya

Bukenya A S et al. (1997) *Oral Literature: a Senior Course*, Nairobi: Longhorn Kenya

Chesaina C (1991) *Oral Literature of the Kalenjin*, Nairobi: Heinemann - Kenya Limited

Kipury N (1983) *Oral Literature of the Masai*, Nairobi: East Africa Educational Publishers Ltd.

Lo Liyong T (1991) *Culture is Rutan*, Nairobi: Longman Kenya Ltd.

Masinjila M & Okombo O (1994) *Teaching Oral Literature*, Nairobi: Kenya Oral Literature Association

Mbarwa H R (1996) *Your Oral Literature*, Nairobi: Eagle H Publishers

Miruka O (1994) *Encounter with Oral Literature*, Nairobi: East African Educational Publishers Ltd.

Nandwa J & Bukenya A (1983) *African Oral Literature for Schools*, Nairobi: Longman Kenya Ltd.

Odaga, Asenath Bole (1985) *Literature for Children and Young People in Kenya*, Nairobi: Kenya literature Bureau

Okinda E (1994) *A Simplified Introduction to Oral Literature and Poetry*, Nairobi: World Press Publishers

Schmidt, Nancy J (1975) *Children's Books on Africa and their Authors: An Annotated Bibliography*. New York: Africana Publishing Co.

Schmidt, Nancy J (1976) 'The Writer as Teacher: A Comparison of the African Adventure Stories of G A Henty, Rene Guillot and Barbara Kimenye' *African Studies Review* 19, September 1976, pp69-80

Sesnan B (1997) *How to Teach English*, Oxford, University Press

Sunkuli L O & Miruka S O (1990) *A Dictionary of Oral Literature*, Nairobi: Heinemann Kenya Ltd.

Wario L H (1989) *Ways of Teaching Primary English*, Nairobi: Macmillan

The Teaching-Story™ from Afghanistan

Robert Ornstein

I will begin with the synopsis of a Teaching-Story by Idries Shah:

Neem the Half-Boy

The Queen of Hich-Hich (which means 'nothing at all') wants a son. The fairies ask the wise man how she can have one, and Arif the Wise Man gives them an apple for the queen. If she eats the apple, he says, she will have a son. But the Queen is distracted and eats only half the apple, and so she gives birth to a half-boy. Neem the Half-Boy grows up to be very clever, but he wants very badly to be a whole boy. Once again, the fairies go to the wise man and ask him how Neem can become whole.

Following Arif the Wise Man's advice, Neem goes to visit the dragon Taneen, who breathes fire all over everyone but who has, in his cave, a wonderful medicine that will make Neem whole. Neem goes to tell the dragon that he must drive him away because the people don't like all the fire he breathes over them. Taneen explains to Neem that he can't help breathing fire because that's how he cooks his food, since he hasn't got a stove. Neem says he can get him a stove, but he still has to drive him away since Taneen has the medicine that will make him whole in the back of his cave.

The dragon suggests that he give Neem the medicine so that he can become whole, and then Neem can go and get him a stove so that he no longer needs to blow fire all over people. And that's what happens, and all the people are very happy. And from then on Neem the Half-Boy is called Kull, which means 'the whole boy' in the language of Hich-Hich.

The Value of Stories

Since the 20th century, a good deal of research has been done into trying to find out how children learn to locate themselves into the world; how they learn the way things operate in the world; how they learn to connect things in order to make sense of them. There are many things to think about:

- How do you get dressed to go to school?
- Why do you wear different clothes at different times?
- How do you eat breakfast, lunch and dinner?

- Do you have sweet stuff before sour stuff?

- How do you sing?

- How do you act towards people you know versus people you don't know?

If you actually think about what you do, you realise that you have hundreds of different routines in your mind about how to act. Most of the initial research has been on simple association: hit – ball, dog – bark, etc. While it is important at an early age to be able to make connections like these, this research doesn't really tell us about so many other aspects of life, about how to operate in the world, for example:

- How to get on the bus to go to school.

- How to read a book.

- When to talk.

- When you're free to scream and run around.

- When you're free not to.

- How to deal with unexpected challenges.

- How to deal with your family as opposed to other people.

Many psychologists and psychiatrists have begun to feel that the way in which people learn is through stories. They may be simple stories like how to go to the drugstore and buy something. They may be complicated stories such as 'What do I have to do in order to get married' or 'What do I have to do if I want to be a fireman?' But they are still stories. They link events together in a meaningful way, and they are really **not** very simple.

While it is very important to know how to read and to use language, it is also very important to know how all these words and concepts come together to make something meaningful. The best way to do this is through stories. We have stories about ourselves and about other people; we have stories about our life; we have stories about our country's life, about political life, and so on. We revise and maintain these stories, and we tell them to each other all the time. So it's no accident that stories have been found to be very important in cognitive development.

What is a Teaching-Story?

Certain stories, though, are a little different than just the 'put your clothes on before you go to school' type. They are known as Teaching-Stories. They've occurred and recurred throughout the world and have been shown, for instance, by the author Idries Shah, to occur in culture after culture with pretty much the same structure. There is a Cinderella story invented and told by the Algonquin Indians for example. These stories are universal throughout all cultures, and hundreds have been collected by Shah (1978, 1991), especially for current learning and teaching.

These universal stories are important because they contain vital elements of learning for children and for adults, elements that are not really replaceable in any other way. Their very universality shows that they are very important to the basic process of becoming human.

This special kind of story, the Teaching-Story, is a form of literature not very well known nowadays in the West, but still common in the Middle East and Central Asia, especially in countries such as Afghanistan. Teaching-Stories are specifically designed to help develop thinking skills and perceptions because they introduce children and adults to events in unusual combinations.

The psychological significance of these stories has only recently been rediscovered in the West. They contrast with the more conventional kind of stories: those that might contain a moral, or tell children how to act, how to behave, or how to be a proper person. These Teaching-Stories tell you a little more about yourself, how to see yourself in unfamiliar situations. They prepare children for the many unfamiliar events that may happen later in life, and they develop the mind in unexpected ways.

Teaching-Stories often appear to be little more than fairy tales or folktales, and their entertainment value has ensured that they remain in cultures. In fact, many fairy tales and folktales we know today have Teaching-Stories at their origin. But Teaching-Stories in their original form are designed to embody – in their characters, plots and imagery – patterns and relationships that nurture a part of the mind that can't be reached in any other way. Familiarity with these stories increases our understanding and our breadth of vision. Stories like *Neem the Half-Boy*, involve unusual happenings and constructive ways of dealing with a situation, such as how Neem confronts the dragon.

Most of our daily life is pretty predictable. We have ordinary routines. We get up, children go to school, they learn at school, they come home, they

255

have their games, and they have their life events. Through exposure to stories like these, we can introduce children to unusual events, occurrences that normally do not happen, even in the safe and comforting harbour of the story-telling situation. When we do this, we prepare their minds to develop more flexibility and to understand the complexities of the world a little better. Obviously, most young children have not encountered that many unusual situations, but these stories prepare them, they enable them to look at the world in a more complex way, and in a way in which they can develop more context. Here is the synopsis of another Teaching-Story from Idries Shah.

The Clever Boy and the Terrible, Dangerous Animal

For the first time, a boy goes on his own to visit a nearby village. As he approaches it, he sees all the villagers looking fearful and saying 'Oooo', 'Ahhh', and 'Ohhh!' He asks them why they are afraid; they tell him, and then show him a terrible, dangerous animal in their field.

The boy sees that it is just a watermelon. He laughs and tells them that it isn't a terrible, dangerous animal. But they don't believe him, so he offers to kill the terrible, dangerous animal, and he cuts a slice out of it. The people then think he's very brave, until they see him take a bite out of the slice, then they think **he's** a terrible, dangerous boy and become frightened of him, too.

At this, the boy laughs and tells them that it's just a watermelon. He has lots in his village, and they are really nice to eat. Finally, the people become interested and ask him how to grow watermelons. The Clever Boy shows them, and now in that village they have lots of watermelons. They sell some, they eat some, and they give some away. And that's why their village is called 'Watermelon Village': all because a clever boy was not afraid when a lot of silly people thought something was dangerous just because they had never seen it before.

Teaching-Stories and the Brain: Scientific Research

In order to see how different these stories are from ordinary reading and writing, I set up a series of studies to see what happens inside the brain when people are listening to them. What I found was that when people are reading Teaching-Stories, the right side of their brain is activated much more than it is when reading ordinary prose. So, for anyone reading stories like these, filled with vivid imagery and with unusual occurrences, the right hemisphere of the brain gets more active than if they are reading, say, a history of the Peloponnesian War.

There have for a long while been many theories about how the two sides of the brain work. To see the right hemisphere as the really good side and the left as the bad side is much too simple. The difference may be seen as one between text and context. When you are reading something, you need to know what each and every word means: for instance you may need to know where Paris is or what an aeroplane is and how the word for it is spelt. But, unless you can put everything together, you don't have any context; you just have a bunch of simple words. If you're looking at a room, what you see is a bunch of lines up and down, left and right. But they don't come together to make a room unless you know that you are in a room. A number of studies show that the left hemisphere of the brain deals with the elements of a situation: for instance, the lines that make up a room or the individual words that make up a sentence. The right side of the brain deals with context: how these words are put together, how the lines assemble together to make a room, where you are in space, etc.

Meaning is not part of one side of the brain or the other. You can't have a story without words. You can't have a story, also, without knowing what the words mean and how they fit together. Teaching-Stories stimulate the area of the brain that has to do with context, with putting words together, and with putting things together in relationship to oneself. This is one reason why they are so important.

If you buy a bicycle by mail order, it arrives looking quite unlike the one in the picture. What you have received is a bunch of pieces. They are all laid out. There is a set of instructions. But you can't ride it, you can't go anywhere with it, you can't do anything with it as it is. 'Some assembly required,' it says. It's the pieces of a bicycle, but it's not a bicycle. In the metaphor that I'm using, what the left hemisphere does is analyse and lay out the pieces. There is a lot of work producing the pieces of the bicycle, but it's still not a bicycle until someone knows how to put it together.

The right side of the brain is the side that puts together the pieces of the puzzle of life. It puts together things into an organised whole wherein we can operate, we can live our life, we can be prepared to know how to act in different situations. Some of these situations may be unexpected; some of them may be just routine. But, without the right hemisphere, we wouldn't know where to go, we wouldn't know how to go; it would be just like having a bunch of pieces unassembled into a bicycle.

This is context. What these stories provide is how to link items together. This gives children or adults pictures of what's going on, how to act and what may befall them in the future. The act of reading stories to children also affects the adults involved. These stories are designed to have effects on both the reader and the person who is being read to. Children may learn to anticipate what's going on in this and many other stories, but the adults may also have their minds taken along some unfamiliar lines.

Analogical Thought

Not only do these stories enrich contextual and intuitive thinking, they also enhance analogical thought, since the right hemisphere is best at recognising the relationships between entities and this process is at the core of analogy. Children can be encouraged to extrapolate from the events and characters in these stories to those in their own lives. When we encourage analogical thought in children, we help them develop flexible, inventive minds that are able to meet the challenges of life in and out of school.

Holyoak and Thagard (1996) give an example of a child's ability to think analogically. Neil is a four-year-old who is pondering the deep issue of what a bird might use for a chair. He initially decides that the tree branch might be the bird's chair, and his mother praises him for his answer, adding that the bird could sit on its nest, as well, which is also its house. Several minutes later (and time is an important factor in this process), Neil has second thoughts and says that the tree is not the bird's chair, it is its backyard. Neil here makes a mental leap. He is now trying to understand the entire world of the unfamiliar in terms of his own familiar world. He is thinking analogically.

Here Neil's everyday world is his only reference, a known world that he already understands in terms of familiar patterns. He knows that people sit on chairs, and that houses open onto backyards. The bird's world is a relatively unfamiliar one that Neil is trying to understand through his own familiar one. Holyoak and Thagard show that young children without any formal training have a natural capacity to reason by analogy. We need to help them expand upon this natural ability because in this way they can increase their contextual knowledge of their world. Children are able to make simple analogies as early as the age of two; children may play with their dolls as if they were the mothers and the dolls the babies. This new experience enables them to understand, integrate and empathise with their own mothers, with mothers and caregivers in general, with mothers of any nationality or even species, and so on.

Learning requires the brain to construct meaning, that is to make connections between new information and the experiences already known to learners. The brain naturally constructs meaning when it perceives relationships[1], and those relevant or meaningful connections motivate the brain to be engaged and focused. Constructing meaning is the major requisite to learning and the core of intellectual processing.[2] When children make analogies, they are constructing meaning by relating something that is both emotionally and intellectually familiar to them with the new information. This is a very powerful way to learn.

Analogical thought provides a powerful mechanism for understanding ourselves and our world, our origins and our destiny. Analogy is used in building scientific theory and in writing poetry. It is used in myths and legends. Coming to an analogical insight – an 'Ah-Ha!' moment – is a fulfilling experience; it feels good no matter how young or old we are. It is this innate ability that we encourage and build on when we use the Teaching-Story. Holyoak and Thagard claim that Teaching-Stories, of which there are many hundreds published for people of all ages, provide the richest 'source analogs' available for the development of our own and our children's potential. As parents use these tales with their children, they too may come to new, more sophisticated insights. By allowing children to juxtapose situations, characters and events that occur in Teaching-Stories with those that occur in their own lives, we enhance their ability to understand, through analogy, aspects of their lives that may otherwise perplex or confuse them. When children start to think in this way with these stories, they begin to experience social and emotional growth. This will continue: as their experiences increase, they will concurrently gain additional analogical insights from each tale.

If we look again at the first story, we note that though there are many stories where the hero fights and defeats the dragon, this story is different: Neem tells the dragon he'll have to drive him out of his cave because the dragon is breathing fire over everyone. Then the dragon explains what's happening. He recognises his problem and he even knows the solution, but he needs help. The dragon knows he needs help to stop breathing fire over everyone, and he knows that Neem can help him once he's whole.

At one level this is about helping each other through negotiation and cooperation, rather than using confrontation. It's a different way to look at resolving conflicts. It may also provide a different insight into the way people are structured. It could be that someone, for instance, who has a lot of energy or anger is lacking a place to put that force, but there are many other interpretations. This story offers a slightly different way of looking at things. The watermelon story, as well, gives a different way to look at something that might be considered dangerous.

These kinds of considerations are obviously very important for both children and adults in today's world. These stories are so continuously interesting and so continuously rewarding because, as we work more and more with them, we see their relevance to changing circumstances in our own lives and in the life of our culture. They not only have an effect on the mind and cognitive development, but on the brain and on our future actions and those of our children.

Conclusion

Educators can enhance learning by using Teaching-Stories in the early childhood classroom. Children can improve their contextual and analogical thinking by working with these stories and engaging in open-ended discussions about them. Through these stories they will discover alternative ways of seeing and coping with their complex world.

By helping our children make these Teaching-Stories their own, through repeated readings and open-ended questions that encourage analogical thought, we help each child learn the story 'by heart', as they would a nursery rhyme or mnemonic, and so provide them with an analogical and contextual source for life. These stories can help them better understand human behaviour and motivation, and so promote their social and emotional development. They are tools to help them solve problems, improve their predictive, intuitive and perceptive skills, and lead happy, productive and meaningful lives. The use of Teaching-Stories in our classrooms can provide endless possibilities for our early childhood learners. This is learning that lasts.

Notes

1.　See Caine & Caine (1994)

2.　See Jackson (2001)

Bibliography

Caine, R N & Caine, G (1994) *Making Connections: Teaching and the Human Brain*, Rev. Ed., New Jersey: Dale Seymour Pubs.

Gladwell, M (2002) *The Tipping Point*, New York: Back Bay Books

Holyoak, K J & Thagard, P (1996) *Mental Leaps: Analogy in Creative Thought*, Cambridge, Massachusetts: MIT Press

Jackson, Y (2001), National Urban Alliance for Effective Education, 'Reversing Underachievement in Urban Students: Pedagogy of Confidence' in Costa, A, *Developing Minds: A Resource Book for Teaching Thinking*, ASCD

Ornstein, R (1997) *The Right Mind*, New York: Harcourt Brace Jovanovich

Shah, I (1978, 1991) *World Tales*, London: Octagon Press, Ltd.

Teaching-Stories™ for children by Idries Shah are available from Hoopoe Books and distributed in the UK by Ragged Bears (www.raggedbears.co.uk), additional Teaching-Stories for adults are available from Octagon Press, Ltd. (www.octagonpress.com)

Biographical Notes on Contributors

Sarah Adams was born in Brussels in 1970, and has spent the last ten years living in Brixton, London. As a journalist and arts critic she has reported on cultural melting pots from Harlem to Marseille, and her work has appeared regularly in *Time Out*, *The Guardian*, *The Observer*, on BBCi and more recently on radio. She has been translating from French for both adults and children since 1998, including the ghetto adventure series 'Golem' by the Murail siblings, and three of Daniel Pennac's works of children's fiction, all for Walker Books. Her translation of Pennac's *Eye of the Wolf* was chosen for the IBBY 2004 Honour List and won the 2005 Marsh Award. She has a special interest in immigrant culture and in translating urban and youth slang.

Dorothy Bedford is a senior lecturer at Roehampton University. She is Programme Convener for the Professional Development Programme in the School of Education Studies and co-manager of the Student Associate scheme. She also co-ordinates international professional development courses for art teachers. Her research interests are in art and craft education, and the professional development of teachers.

Anthea Bell was educated at Oxford University and is a translator, mainly from German and French, of works of fiction, non-fiction, and books for young people, including the *Asterix the Gaul* series (with Derek Hockridge). She has received a number of translation awards, including the 2003 Independent Foreign Fiction Prize (with the author) for W G Sebald's *Austerlitz*, and the 2003 Austrian State Prize for Literary Translation.

Patricia Billings is Director of Milet Publishing, the leading publisher of bilingual children's books, with over 350 bilingual editions in English and 25 languages, as well as artistic children's books, many translated. Before founding Milet with her partner Sedat Turhan in 1995, Patricia worked as a journalist, editor and researcher on Middle East and human rights issues. Her academic background includes a degree in Political Science and Middle East Politics and post-graduate work in Arab Studies and Film Studies.

Tricia Brown is the acquisitions editor for Alaska Northwest Books and WestWinds Press, two imprints of Graphic Arts Center Publishing Company in Portland, Oregon. She is the author of books for young readers, including the award-winning *Children of the Midnight Sun: Young Native Voice of Alaska* and *Groucho's Eyebrows*, as well as numerous nonfiction books for adults. She began her career in newspaper journalism, and also served as editor of the widely read *Alaska* magazine. She has travelled extensively throughout the Alaska bush, and has been immersed in various Native American cultures across this vast state. She holds a bachelor's degree in journalism from the University of Alaska, Fairbanks, and a master of fine arts degree in creative writing from the University of Alaska, Anchorage.

Michał Borodo is an academic teacher at Kazimierz Wielki University, Poland. In 2003 he received his MA in English studies from Nicholas Copernicus University, Poland. He is currently working on his PhD thesis in the field of children's literature translation. His research interests include children's literature translation in turn of the century Poland, power relations in translation, and children's literature translation history, and he has participated in recent conferences in this area.

Belén González Cascallana holds a PhD in Translation and Interpretation (University of León, Spain) and an MA in Translation Studies from Warwick University. Her main field of research is translation of children's literature with a special interest in multiculturalism. Currently she is the Director of Learning Support at Sotogrande International School (Cádiz, Spain).

Mieke K T Desmet is Flemish, but is currently working as an Associate Professor in the Foreign Languages and Literature Department of Tung Hai University, Taichung, Taiwan. She holds a PhD in Comparative Literature from University College London (UCL) on the translation of English narrative fiction for girls into Dutch. She also has an MA in Comparative Literature from UCL and an MA in Children's Literature from the Roehampton Institute, University of Surrey. Her main research interests are the translation of children's literature, fiction for girls, visual texts, alphabet books and children's literature in Taiwan. Her most recent paper, 'Connecting Local and Global Literatures or Driving on a One-Way Street? The Case of the Taiwanese Grimm Press', was published in: Reynolds, K, O'Sullivan, E & Rolf, R (eds.) (2005) *Children's Literature Global and Local: Social and Aesthetic Perspectives*.

Annette Goldsmith is a doctoral student at the Florida State University College of Information. She has long been interested in international children's and young adult books through her work in the Canadian book trade (bookselling, publishing, librarianship), as a member of IBBY, and as founding editor of *The Looking Glass* (www.the-looking-glass.net).

Neal Hoskins founded Winged Chariot Press in 2004. Previously he worked in educational publishing at Oxford University Press. He now sees picture books as a perfect conduit for European co-operation, understanding and enjoyment.

Isabel Hoving won The Golden Kiss Award (2003), the most prestigious book award in the Netherlands, for her ground-breaking novel *The Dream Merchant*, published by Walker Books in March 2005. She currently works at the University of Amsterdam, as a comparative literature specialist and cultural analyst, focusing especially on post-colonial writing and issues of immigration.

Margherita Ippolito is a PhD student in Translation Studies at the University of Bari, Italy, and teaches in a primary school there. She is currently working on the translation of children's literature into Italian, with particular reference to Beatrix Potter's tales.

Abasi Kiyimba is a Senior Lecturer in the Department of Literature, and Deputy Dean of the Faculty of Arts at Makerere University. He holds a BA in Literature and Language from Makerere University, a Master of Letters Degree from the University of Strathclyde, Glasgow, and a PhD in Literature from the University of Dar es Salaam in Tanzania. His publications include *A Ugandan Without a Tribe*; *Indigenous African Writers Versus Expatriat Writers on the African Scene: A Clash of Perspective*; *The Ghost of Idi Amin in Ugandan Literature*, and *Tribute to Ngugi Wa Thiongo*.

Maria-Venetia Kyritsi has an MA in Literary Translation from the University of East Anglia and the Diploma in Translation from the British Council in Athens, Greece. She translates primarily between English and Greek, with a research interest in the translation of children's literature. She is researching the Grimms' Tales for a PhD at UEA, while working as a free-lance translator, Greek language teacher and production editor for the translation journal *The Norwich Papers*.

Vasiliki Labitsi is a Greek children's book illustrator and primary teacher specialising in art education. She is assistant editor of the *International Journal of Education through Art* and a member of the board of the International Association of Greek Illustrators of Children's books. Currently she is researching visual narrative in children's books and drawings for a PhD at Roehampton University.

Gillian Lathey is Reader in Children's Literature at Roehampton University and Acting Director of the National Centre for Research in Children's Literature. She was for many years an infant teacher in north London, and combines interests in children, childhood and literature by teaching on the MA in Children's Literature at Roehampton University, supervising doctoral students in Children's Literature, and researching the practices and history of translating for children. She also administers the biennial Marsh Award for Children's Literature in Translation.

Darja Mazi-Leskovar is assistant professor at Maribor University, Slovenia. Her research interests are: translation of children's literature, books read by a dual audience of children and adults, and issues connecting culture and

264

literature. She is a founder member of the Slovenian Literature and Cultural Studies Special Interest Group (IATEFL) and its current coordinator.

Márta Minier graduated in English and Hungarian studies from the University of Debrecen, Hungary in 2000. She has recently completed her PhD thesis on the translation of *Hamlet* into Hungarian culture at the University of Hull, UK. Her main research interest is translation and rewriting in an Anglo-Hungarian context, with an emphasis on Shakespeare, women writers and children's literature. She has published articles and interviews both in English and Hungarian.

André Muniz de Moura has completed a MSc in Literary Theory at the Federal University of Rio de Janeiro. He is currently studying for a Ph.D. on Fantasy as an epistemological tool in Secondary Worlds, while working as a freelance Children's Literature critic for many publishing houses in Brazil.

Sue Neale is a postgraduate student at Oxford Brookes University with an enthusiasm for contemporary French writers. Professionally she has worked as an art director for educational and children's books. Her interest in Pennac stemmed from his crime fiction, her main area of academic study.

Robert E Ornstein is an internationally renowned psychologist and author, who has written more than 20 books, among them *The Psychology of Consciousness*, *The Roots of the Self* and *The Amazing Brain*. He has taught at the University of California Medical Center and Stanford University and has lectured at more than 200 colleges and universities in the U.S. and overseas. He is the president and founder of the Institute for the Study of Human Knowledge (ISHK; www.ishk.net).

Pat Pinsent, having been for many years a Principal Lecturer, is currently a Senior Research Fellow at Roehampton University. She has been responsible for the production of Distance Learning materials for the Roehampton MA in Children's Literature. Her books include *The Power of the Page: Children's Books and Their Readers* (1993) and *Children's Literature and the Politics of Equality* (1997), together with a number of edited compilations of conference proceedings. She edits the journal of the British Section of the International Board on Books for Young People, *IBBYLink; Network,* a journal devoted to feminist spirituality and theology; and *The Journal of Children's Literature Studies*.

James Riordan studied Russian in the RAF and at Birmingham University. He worked and studied in Moscow for five years, as Senior Translator at Progress Publishers. He has translated a number of Russian children's classics, including Turgenev's *Mumu*, Chekhov's *Vanka*, Pushkin's *Fairy*

Tales, and Tolstoy's *Stories for Children*. His prize-winning novels for young people include *Sweet Clarinet, Match of Death* and *The Gift*.

Teri Sloat has worked with native Alaskan translators to develop a first-language bi-lingual programme in Alaskan schools, and also a programme for publication of trade books in small runs for indigenous languages. She is the author and illustrator of over 20 books for young children, including many published in the UK.

Gaby Thomson-Wohlgemuth holds an MA in Translation studies and is at present writing a PhD thesis in the area of translation of children's literature. Her publications focus on indigenous East German children's and youth literature, translation of English children's books in the former East Germany, as well as on general issues regarding translation, the publishing industry and cultural/literary politics in the German Democratic Republic.

Stefania Tondo is a researcher in English Literature at Suor Orsola Benincasa University, Naples, where she teaches English literature (the subject of her doctorate at La Sapienza, Rome). She has published on Shakespeare, Victorian fantasy, children's literature, *Alice*, and Henry James and the art of letter-writing.

Elena Xeni is a Teaching Assistant at the Department of Education of the University of Cyprus. She holds a Diploma for Writing for Children and Young Adults, a Master's Degree in Translation Studies from the University of Surrey, UK), Degree in Primary Education from the University of Cyprus. Her research interests focus particularly on the translation of literature for children and young adults. She has worked in schools and as a free-lance translator.